WHAT THE EXPERTS ARE SAYING ABOUT

THE QUICK & EASY ORGANIC GOURMET

You can gauge a people's overall condition by the quality of its food. Americans typically allow themselves ill-prepared, ill-presented, fast, neurotic, unhealthy, and tasteless food. Leslie Cerier's book offers imaginative ways to restore health and taste, providing practical information, great recipes, and a fresh vision of what eating could be.

Thomas Moore, author of *Care of the Soul* and *The Re-Enchantment of Everyday Life*

This is an invaluable resource both for beginners looking for an introduction to cooking with natural foods, and for experienced cooks in search of new ideas and inspiration. Her variations on the classic themes — vegetable and grain dishes, soups, sauces, seasonings, and cooking methods — seem endless. Leslie also provides, in a charming manner, excellent instruction in creating healthy, balanced, delicious, aesthetically appealing meals. Included in the book are sections on how to read food labels, order organic foods and high-quality cookware by mail, and a special guide to common pesticides that are particularly dangerous to children. All in all, for cooking organically there's no book more comprehensive than *The Quick & Easy Organic Gourmet*. If you can only buy one cookbook this year, make it this one.

Tom Monte, author of *World Medicine: The East West Guide to Healing Your Body* and, with Dr. Joel Robertson, *Peak Performance Living*

The recipes in this fascinating book are ideal for anyone wishing to prepare healthful meals without meat, wheat, or dairy.

Gene A. Spiller, Ph.D., author of *Nutrition Secrets of the Ancients* and *The Superpyramid Eating Program* and Director of the Health Research and Studies Center in Los Altos, California.

THE QUICK & EASY
ORGANIC GOURMET

DELICIOUS, HEALTHY MEALS
WITHOUT
MEAT,
WHEAT,
DAIRY,
OR
SUGAR

LESLIE
CERIER

STATION HILL OPENINGS
BARRYTOWN. LTD

Published by Barrytown, Ltd., Barrytown, New York 12507 for Station Hill Openings

Cover and book design by Susan Quasha

Typesetting by Vicki Hickman with Alison Wilkes

Drawings by Carolyn Y. Kibe: front cover, title page, and pages 1, 11, 72, 97, 106, 123, 131, 146, 182, 198, 220, and 241

Photo of the author by Ron King (Naresh), page 316

Photo of "Emily cooking at age 3," page xx by the author

Distributed by Consortium Book Sales & Distribution, Inc.
1045 Westgate Drive, Saint Paul, Minnesota 55114-1065.

Library of Congress Cataloging-in-Publication Data

Cerier, Leslie

    The quick & easy organic gourmet : quick, delicious, healthy meals without meat, wheat, dairy, or sugar / by Leslie Cerier.

        p. cm.

    ISBN 1-886449-00-7

    1. Cookery (Natural foods) 2. Natural foods. I. Title.

TX741.C46 1996

641.5'63—dc20

95-15667
CIP

Contents

ACKNOWLEDGMENTS xiv
FOREWORD BY DR. MICHAEL W. FOX xv
PREFACE xvii
HOW TO USE THIS BOOK xviii

1. *The Organic Gourmet* **1**
Engaging the Senses 1
Ecological Organic Foods 2
Where to Buy Certified Organic Foods 3
Community Markets, Coops, and Gardens 4
Shopping Tips: Buying the Best and Spending the Least ... 5
What to Stock and How to Store It 6
Cookware 10

2. *Improvisation: Creating Your Own Themes and Variations* ... **11**
Cooking Methods 11
Cooking With Liquids 15
Making Substitutions 17

3. *Craving and Creating Balance* **19**
The Senses 19
Colors 19
Seasonal Availability 20
Shapes 20
Textures 21
The Five Phases of Food 22
Recipe First Aid 29
Feel Free 30

4. *Quick Meals for Busy People* **31**
Time-saving Tips 31
Common Improvisations for All Recipes 32
Soups With International Themes 33
Cornucopia of Quick Cooking Ingredients 34
Magical Transformations With Leftovers & Garnishes ... 36
Chinese Cabbage and Watercress Soup 38
Japanese Noodles in Tamari Broth 39
Quick and Easy Vegetable Sauce 40

Colorful Ginger Noodle Soup   41

Udon Noodle Soup   42

Greens and Grains   43

Quinoa Veggie Pilaf   44

Quinoa Pepper Pilaf   45

Spanish Dancer   45

Hot or Cold Salad   46

Juicy Ginger Vegetables   47

Ginger Tempeh   48

Stir-fry Vegetables With Tofu   49

Tofu Stroganoff   50

Sweet-and-Sour Tofu   51

Cashew Carrot Curry Sauce   52

Cashew Florentine Sauce   53

Almond Pesto   53

Pasta Salada with Pesto   54

Another Great Pesto   55

Colorful and Crunchy   55

5. *The Art of the Stir-fry and Sauté*   **57**

Guidelines for Stir-fry   57

Common Improvisations for All Recipies   59

Designing an Oriental Stir-fry   60

Szechwan Broccoli   60

Japanese Fried Rice   61

Oriental Express   61

Green Noodle Sauté   62

Fat-free   63

Designing an Italian Sauté   64

Sauté of Garden Greens   64

Country-style Broccoli   65

Designing an Indian Stir-fry   66

Fragrant Indian Cabbage   66

Curried Tempeh with Tomatoes   67

Designing a Mexican Stir-fry   68

High Energy   68

Refried Beans   69

Designing a French Sauté   70

It Looks Like Meat Loaf   70

6. *Around the World with Salads and Dressings*   **73**

Common Improvisations for All Recipes   73

Ancient Goddess Spring Tabouli   74

Italiano Arugola Salad With Cauliflower 75
Len's Sunny Macaroni Salad 76
Cilantro Pesto Pasta 77
Spinach and Potato Salad with Capers 78
Easy Potato Salad 79
Roasted Eggplant and Pepper Salad 80
Babaghanoush 81
Japanese Rainbow Salad 82
Ruby Red Salad 83
Oriental Vegetable Salad 83
    Marinated Sun-dried Tomatoes 84
Special Marinade for Sun-dried Tomatoes 84
Mediterranean Tofu Dip 85
Festive Rice Salad 86
The Ultimate Pasta and Bean Salad 87
3-Bean Dill Salad 88
    Composed Green Salads 89
    Nuts and Nuts — and Seeds, Too 91
    Salad Dressings 92
Creamy Garlic 92
Green Queen 93
Golden Goddess 93
Will's Dressing 94
Pinto Parsley Salad 95
Lemon Fire 95
Tofu Mayo 96
Winds of Japan 97
    Exciting Oil-free Salads 98
Lemony Carrot and Radish Salad 99
    Boiled Salads 100
    Marinated Salads 100
Marinated Tofu 101
    Pressed Salads 102
Pressed Cucumber Salad 103
Pressed Cabbage Salad 103
    Homemade Sauerkraut 104
Sauerkraut with Carrots and Onions 104
Pickles 105

7. Secrets of Soups, Stews, and Sauces **107**
    Stocks: The Basis of Soup, Stew, and Sauce Making 108
    Common Improvisations for All Recipes 109

Fancy French Onion Soup 110
Herb Croutons 110
Sweet Borscht 111
Chinese Hot and Spicy Soup 111
Shiitake Barley Mushroom Soup 112
Invent Your Own Miso Soup 113
Miso Vegetable Soup 114
    Invent Your Own Soups, Stews, or Sauce 116
    Bean Cookery 117
    Using a Ceramic Pressure Cooker Insert (Rice Crock) 118
Basic Beans 119
Autumn Minestrone 120
Thanks, Grandma 121
Red Lentil Asparagus Soup 122
Paradise of India 123
Lentil Soup 124
Sweet Split Pea Soup 125
    Blender Soups 126
Heavenly Potato Leek Soup 126
Creamy Cauliflower Soup 127
Creamy Broccoli Soup 128
Gypsy Bean Soup 129
Brazilian Black Bean Soup 130
French Patty Pan Stew . . . and Soup 131
Sweet Bean Stew 132
It Must Be Chili 133
French Peasant Stew 134
Sunset Casserole 135
Seitan-making Party and Pot Roast 136
Holiday Tempeh 138
Emperor's Sweet-and-Sour Tempeh 139
Sweet-and-Sour Tempeh and Vegetables 140
Sweet-and-Sour Everything 140
    Curried Vegetables 141
Vegetables in Indian Spices 141
Curried Summer Vegetables 142
Curried Vegetables with Cashews 142
Indian Red Bean Sauce 143
Quick Ginger Scallion Sauce 144
Tahini Cream Sauce 144
Ginger Burdock Sauce 145

Mushroom Leek Sauce   146
Creamy Mushroom Basil Sauce   147
Vegetable Gravy   147

8. *Calcium Without the Cow*   **149**
    What to Eat   149
    Common Improvisations for All Recipes   153
Children's Special Soup   154
A Taste of Japan   155
Sautéed Kale with Leeks and Dill   156
Italiano Green Sauté   156
Greens with Shiitake   157
Sweet Vegetables Lo Mein   157
Ginger Vegetables   158
The Works   159
Black, White, and Greens   160
Vegetarian Sushi   161
Chickpea Vegetable Pâté   163
Sunny Mushroom Pâté   164
Chickpeas in Garlic Sauce   164
Greens With Tahini Sauce   165
Tahini Parsley Sauce   166
Tempting Tempeh Casserole   166
    Versatile Tofu   167
Shiitake In the Wok   167
Herb Pâté   168

9. *Cooking For and With Your Children*   **169**
French Toast   173
Good Morning Strawberry Muffins   174
Emily's Strawberry Drink   175
    Cooking Beans For and With Your Children   176
Pinto Beans and Tortillas   176
Roasted Potatoes   177
    Steamed Vegetables   178
Steamed Cauliflower   178
Garlic Bread   179
Coffee Cake and Cupcakes   180
Pickles   181
    Other Recipes Your Children Will Love   181

10. *Fish Cookery*   **183**
New England Fish Chowder   188

Smoked Fish Hors d'Oeuvres   189
Smoked Fish Salads   190
Japanese Poached Salmon   191
Chinese Stir-fry   192
Honey Shrimp Kabobs   193
Dorothy's Steamed Bay Scallops   194
Broiled Farm-raised Trout   194
Striped Bass, Trout, or Tilapia
   Stuffed with Herbed Croutons   195
Quick-fried Bass With Tartar Sauce   196
   Pan-fried Fish   197

11. *Grain Cookery*   **199**
   Special Ways of Cooking Grains   202
Basic Brown Rice   204
A Taste of India   204
Barley Rice   205
Short and Sweet   205
Spelt Good   206
Wild and Wonderful   207
Three Sisters Grains   208
Freckles   208
Aztec Two-step   209
King Tut Special   209
Sunny Mountain Rice   210
Sweet Millet   211
Millet Apple Raisin Cake   212
Chestnutty Rice   213
Kasha   214
Kasha Cous   214
Couscous and Teff   215
Bronze Delight   215
   Bread Making   216
Rice Bread #1   216
Rice Bread #2   217
Brown Rice and Barley Bread   218
   Bread Making Improvisations   218

12. *Teff: Gem of Grains*   **221**
Basic Teff   223
   Teff Plus Other Grains   223
Fritters   224

Millet and Teff with Squash and Onions 225
Deluxe Morning Breakfast 226
Elegant Vegetable Quiche 227
Coffee Apricot Tofu Pie 228
Teff Applesauce Cake 229
Lemon Poppy Seed Cake 230
   Wheat-free Baking With Teff Flour 231
Dessert Pie Crust 231
Super Chocolate Chip Cookies 232
Apple Crumb Pie 233
Topless Blueberry Pie 234
Berry Good Tofu Pie 235
Bananarama Tofu Pie 236
Espresso Scones 236
Peanut Butter Cookies 237
Hazlenut Butter Cookies 238
Fruit Paradise 238
Vanilla Hazelnut Granola 239
Scrumptious Muffins 239
Chocolatey Pancakes 240

13. Guilt-free Desserts **241**
   Sweet Alternatives and Unrefined Sweeteners 241
   Spelt and Kamut Whole Grain Flours 243
   Pies and Pie Crusts 244
Banana Date Tofu Pie 244
Luscious Strawberry Pie 245
Creamy Chocolate Truffle Pie 246
Walnut Pie 247
   Cookies 248
Chocolate Chip Cookies 248
Carob Cookies 249
Fruit Cake Cookies 249
Apple Date Crisp 250
Exotic Pear Crisp 251
   Cakes 252
Ginger Bread Cake 252
Corn Bread Cake 253
Mocha Walnut Cake 254
Banana Cake 254
   Layer Cakes 255
Carrot Coconut Cake 255

Coconut Icing   256

Carob Fudge Layer Cake   256

Caramel Icing   257

Carob Fudge Icing   257

Chocolate Cake Supreme   258

Cocoa Fudge Icing   259

Outrageously Delicious Hazelnut Cake   259

Hazelnut Butter Icing   260

Chocolate Hazelnut Pudding or Frosting   260

Kanten (Vegetable Gelatin)   261

Apricot Compote   261

Hot Carob Fudge   262

APPENDIX 1

    Pesticides That Pose a High-risk for Children   265

APPENDIX 2

    The Ten Commandments   272

APPENDIX 3

    Reading Labels   274

APPENDIX 4

    Organic Mail Order Guide   276

APPENDIX 5

    Grow Your Own Herbs   284

GLOSSARY   286

INDEX   295

Acknowledgments

I want to acknowledge and appreciate the many people who supported me while writing this book.

Thank you to my husband Len, a great father to our two daughters, for his patience, computer instruction, and technical support, especially when the computer crashed and I did not have a printout of this book.

Thank you to my oldest daughter Emily, age 13, for her recipe, "Emily's Strawberry Drink," and for helping me create the "Coffee Cake" recipe while teaching a mother-and-child cooking class with me; and thankyou Michelle, my youngest daughter, age 6, for your great assistance in baking and preparing meals.

Thank you to Paula, my dear mom, for teaching me to be flexible and creative in everyday life, and to my brother Steve, who rooted for me all the way.

Thank you to Maurice, my father, whose sudden, unexpected, grave illness inspired my learning macrobiotic cooking, thus opening the door switching from candid photography to my career as a creative cook and caterer.

Thank you to Sylvia Staub for her "labor support" in helping me give birth to this book on paper.

Thank you to Amy Shornstein for reading all my first drafts, and for cooking and tasting with me as I invented and refined many of these recipes.

Thank you to Julie Maloney and Kathy Dyer for encouraging me to "go for it" and write this book.

Thank you to all my cooking clients and students, especially Judy Hooper, for their trust; and for letting me create whatever savory meals I wanted with local, seasonal, organic produce.

Thank you to Carol Holzberg-Pill for her kind and generous computer support; as an improviser, I often called upon her to tell me how my computer really worked. She was there when Len was not home.

Thank you to Alyse Bynum, bicycling and walking partner, for her grace, wit, and intelligence in fielding my many editing questions in the midst of our many walks and bike rides.

Thank you to Bronwyn Mills for her creativity and humor as we wrote about teff.

I am very grateful to P. J. Lorenz, my editor, for shining up my diamond-in-the-rough manuscript, for fielding all of my questions so graciously, and for being like a friend during the process.

Many thanks go to Mollie Katzen for reading what I thought was the final draft and offering constructive changes.

Thank you to Annemarie Colbin for giving generously her permission to reprint four pages from her cookbook *The Natural Gourmet,* her chart of the five phases of food and the passage that I excerpted in"Recipe First Aid." These appear in chapter 3, "Craving and Creating Balance."

Thank you Verena Smith, my acupuncturist, for her keen understanding of the five elements and her fine job of editing my writing about them, and for putting me in contact with Station Hill.

Thank you to Wendy Gordon from Mothers and Others for giving me permission to reprint her information on pesticides that are high risks for children that appears in appendix I. I am grateful for your work and for Mothers and Others' work informing the public about dangerous pesticides and increasing the national marketplaces for organic foods.

Thank you to Ellen Haas and the CHEFS Coalition for sending me such great pamphlets on seafood safety and inspiring my chapter 10, "Fish Cookery."

Thank you to Michael Fox; your introduction to this book is passionate.

Thank you to all the farmers and distributors of organic foods; may you grow and prosper.

Thank you to everyone at Station Hill for providing me with the opportunity to write this book and for gently making demands that made me a better writer and a cook.

Foreword

It was an unexpected pleasure for me to read this book after Leslie Cerier asked me if I might like to write a foreword to it. I never expected such a highly informative cookbook that offered not only some of the most delectable recipes from around the world, but also well-documented nutritional information and sound advice on avoiding chemically contaminated foods from our seas and soils.

Good nutrition is one of the cornerstones of physical and psychological well-being, and an essential ingredient for health maintenance for young and old alike. We are, with the advent of fast, convenient, frozen, microwaveable, genetically engineered, irradiated, and otherwise processed and adulterated (even analog) foods, in urgent need of a book like this. We are losing that cultural wisdom, developed over generations and passed on from one generation to the next, regarding how properly to select, store, cook, and serve nutritious foods and thrive on a wholesome diet. *The Quick & Easy Organic Gourmet* is a book of culinary conservation and restoration, salvaging this wisdom from many different cultures. Recipes from around the world help us understand and enjoy the ethnic differences and subtleties of other peoples, turning our kitchens into a veritable United Nations. What better way to world peace than through such understanding and appreciation?

This book takes the reader step by step through the art and science of gourmet cooking, and, in the process, helps us turn our kitchens into what they should be and used to be: hallowed and hallowing places wherein we can pride ourselves in becoming more and more independent from the agribusiness food and drug industry complex. This industrial cpomplex — with its tax breaks and subsidies — spends billions of dollars on encouraging consumers to eat unhealthy, refined, processed, and chemically contaminated foods high in sugar, salt, animal fat, and protein, and then profits doubly by selling diet foods and pharmaceuticals when we get sick.

In transforming our kitchens and our food purchasing and eating habits, *The Quick & Easy Organic Gourmet* also enables us to support those good farmers, food wholesalers, and retailers who are committed to providing organic, natural foods from ecologically sound and sustainable farming systems. The greater diversity of grains, fruits, and vegetables people seek out, the more farmers will produce. This will naturally lead to a more diversified agriculture locally, nationally, and internationally, which is intrinsically more ecologically sound, sustainable, and biodynamic. Conventional agriculture, with its commodity crops of corn and soybeans raised primarily to feed farm animals incarcerated in cruel factory farms and feedlots, is causing global ecological damage, from loss of topsoil and soil nutrients to loss of genetic and biological diversity.

While freshwater fish and various seafoods are highly nutritious, as Ms. Cerier points out, our waterways and oceans are heavily polluted and overfished. Regrettably, most farmed fish and other aquaculture products, like shrimp, come from producers who rely upon a host of hazardous drugs to maintain the animals' health and productivity. If there is no verified organic certification accompanying such produce, I would advise against supporting this nascent global industry that feeds the rich, starves the poor, and damages the environment. (Cold-pressed organic flaxseed oil is a good alternative source of Omega-3 fatty acids, one of the touted benefits of seafoods.)

In helping establish a New Covenant between urban consumers and rural producers, this book helps lead the way for all who want to farm without harm and eat with conscience. It's good for you — and good for all! And it shows that being a gourmet has as much to do with ethics (and the politics of food) as it has with esthetics.

DR. MICHAEL W. FOX
Vice President
Bioethics and Farm Animals
The Humane Society
    of the United States
2100 L Street, NW
Washington, DC 20037
Tel: (202) 452-1100

Preface

Before I became a professional cook, I was a photographer spontaneously capturing the moment on film. I took my camera everywhere. I photographed creative dance, my family, and nature. Then in 1987, after building my home with non-toxic building materials, working in a darkroom with toxic chemicals no longer made sense to me. I couldn't do it. I had always gone out of my way to buy organically grown food, so I turned my creative attention to cooking.

When earning my master's degree in physical education at Teacher's College, Columbia University, during the '70s, I came to reject competitive sports in favor of creative movement, relaxation techniques, body awareness, experimental theater, and vocal improvisations. I began teaching sports focusing more on body alignment and the joy of movement than on winning the game.

In *The Quick & Easy Organic Gourmet* I present my approach to cooking as a creative sport! Though, of course, I do present hundreds of exciting recipes, in writing this book I wanted to give you more than rote directions to follow. I wanted to show you what it really means to be a "gourmet" of organic foods and to inspire you to use your intuition and engage your senses in inventing infinite variations to suit your moods, cravings, and busy schedules. While most cookbooks are collections of recipes, this one is also a tool for self-expression.

Written so that both the novice and the seasoned cook can use it, *The Quick & Easy Organic Gourmet* is for everyone: those who need quick meals, vegetarians, vegans, macrobiotic practitioners, dieters in search of rich, satisfying, low-calorie meals and snacks, people with wheat, dairy, or sugar allergies, those in transition from high-fat diets because of ill health, athletes needing foods that build stamina, creative cooks who already love to invent and improvise, and those that simply love to eat! Please trust your sensibilities and feast on this dairy-free cuisine of naturally farmed fish and organic vegetables in all its glorious diversity.

As nutritionists tout the benefits of high-fiber, low-fat diets, and ecologists advocate organic farming and sustainable agriculture, *The Quick & Easy Organic Gourmet* also supports the ecological and sensual benefits of organic cooking. The time is ripe for creative cooking with organic foods.

How to Use This Book

The Quick & Easy Organic Gourmet offers methods for creating your own recipes, for substituting ingredients or cooking methods in the recipes provided, and for learning from one surprise to create another.

Say you are cooking with carrots, for example. Varying the combinations of vegetables, grains, pasta, herbs, beans, fish, and spices cooked and served *with* carrots changes the "culinary theme." (Once you have created a dish you enjoy, you might even try substituting one or more vegetables for the carrots!) Changing even one ingredient, especially if it is a seasoning, will affect the flavor and possibly the ethnic character of the dish.

If you switch cooking methods while keeping the ingredients the same, you alter the texture and taste, thereby creating another variation on the same theme. For example, if you have been steaming carrots, stir-frying them will change their character, producing a different culinary result.

In chapter 1, "The Organic Gourmet," you will learn where and how to buy the best and spend the least, what to stock and how to stock it, and the ecological and aesthetic benefits of cooking with organic foods. In addition, you can refer to the five appendices at the back of the book for useful data and further information on these topics.

Chapter 2, "Improvisation: Creating Your Own Themes and Variations," teaches you how to cook, mix and match ingredients, vary seasonings, alternate cooking methods, and improvise with whole foods to create an endless assortment of balanced meals.

Chapter 3, "Craving and Creating Balance," demonstrates how to design sensuous meals with seasonally available, colorful foods. You will work with food shapes and textures and explore the creative use of the flavors: sweet, salty, bitter, sour, and spicy. The "Kitchen First Aid" section will help you repair improvisations that didn't work. Using the five phases of food — the Oriental system of food classification presented in this chapter — is a fun way to help you balance your meals and understand your food cravings.

Chapters 4 through 13 include dozens of recipes, each chapter presenting a different culinary theme. Each recipe is accompanied by suggested variations and options. Each chapter includes a page with common substitutions for all recipes offered within it.

Appendix 4: "Organic Mail Order Guide," in the back of the book will help you acquire organic ingredients, cookware, and additional information about organizations concerned with food safety.

I want particularly to call your attention here to appendix 1: "Pesticides That Pose a High Risk for Children." Though placed in the back for ready reference, its concerns are really a big part of the soul of this book. These pesticides are probable carcinogens, substances toxic to the nervous and/or reproductive/development systems, or that may have other adverse health effects. The list of fruits, vegetables, nuts, seeds, and other foods normally produced using these toxic pesticides is enormous. I hope that studying this list will intensify your motivation for becoming an environmentally savvy cook — an "organic gourmet" who creatively plans their meals around fresh, regional, seasonal, organic foods.

I have also included an appendix to help you understand how to read labels so you will not be fooled by deceitful practices (appendix 3); an organic mail order guide (appendix 4); and an appendix providing basic tips for growing your own herbs (appendix 5). In addition, I have also included a glossary.

Let your imagination and intellect soar. As you become fluent in the different cooking methods, you can improvise just for the fun of it. Using different cooking methods is just the ticket for transforming that same old stew into a succulent braised dish.

Cooking is a kind of free play that offers everyone who enjoys good food an unlimited field for healthy and environmentally responsible self-expression.

*This book is dedicated
to my daughters Emily and Michelle*

1

The Organic Gourmet

An organic gourmet prepares colorful organic foods, creates numerous soft and crunchy textures, and skillfully uses many cooking methods. Sweet, pungent, bitter, sour, and salty flavors create mouth-watering, well-balanced meals and snacks. It's fun serving low-fat, high-fiber foods in style.

An organic gourmet sees fresh options and changes boring eating habits. There is always a fresh way to make something tasty. Centered and focused in the kitchen, with a well-stocked pantry or the little that is handy, she/he is ready to improvise.

Let your imagination and taste buds guide you. Sharpen your culinary skills. Get ready to elevate every organic food to haute cuisine.

Engaging the Senses

Trust your instincts to make lively choices. Engage your senses when food shopping, meal planning, and cooking. Be like a child. See, smell, taste, touch, and listen to everything around you. New pleasures await. Choose what delights your palate.

Select vegetables, herbs, fish, and fruits by their color, smell, and texture. Feel them. Are they firm or soft? Examine them. Are they ripe? Are they spoiled or moldy? Do they smell fresh? Is their color vibrant or dull?

Choose an exciting variety of organic grains, beans, pasta, oils, herbs, spices, salty seasonings, cooking liquids, nuts, seeds, sweeteners, flours, fresh fruits, and vegetables. Select those with different shapes than you already have at home: round, flat, straight, curvy, curly, tiny, big, long, and short. These will give you an assortment of quick- and long-cooking foods. (If your budget is tight, choose one or two foods from each of the above categories. Make your selection based on your craving for a particular ethnic cuisine, special texture, color, etc.) Using different cooking styles, as defined in chapter 2, you can turn these foods into gooey, chewy, soft, light, crunchy, pungent, full-bodied, sweet and sour appetizers, soups, stews, side dishes, casseroles, desserts, snacks, or whatever you desire. Be adventurous. Perhaps buy something you have never tried before. See "What to Stock and How to Stock It" at the end of this chapter on page 6 for more ideas.

While trying recipes from chapters 4-13, tune in to the **aromas** and **sounds** of the kitchen, of sizzling vegetables, baking cakes, and simmering soups. Can you tell by its appearance or smell if something is ready?

Always **taste** each recipe before serving and, if desired, adjust the seasonings.

In chapters 12 and 13, roll up your sleeves and touch the cookie dough; like a child or master baker, feel the size, shape, and weight of it.

Do you want to feast or nourish? Are you in the mood for something simple or elegant? The aesthetic, visual presentation of a meal, appetizer, or bowl of garnished grains depends on natural colors, contrasting textures, beautiful forms, and delicious flavors. Let inspiration come from chapters 2 and 3. Using your senses, you can create a culinary masterpiece. Trust your intuition. Cook with your inner desires.

Ecological Organic Foods

Environmentally savvy cooks shop, buy, and cook organic foods. They shop with their own shopping bags and baskets and think about the recycling potential of the containers of products they purchase.

According to the Environmental Protection Agency (EPA), farmers use 845 million pounds of pesticides yearly. As crops and pests develop resistance to these pesticides, chemical companies invent new pesticides instead of questioning their use.

The chemical assault on farmland is so enormous that it has contaminated ground water and destroyed natural vegetation. Pesticides do not die. Winds carry them into the air, to other fields, and to bodies of water, causing billions of dollars of loss and poisoning human beings, fish, livestock, and wildlife.

Many pesticides are systemic. They penetrate the skin and outer leaves. They go straight into the hearts and tissues of fruits and vegetables and into the children and adults who eat them. They are not lost by washing with detergent, or by peeling or cooking.

See appendix 1 for "Pesiticides That Pose a High-risk for Children," a list of pesticides found in ten or more foods heavily consumed by children that are likely carcinogens, neurotoxins, reproductive/developmental toxins, or may have other adverse health effects.

Organic foods promote ecology and sustainable agriculture. Organic farmers practice crop rotation, mechanical cultivation, and biological pest control (bringing in friendly insects). They fertilize the soil with manure, compost, kelp, green manure, and mineral bearing rocks. (Green manures are mineral rich crops like buckwheat, alfalfa, peas, beans, clover, and rye that hold nitrogen in the soil and add more to it when plowed under at the end of the season.) Building soil fertility rather than depleting it, organic farming is very productive, energy efficient, and conserving of natural resources.

See appendix 3, "Reading Labels," for how to recognize safely grown foods.

Organic foods taste better. The food's true flavor comes through without dyes, waxes, soil fumigants, synthetic fertilizers, pesticides, and formaldehyde. Organic farmers select and cultivate their plant seeds and harvest their crops with the peak flavor in mind.

Minus the risk of ingesting toxic substances, organic foods bring us strength, not disease. Though they generally cost more than conventionally grown foods, they are the cheapest health insurance around for you, your family, and the environment.

Where to Buy Certified Organic Foods

Snazzy natural food supermarkets and natural foodstores, co-ops, and buying clubs sell certified organic produce and products. Even ordinary supermarket chains are stocking their shelves to meet the growing demand.

Whole Foods Market has 44 stores in thirteen states: Massachusetts, Texas, California, Rhode Island, North Carolina, Illinois, Michigan, and Louisiana, New York, Virginia, Wisconsin, Pennsylvania, and Washington, D.C. They own Bread and Circus stores in Massachusetts, New York, Virginia, Wisconsin, Pennsylvania, Washington, D.C., and Rhode Island; Wellspring Groceries in North Carolina; and, Mrs. Gooch's in California.

Fresh Fields Natural Food Supermarkets has 23 stores in eight states: Pennsylvania, Virginia, Maryland, Washington, D.C., New Jersey, New York, Connecticut, and Illinois.

Nine J.B. Pratt Foods stores in Oklahoma sell certified organic foods along with everyday grocery items. J.B. Pratt provides attractive, large displays and brochures to educate consumers about organic produce and products.

In New York City, Whole Foods is in Soho and on the upper West Side.

If you live in the middle of nowhere, check the mail order section (appendix 4) for several organic wholesalers and retailers that ship cross-country.

Community Markets, Coops, and Gardens

There are many farmers' markets in cities and in rural neighborhoods. Come out and meet your local organic farmers. Buying direct from the farmers can save you money, too.

Community-Supported Agriculture (CSA) and subscription purchasing support the local farmer in growing safe, sustainable food for his or her local community. CSA members buy shares in the farm's harvest. They perform farm chores, publish a newsletter, recruit new members, build greenhouses, etc.

At subscription farms or farm coops, gardening by members is optional. At mine, I can volunteer if I want to, and I often do. Gardening is a centering and grounding experience, relaxing, and very good exercise. Children usually love to garden, too. They love to put their hands in the soil, plant the seeds, spray water on them, and watch the growing progress of their favorite vegetables.

Several membership options are available at subscription farms. Full memberships allow you to enjoy unlimited use of the produce all year round so you will be able to can, dry, and freeze. A limited membership is less expensive, and it entitles the member to fresh use only. Seasonal produce is available without extra quantities for putting foods by.

Some CSAs and garden subscriptions have farm shop hours. Others are always open with a cooler stocked with fresh harvested vegetables so that members can pick up their produce at their convenience. Some let their members go out into the fields to pick their own produce. Some have a root cellar; others have walk-in refrigerators to store cabbages and root crops for members during the winter months. Some distribute all the produce after the last harvest, and it is up to each member to store it.

Financially, my garden subscription saves me money. I pay $56.50 a month for my family of four. That is fifty cents a day per person. It is a bargain. Furthermore, I know that the vegetables are really organic. The community spirit and socializing among the members is very dear to me, too.

For more information about local CSAs and farm subscriptions, check local newspapers and bulletin boards and talk to friends and neighbors. Individual financial arrangements and apprenticeships are often available, too.

To start up your own CSA, survey your neighborhood for other interested residents. Ask at the local elementary school. Do some research. Is there a local farm that is already organic and that wants to become a CSA? Is there a local farm that needs financial support from its community to convert to organic agriculture? Is there a local restaurant that the community would support if it served organic foods?

Surveys indicate people are willing to pay more for certified organic foods. Convince your local supermarkets and produce stands to stock them. Let them know that if they stock certified organic foods, they will have customers to buy them. Enlist your neighbors, friends, and local civic leaders and organizations. Group buying power speaks loudly and often drives prices down. Availability and convenience are the key.

See appendix 5 to learn how to grow your own indoor herb garden.

Shopping Tips:
Buying the Best and Spending the Least

Go for freshness and quality. Shop in stores with a quick turnover. It makes a difference in flavor and freshness. If possible, plan your shopping days and times around the fresh fish and produce delivery schedule.

Buy the best and the freshest by asking for it. If you do not see what you want or you suspect there are fresher produce or fish in the back, ask for it. Befriend the produce and fish salespeople. They may even cut you a better deal.

Select beans that are uniform in size, smooth skinned, full, and shiny. Avoid beans split at the seams, wrinkled, spotted, or streaked. Avoid dented, deformed, or broken whole grains.

Do not buy nuts in small pieces. They are usually rancid. (A rancid nut is sour, rubbery, or moldy.) All nuts and seeds, except cashews and Brazil nuts, are fresher and cheaper in their shells.

Save money with bulk buying. Many natural food stores, coops, buying clubs, and supermarkets sell beans, grains, pasta, flour, oil, herbs, spices, sweeteners, laundry soap, etc. in bulk and prepackaged. Bulk foods are generally cheaper than packaged items. Be adventurous and spontaneous. You are in control at the bulk bin. Choose a little of a new food you have never tried, small amounts of a variety of items, or buy a lot from a bulk bin.

Bulk buying is more ecological. Bring your own bags and refillable containers. Reduce solid wastes by eliminating unnecessary packaging. This also saves trees and fuel. Bulk packaging weighs less and takes up less room when being transported.

Buy locally grown fruits and vegetables in season. They are the most flavorful and least expensive.

Join a coop or buying club. Coops and buying clubs have very little markups on food. Generally, prices are lower than supermarkets.

Buy by the case. It is cheaper.

Take advantage of special sales. Stock up on items that keep, or ask neighbors and friends to split the case with you.

Comparison shop. Have more than one source for all your staples. I belong to a food buying club, a food coop, and a subscription farm. I also shop at a nearby natural supermarket. I keep my eyes and ears open for other organic gardeners and farmers, who may grow different crops or harvest sooner, have a longer growing season for a particular crop, or get a better yield than my subscription farm does.

Pick your own. Many organic farms let you pick your own produce, such as apples and strawberries. It's fun and cheaper to pick your own.

What to Stock and How to Store It

Try to stock an exciting variety of organic foods. Use recycled glass bottles, ceramic crocks, and quart/pint mason jars for all natural foods except produce.

Understand your shopping rhythms. If you live far away from your source, stock up each time you shop. If you live close by and shop once or twice a week, buy only what you need till the next time you shop, plus a little more for unexpected guests and spontaneous dinner parties.

Unless noted, store these ingredients for up to one year. Stock up again with the new harvest. Check the following list for unfamiliar ingredients, and to remind yourself of what you wish to stock.

Grains: short, long, medium, sweet, and basmati brown rice, millet, barley, barley flakes, whole oats, rolled oats, teff, spelt grain and flakes, kamut grain and flakes, buckwheat groats (kasha), wheat berries, whole wheat couscous, bulgar wheat, spelt cous, corn grits, whole corn, rye flakes and berries, wild rice, quinoa, amaranth

Storage Tips: Store grains in a cool, dry, shaded place. Putting a bay leaf in the jar also keeps bugs away. If your kitchen or pantry is hot, it is best to store your grains in the refrigerator, dry basement, or in a bag in the freezer.

Beans and Legumes: chickpeas, pinto beans, kidney beans, anasazi beans, navy beans, green and yellow split peas, red and brown lentils, black beans, lima beans, aduki beans, black-eyed peas, great northern beans, mung beans
Storage Tips: Store beans and legumes at room temperature or in a cool, dry, shaded place.

Pasta/Noodles: whole wheat, kamut, spelt, quinoa, corn, rice, amaranth, buckwheat (soba), vegetable, herb and spice varieties, red, yellow, green, brown, elbows, spirals, shells, ribbons, trumpets, confetti, bowties, corkscrews, ziti, thin, thick, long, wide, short, flat, somen, angel hair, udon, spaghetti, fettuccine, lasagna
Storage Tips: Keep in jars or other well-sealed containers.

Flours: whole wheat bread flour, whole wheat pastry, spelt, kamut, teff, cornmeal, blue corn, brown rice, barley, oat, soy, rye, quinoa, arrowroot powder
Storage Tips: Store flours in a cool, dry place, such as crocks on the counter, jars or well-sealed containers in the basement, refrigerator, or freezer. For best results, warm flours before baking by leaving out at room temperature.

Sea Vegetables*: nori, ocean ribbons, sweet kombu, kombu, sea palm, alaria, wakame, digitata, dulse, arame, hijiki, agar agar
Storage Tips: Store sea vegetables in jars or plastic bags. Keep them cool, dry, and dark. They keep for years.

Nuts* and Seeds*: almonds, filberts, walnuts, pistachios, pecans, peanuts, chestnuts, cashews, soy, pine nuts, sunflower seeds, sesame, pumpkin, poppy, flax, and alfalfa and radish for sprouting
Storage Tips: Store nuts in shells for up to one year in a cool, dry, dark place. Shelled nuts and seeds will keep for up to four months if refrigerated and up to one year if frozen.

Nut and Seed Butters: almond, peanut, hazelnut, cashew, tahini, sesame, sunflower
Storage Tips: Refrigerate after opening for up to four months.

Dried Fruits*: apples, raisins, peaches, nectarines, pears, apricots, dates, figs, prunes, currants, bananas, cherries, kiwi, persimmon, mango, pa-

---

* Leave dulse, toasted nori, fresh fruits, dried fruits, nuts, and seeds out during the day for snacks. Then at night store them in the appropriate places.

paya, pineapple, shredded and flaked coconut, sun-dried tomatoes
Storage Tips: For immediate or quick use, store them on a cool kitchen shelf in jars or other airtight containers. If your kitchen or pantry is hot, you can store them in a basement or refrigerator for up to six months. Soak in warm water for one hour to soften them before eating, if desired.

Herbs and Spices: basil, bay leaves, caraway seeds, cayenne, cilantro, celery seed, chili powder, chives, cinnamon, cloves, cumin, curry, dill seed, dill weed, garlic, ginger, mustard seed, nutmeg, oregano, paprika, parsley, rosemary, sage, savory, sorrel, tarragon, thyme
Storage Tips: There are several methods.

They keep best cool, well ventilated, and moist. Fresh picked herbs can keep for five-seven days in the refrigerator.

You can refrigerate some fresh herbs with long, stiff stems, such as parsley, basil, lovage, and mint, in a container of water, or sprinkle a little water on fresh herbs before putting them into a plastic bag. Then close the bag, leaving plenty of air inside so the herbs are in less contact with the plastic, or refrigerate fresh herbs in a closed plastic bag with a few holes poked in it for ventilation. There are two exceptions: cilantro keeps better in the refrigerator out of a plastic bag or in an open one; and basil is best stored on a cool counter (refrigeration turns hydroponic basil black).

Store garlic and ginger at room temperature, just as you see it displayed in the store.

Put dried herbs and spices in small, dark jars or in tightly sealed containers away from the light. Store them in a cool place and close to the stove, if possible. (I store mine on a long shelve running underneath my overhead kitchen cabinets.)

Oils

for sautéing: extra virgin olive, sesame, walnut, hazelnut, almond, sunflower, and peanut

for baking: canola, corn, safflower, high-oleic safflower, almond, and hazelnut

for salads: extra virgin olive, sesame, toasted sesame, canola, safflower, high-oleic safflower, sunflower, hazelnut, pistachio, pumpkin, flax, and walnut

Storage Tips: Store extra virgin olive, sesame, and toasted sesame oil in a cool place in the kitchen, unless your kitchen is very hot. Once opened, other oils keep best in the refrigerator for up to four months.

Beverages: herbal teas, grain coffee, soy milk, rice dream drink, fruit juice, amasake

Storage Tips: Store herbal teas and grain coffee at room temperature or, if you have a lot, store some in a cool, dry place. Store opened soy milk, rice dream drink, and fruit juice in the refrigerator. Some brands of amasake always need refrigeration. Some do once opened. If you bought it refrigerated, store it that way.

Salty Seasonings: sea salt, tamari, shoyu, sesame salt (gomasio), miso, umeboshi (plums, paste, and vinegar), Bragg Liquid Aminos, sauerkraut, pickles

Storage Tips: Only the miso needs refrigeration; the others are fine at room temperature. Once opened, sauerkraut and pickles need refrigeration. If they are homemade, they may require refrigeration after pickling. See recipes on pages 104, 105.

Other Condiments: apple cider vinegar, balsamic vinegar, rice vinegar, mustard, soy mayonnaise (nayonnaise), salsa, ketchup

Storage Tips: Store vinegars at room temperature and refrigerate everything else after opening.

Sweeteners: maple syrup, rice syrup, barley malt, date sugar, sucanat, honey, molasses

Storage Tips: Store opened maple syrup in the refrigerator. Everything else keeps well at room temperature unless your kitchen is very hot. Opened barley malt sometimes needs refrigeration, unless you use it up quickly.

Miscellaneous: vanilla, baking powder, dried shiitake mushrooms, dried chestnuts, dried lotus seeds, dried burdock

Storage Tips: Store them at room temperature in jars.

Dried shiitake mushrooms store well in jars in a cool dry place for months. Store fresh shiitake mushrooms for 7-10 days in the dark in the refrigerator in either an opened plastic bag in the crisper or in a cardboard box, not tightly sealed. Use them like fresh white mushrooms.

Vegetables and Fruits

Storage Tips: If you're not sure of how to store an item, copy the display in the supermarket or produce store. Berries and grapes are the exceptions. Take off the plastic wrap and refrigerate them.

Potatoes, onions, winter squash, and yams keep best in a dark, dry, cool place, like a root cellar or basement. Make an exception for small amounts of onions, winter squash, and yams. Leave some for everyday use on a counter or in a hanging basket in the kitchen. Put the potatoes in a paper bag because they turn green from light and become poisonous. (If a potato has a small green spot, cut it off. It is safe to cook and eat the rest.)

Green leafy vegetables such as lettuce, kale, and collards keep best in a moist, cold climate. Stores spray them a few times a day with a mist of cold water. To retain moisture, wrap a damp paper towel around the base of green leafy vegetables and cabbages and store in your refrigerator. Put them in closed plastic bags poked with a few tiny holes for ventilation. Do not leave them in a bag of water or they will rot. Optional: Mist leafy greens everyday. To revive leafy greens, give them a bath in icy water.

Whenever possible, use the whole vegetable at once rather than storing the leftover parts in the refrigerator. Plastic wrap is no substitute for the vegetable's own outer leaves or skin. Cabbage stays fresher when you use the outer leaves first, rather than slicing it through the middle.

Cookware

An organic gourmet enjoys using cast-iron, stainless steel, ceramic, and glass cookware.

Ceramic cookware is very attractive for cooking and serving. It conducts heat slowly and evenly and keeps foods warm for hours.

Cast-iron pots and pans are known for slow, even cooking and for releasing small amounts of iron into the food, which is nutritional.

Glass cookware is excellent for watching foods cook and bake inside. They retain heat for a long time.

Stainless steel cookware is lighter than cast iron and just as versatile. Be sure to buy those with heavy gauged bottoms. Although more expensive, you are less likely to burn the foods cooked inside.

Avoid aluminum and copper cookware. Aluminum pots are thin, causing foods to cook unevenly and burn. Some research indicates that eating foods cooked in aluminum cookware causes indigestion, constipation, heartburn, gas, headaches, and may contribute to Alzheimer's disease. Do not select pots where copper can come in contact with food, because small amounts of copper may be released into the food. Stainless steel pots with copper bottoms are okay.

Avoid Teflon-coated or other metal cookware with non-stick surfaces. They scratch easily and release bits of plastic into foods during cooking.

2

Improvisation: Creating Your Own Themes and Variations

This chapter deals with cooking methods, cooking liquids, and how to substitute ingredients. Grasp these concepts and you can follow any recipe, as well as create one-of-a-kind dishes to suit any mood, craving, and schedule. A little knowledge of kitchen basics and some courage and confidence is all you need to improvise.

Once you understand the proportion between wet and dry ingredients in any recipe (soups, stews, pancake, and cake batters), you can cook from intuition and easily invent your own variations. You are free. Without even measuring, you can mix up a batch of pancakes. You know the consistency, the flavor, the texture that you are looking for. Engaging your senses, you can improvise. Add a little of this or a lot of that. Grandma did it without a measuring cup or spoon. With this cookbook, you too can cook from inspiration.

Although I have measured the ingredients carefully before writing down the amounts, feel free to use the list of ingredients (in the recipe sections) as a guide. If a recipe uses an herb or a vegetable you don't like or have, omit it or add something else.

Cooking Methods

Baking squash, root vegetables, beans, casseroles, breads, and pastries is especially delightful in winter, when the aromas linger in a warm house. Baking is a slow and even process that dries foods out a bit, so their flavor becomes more concentrated.

Cook's Tip: Bake tofu and seitan in a covered pan; these foods have no oils and will dry out.

Blanching is quick. Briefly plunge green leafy vegetables into boiling water for 15-30 seconds and remove them quickly. Blanch thinly sliced root vegetables for a slightly longer time. Blanching preserves color, texture, and nutritional value.

Boiling foods in a pot of rapidly moving liquid is great for cooking pasta or as a leading step to other cooking methods such as simmering, steaming, and blanching. Boiling wastes the minerals and flavors of vegetables, unless you use the boiling water in your recipe.

Eco Tips:

❖ Steam vegetables or other ingredients of the meal in a large bamboo steamer on top of a pot of boiling noodles.

❖ You can use the hot water from the cooked noodles for steaming, simmering, baking, blanching, poaching, parboiling, or pressure cooking. You can also refrigerate it for later use in making grains, beans, soups, stews, and sauces.

Braising uses a combination of cooking methods: sautéing, simmering, baking, and steaming. First, sauté vegetables, fish, tofu, tempeh, or seitan. Then cover them halfway with a salty, sour, or sweet liquid. Next, the dish bakes in the oven, and simmers and steams. Braising brings out a succulent and tender quality.

Broiling and grilling allow soft vegetables to retain their shape instead of becoming mushy, as they can when boiled. Fish, tempeh, tofu, seitan, and vegetables acquire a pleasant bitter-burnt taste associated with summer when grilled whole or cut into chunks and skewered.

Cook's Tip: Lightly coat vegetable proteins (tempeh, tofu, seitan) with at least enough oil to keep them moist. Marinades add even more flavor.

Deep-frying in lots of oil at high heat creates a crispy coating that quickly seals in all nutritive elements. It is important that the oil be hot before deep frying to prevent foods from becoming soggy or greasy. Fish, vegetables, tofu, tempeh, seitan, and grain croquettes are delicious deep-fried. Top with or serve a sweet-and-sour, spicy, or salty dipping sauce on the side.

Cook's Tip: Strain oil after it cools to remove food particles and store to use again. This prevents the oil from breaking down, which would affect the way in which it fries foods.

Dry roasting magnifies aromas, intensifies colors, and delivers a nutty flavor. Dry roast grains, nuts, and seeds in an unoiled skillet on the stove top, or in the oven on a cookie sheet, pie pan, or baking dish. Stir constantly until they are fragrant and begin to pop. Dry roasting slightly shortens the cooking time of longer cooking grains: barley, kamut, spelt, and whole wheat.

Cook's Tip: For a delicious change of pace and texture, try dry roasting grains before pressure cooking or simmering. They will be fluffy, individual, dry, and chewy, instead of moist and dense.

Marinating saturates and fuses grains, beans, sea vegetables, fish, pasta, and vegetables with a sauce made from several of the following: oil, herbs, spices, vinegar, wine, and salty seasonings.

Pickling is the opposite of boiling, as it removes water and adds minerals. Vegetables, salt, herbs, and spices create crunchy pickles for year-round enjoyment.

Poaching simmers food without first boiling. Try this in the oven or on top of the stove. Cover fish, vegetables, tofu, tempeh, seitan, sea vegetables, herbs, and spices with water, broth, or wine, and cook them just below the boiling point until *al dente*. Poaching adds moisture to food.

Pressure-cooking is an old fashioned time-saver that's making a comeback. Pressure cookers create steam under pressure to cook foods quicker. Pressure cookers today are easier and safer to use than yesterday's. You can choose an airtight stainless steel or an enamel pressure cooker.

Pressure cooking sweetens the flavor of grains and makes them dense. Pressure cook grains and beans alone or in combination with other grains, vegetables, or spices. Adding more water produces great soups, stews, and sauces.

Ceramic pressure cooker inserts, also known as "Ohsawa pots" and "rice crocks," are available in many colors and sizes. They fit inside stainless steel pressure cookers, making it practically impossible to burn any food cooked inside. Foods cook evenly, gently, and without agitation, making layering possible. Breads, grains, beans, stews, and soups need less water than foods cooked in a stock pot on the stove. You can also use this versatile crock for serving, baking, and storing the foods cooked inside. (See chapters 7 and 11 for recipes, and appendix 4 for a list of mail order distributors.)

Refrying embellishes plain cooked grains and beans. Fried rice and refried beans are classic illustrations. Heat pan. Add oil, spices, diced vegetables, herbs, and salty seasonings such as sea salt or tamari. Cook vegetables until they are two-thirds cooked, stir in cooked grains or beans, and continue cooking uncovered until the vegetables are soft and the grains and beans have absorbed the flavorings of the oil and seasonings.

Sautéing and stir-frying are quick cooking methods for vegetables, tofu, tempeh, fish, sea vegetables, seitan, and raw grains. Stir continuously in a wok, pressure cooker, or skillet with a little oil and other liquid seasonings, herbs, and spices. Each piece contacts the oil at the bottom of the pan, sealing in nutrients. Grains come out soft and individual. Sautéed foods are moist and rich in flavor from the seasonings of the pan.

Stir continuously, or the top ingredients will only steam.

Cook's Tips:

- To make a little oil go a long way, first heat wok or pan. Brush on, or pour in a little oil. The heat quickly thins and spreads the oil to cover the whole pan.
- When sautéing vegetables, add onions and garlic first, then firm (root) vegetables before the more tender (leafy) ones.
- Sauté vegetables, herbs, and spices, before adding raw, rinsed, grains. Then add cooking liquid.
- Sautéing is often a preliminary step used in combination with baking, pressure cooking, steaming, and simmering.
- Oil-free sautéing is also an option. Simply replace oil with water and other liquid seasonings.

Searing or frying is similar to sautéing but without continuous stirring.

Simmering and stewing adds tenderness to food. First, bring the food to a boil, then reduce the heat so that just a few bubbles pop to the surface rather than the whole surface rolling. Simmer fruits, vegetables, grains, beans, seitan, tofu, tempeh, sea vegetables, and fish to make a variety of soups, stews, and sauces.

Steaming gives foods a sweet, light, moistness that brings out their true flavors. You can steam vegetables, fish, tofu, and dried fruits. Steaming is a great way to heat breads, grains, and other cooked entrees without drying them out. Place foods in a bamboo or stainless steel basket above the cooking liquid (water, stock, or vegetable juice) in a covered pot. Bring the water to a boil, then reduce heat to a simmer. Serve steamed foods immediately or turn off heat before they are fully done because they will continue to cook from internal heat. Save the steaming liquid for stock or sauce.

Washing and rinsing vegetables thoroughly requires special care.

Eco tip: Place root vegetables, such as potatoes, beets, radishes, and carrots, in the sink or a pot filled with cold water, rather than running water over them. Scrub them individually with a vegetable brush and rinse. To wash leeks, slice off the root, and slice the leek in half lengthwise. Spread the layers and rinse carefully to remove all the dirt. To wash leafy greens, such as kale, lettuce, and collards, separate the leaves first before dunking them in cold water. Swirl them around and use your hands to loosen sand and dirt.

Even though I recommend that you buy all organic vegetables, if this is not possible, add a cap full of Spectrum's organic white vinegar, Heinz distilled vinegar or a liquid castle soap to your rinse water. Heinz is better than some distilled vinegars, which are made from petroleum products. This is also a great way to remove molds and bacteria from the surface of fruits and vegetables.

Cooking with Liquids

There are many options. A diversity of cooking liquids helps you to create different textures and flavors.

Water is neutral in flavor and compatible with all cooking methods. Clean well water and spring water are the best to use.

Flavored and colored waters are variations on the water theme. Add fresh garlic, ginger, bay leaves, whole peppercorns, cinnamon sticks, cloves, dill seeds, caraway seeds, cumin seeds, saffron, cardamom, and or sea vegetables to the water in soups, stews, sauces, fish, bean, and grain dishes to enhance and liven up the taste.

To change its color, add red cabbage, tomatoes, beets, or red wine to the water. A one-fourth teaspoon of turmeric or paprika will change its color, too.

Vegetable stocks are easy to make and add a lot of nutrition and flavor. To learn how to make them, see page 107 in chapter 7, "Secrets of Soups, Stews, and Sauces."

Nut and seed milks are excellent substitutes for dairy milk and cream. Use them when baking, boiling, simmering, and pressure cooking. Their dense texture is excellent for preparing hot, creamy sauces. Naturally, nut and seed milks taste like their ingredients. They are lighter and more refreshing than dairy milks, and some say they are not as likely to produce congestion. Try them for a delicious, cool summer drink.

To Make Your Own: Grind nuts into a meal in a food processor. Then add water, wine, or juice. Blend until creamy. The ratio of nuts to liquid is 1:8 for almonds and 1:3½ for cashews; 1 (part shredded coconut) :2 (parts liquid) for coconut milk; 1:6 for sesame and sunflower seeds. Optional for drinks: add maple syrup, dulse, carob powder, honey, molasses, vanilla, or grain coffee to taste. For sauces, add umeboshi vinegar, umeboshi paste, mustard, mirin, herbs, and spices.

Fruit juice, soy milk, and rice dream are wonderful substitutes for water and dairy milk in baked goods, grain dishes, puddings, and sauces.

Mirin is a sweet rice cooking wine and a popular seasoning in oriental cooking. Mirin gives an exotic, sweet flavor to stir fries, soups, stews, marinades, dips, dressings, sauces, and puddings.

Organic beers, wines, and non-alcoholic beers and wines are fine beverages to occasionally accompany a meal. Dilute their strong flavors with nut milk, water, or stock to create hot and cold sauces and gourmet grain dishes. (They are a natural complement to grain cookery, because they are also made from grains. Their strong, fermented flavor goes well with other strong-flavored grains, such as wild rice, teff, quinoa, and amaranth). Beers and wines are compatible with all cooking methods. Be careful not to use too much red wine; it will turn foods purple.

Vinegars are sour seasonings that add zest to hot and cold sauces. Whether you are marinating a salad or braising a stew, vinegars add accent and balance flavors.

Oriental rice and umeboshi plum vinegars are my favorites. I use them almost exclusively. Umeboshi (also known as ume) has a delightful sour (lemony) and salty flavor and a deep ruby color. I use it in place of tamari or lemon and salt. Unlike other vinegars, ume is alkalizing instead of acidic and aids digestion. Golden brown rice vinegar is also low in acid content, and is my favorite vinegar to use for making sweet-and-sour sauces. For quick, delicious salad dressings, try olive oil and umeboshi vinegar or umeboshi vinegar, sesame oil, and rice vinegar.

Apple cider vinegar smells like apples and has a sweet-and-sour flavor. American cuisine uses apple cider vinegar to accent its dishes. It is 5% acid.

Wine vinegar infused with fresh fruits, herbs, and spices preserves the natural flavors of fresh fruits, herbs, and spices when they are not readily available. It is easy to create elegant salad dressings with a tarragon or other herbal vinegar. For a Mediterranean-style sauce or dressing, use wine vinegar and add herbs and olive oil. Wine vinegars are generally stronger in flavor than grain vinegars with more acidity, about 6%.

Italian **balsamic vinegar** is rich and slightly sweet. Try it in salad dressings and sauces. I like to use it in Oriental marinades.

Making Substitutions

The possibilities are endless. You can substitute one vegetable for another, a grain for pasta, one bean for another bean, herbs for spices, one grain for another grain, and on and on. Here are ideas to consider when you are inventing recipes or substituting ingredients:

Colors: Foods come in many colors and shades of red, orange, white, green, purple, black, yellow, and brown. You can change the visual presentation of a dish by changing the color of one or more ingredients. Also, there are many foods that are the same color. The colors of the dish can stay the same, but the ingredients can change.

Yams, carrots, and winter squash can substitute for each other in a soup or stew. Potatoes are also delicious in soups and stews, and they are a different color. It is fun changing the colors of soups, salads, sauces, and stews by changing one or more ingredients. Change the color of a salad by substituting purple cabbage for green cabbage, red peppers for green peppers, mustard greens for radishes.

Cooking Times: Bok choy takes less time to cook than collards. It also cooks down more. Try substituting green cabbage for collards in a vegetable stir-fry or stew. It cooks in the same amount of time as bok choy. If you want to substitute bok choy for collards, just remember that bok choy takes less time to cook.

Texture: Raw carrots, celery, and string beans are crunchy. Tomatoes are soft and juicy. Substitute tomatoes for carrots in a salad, and the color and the texture change. Substitute other crunchy vegetables, such as cauliflower, broccoli, string beans or peas, for carrots to keep the texture the same.

Flavor: Substitute leeks and shallots for onions. Leafy greens have different flavors. Chicory, watercress, arugola (also spelled "arugula"– I am using the Italian spelling), escarole, spinach, and mustard greens are stronger in flavor than lettuce. They are all wonderful in salads, but the flavor of a salad changes when you substitute even a few mustard greens for lettuce.

Volume: Leafy greens such as collards and kale cook down more than broccoli or string beans. Take this into account when you are steaming or stir-frying. Green leafy vegetables shrink more than root vegetables.

Seasonal Availability: Cooking in harmony with the seasons means planning menus around the local produce in season. For example, when I make a fruit pie in the fall, I use apples and pears. In the summer, when the blueberries are fresh, I make the same pie crust, but use blueberries instead.

All the recipes in this book are flexible. Substitute seasonal, regional, organic ingredients as you like. From the earth to the table, what excites your palate today? Be inventive.

Successful improvisers are bold and confident. Cook with your intuition. You are only limited by your imagination and what you have in stock.

3

Craving and Creating Balance

Think of yourself as an artist creating a culinary masterpiece. Your plate is your canvas. Your stove is your palette. Fill your refrigerator and cupboards with a rainbow of colors, shapes, textures, and flavors. Using a variety of cooking methods, we will mix and match organic foods, blending and contrasting colors and textures to create an endless assortment of meals with sweet, sour, bitter, pungent, and salty flavors.

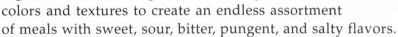

Improvising with seasonal foods, a creative cook can achieve unlimited choices to satisfy any palate. If you are very imaginative, you may never have to serve the same meal twice, unless you want to.

The Senses

Use your senses to make lively choices. Employ them when you select foods, rinse, chop, stir, blend, season, and taste. Listen to your inner voice. Our instincts let us know what and how much we want without measuring. As you create, relax and breathe. In these moments when the mind is open and the senses are alert, we have the greatest potential opportunity for improvisations with food.

Detached from failure, there is only the creation of the meal in the moment. Love transforms the process into a passionate state of being. At one with food, conscious, awake, and present in the moment, we intuitively satisfy our cravings and hunger with nourishing foods.

Colors

To me, the easiest way to balance a meal is by color. Instinctively, many cooks prepare colorful meals, including something white, red, orange, brown, and green. Though greens have a healthy reputation, a meal of green split pea soup, green cabbage salad, and steamed kale is visually boring. However, when you add orange yams and carrots to the soup and red onions and radishes to the salad, the meal becomes colorful and visually pleasing. Substituting cauliflower for the kale or purple cabbage for green cabbage are other colorful solutions. Colorful serving bowls, platters, and dinnerware enhance healthy appetites, too. A white tofu dip garnished with red radish flowers served in a red bowl is sure to catch your eye.

Seasonal Availability

Select ingredients by seasonal availability and abundance. I created *Autumn Minestrone* (see page 120) inspired by the magnificent New England fall foliage I witnessed on my bike ride that morning. The soup was full of tomatoes, carrots, and celery. These seasonal vegetables, abundant and colorful, complemented the flavor of red kidney beans to mirror the glorious fullness of the outdoors.

Seasonal availability also means lower prices. Locally grown foods in season are fresher and less expensive than the ones shipped cross-country or flown overseas. We must be willing to adapt to seasonal availability of locally grown foods. It supports the local economy and is more energy efficient, too.

Shapes

I buy the freshest, best looking, organic ingredients. Often I plan my shopping sprees on the same day the store gets its deliveries, or on the days that my subscription farm harvests its vegetables. I touch, smell, and, if in doubt, even nibble a piece of the produce. I buy a colorful assortment of edible multi-shaped minerals and vitamins, namely organic vegetables: curly, flat, long, broad, round, and cylindrical vegetables. I make my choices based on what is organic, fresh, and in season, and what smells and looks the best.

I am free to slice, cook, mix, and match my bounty in many ways. Depending on the season, I could slice the ingredients immediately into a salad; simmer them for hours in a soup or stew; pressure cook them with grains; marinate them with cooked beans; or pickle the vegetables to preserve them. There are many options and factors to consider: the season, my mood, what my family wants to eat, how quickly we want to eat, what we ate yesterday, etc.

Pasta, too, has many colors, shapes, and sizes: green, yellow, white, red, brown, spirals, elbows, thin, thick, wide, cylindricals, long, and short. Likewise, there is an array of beans, grains, and fish. For spontaneity, I try to stock them all (except fish, which I buy the day I cook it, unless it is a smoked variety, which stores well). However, stocking just a few varieties of grains, beans, and pasta is really adequate, unless you live very far from your shopping source.

Textures

Contrasting textures, prepared at different temperatures, give zest to the meal. Creative cooks balance a meal with contrasting textures: crunchy, creamy, fluffy, light, dry, heavy, juicy, gooey, chewy, soft, and crisp.

It is not enough to have one hundred and one stir-fry recipes. If you always rely on one or two cooking styles or condiments, your dishes will have similar textures, and you probably will crave the textures missed.

Influencing Textures

Cooking Times: Uncooked vegetables are crunchy. Long simmering, steaming, pressure cooking, and sautéing make foods soft. Quick stir-frying also keeps vegetables crunchy. Quickly roasting and toasting nuts and seeds makes them crunchy, too. Fast grilling and deep-frying foods make them crispy on the outside and soft inside. Perk up appetites by including a mixture of uncooked, long cooked, and fast cooked foods in your daily menus.

Measurement of Cooking Liquids: If you simmer brown rice with twice as much water, it will be heavy and chewy. If you cook brown rice with five times as much water, it will be creamy and similar to a pudding. The more cooking liquid you use, the softer the food becomes.

Cooking Temperatures: The way you bring the grain and water together influences the texture. If you heat the grain in a pan first (dry roasting) and then add boiling water, the grain will come out light, fluffy, dry, individual, and great for a pilaf. If you add cold cooking liquid or water to a hot roasted grain, it will come out light, sticky, and somewhat individual and chewy. If you start with a cold grain (room temperature, like rolled oats) and cook it with a cold liquid, it will be heavy and sticky, which is just what you want in an oatmeal. If you pour boiling water on a cold grain, it will come out with the standard grain texture, neither heavy nor light.

Cooking Methods: Grains cooked in ceramic pressure cooker inserts are moist and stick together. To make them lighter and drier, first dry roast and then simmer them in a cast iron skillet.

If you sauté uncooked grains and then either simmer, bake, pressure cook, or braise them in cooking liquids, they come out soft, moist, individual, and rather heavy. If you presoak grains before simmering, pressure cooking, baking, or braising, they will come out very soft, heavy, and sticky. If you add dried fruits and seasonings, they will not be so bland.

Cook's Tip: Bond vegetable flavors and spicy seasonings to grains by first sautéing grains with vegetables and spices.

Contrasting Combinations

In Texture: Pair opposite textures in the same dish. For instance, add sunflower seeds to a macaroni salad. Garnish hot soups or grains with fresh sprigs of parsley or raw slices of scallions.

In Size: Chopping and slicing foods into different thicknesses can make a difference. Thinly sliced vegetables will cook faster than chunky style. Diced vegetables cook faster than thick slices. You may want to bake some vegetables such as potatoes, winter squash, yams, or sweet potatoes, whole. Some people enjoy eating foods cut into chunks. Others like to eat small pieces. The shapes of cut vegetables can affect the aesthetics of the dish as well.

The previous sections dealt with colors, shapes, senses, textures, seasonal availability, and what influences the textures of foods. The next section deals with something more abstract.

The Five Phases of Food

The five phases of food, also known as the five transformations, or the five elements, is the Chinese system of meal balancing and food classification. The basic idea is to eat equal amounts from all five phases at each meal, or at least over a three-day period. Colors, senses, seasons, organs, flavors, emotions, and much more correspond to each phase. When we eat equally from each phase, food cravings are rare. Our meals are colorful and flavorful with complementary proteins. A variety of cooking techniques elicits multiple textures and shapes. Then each phase flows into the next one without blockages or haste, and we feel in balance. In reality, people have different constitutional attractions to certain foods and disinclinations to others. Sometimes this results in overeating or undereating from one or more of the food phases.

The following chart for the five phases of food is easy and fun to use. You may wish to post it on your refrigerator. Keeping a written record of what you eat for a week is enlightening. You may find that you are eating most of your foods from just two or three phases and using only two or three cooking techniques.

Foods Categorized According to the Five Elements

In this order: 1) grains and tubers; 2) dry beans and legumes; 3) vegetables; 4) fruits; 5) seeds; 6) herbs; 7) nuts; 8) dairy products; 9) seafood; 10) fowl; 11) meat; 12) miscellaneous; 13) cooking techniques.

WOOD

1) barley, oats, rye, triticale, wheat, kamut, spelt
2) green lentils, mung, black-eyed peas, split peas, peanuts
3) artichoke (globe), bell pepper (green), broccoli, carrot (raw), knotweed, lettuce (Bibb, Boston, romaine, curly), parsley, green beans, green peas, rhubarb, summer squash (pattypan, zucchini)
4) apple (sour), cherry (acerola), avocado, currant (sour), coconut, crab apple, grapefruit, kiwi, lemon, lime, orange (sour), pineapple, plum, pomegranate, quince
5) alfalfa
6) alfalfa root, saffron, caraway, cumin, marjoram, bay leaf, dill, nutmeg, tarragon, cloves, gumbo filé
7) Brazil nuts, cashew nuts, litchis
8) butter, cream, egg yolk, mayonnaise, sour cream, yogurt (sour)
9) freshwater clams, softshell crabs, eel, trout, mackerel
10) chicken, liver (chicken)
11) fats, liver (beef, lamb)
12) lard, nut butters, oils, olives, sour pickles, sauerkraut, seitan (wheat gluten), vinegar, wheat bran, wheat germ, wheat grass, yeast
13) frying

FIRE

1) amaranth, corn (yellow), popcorn, sorghum, quinoa
2) red lentils
3) asparagus, arugola, bell pepper (red), bok choy (greens), broccoli rabe, Brussels sprouts, chicory, chives, collard greens, dandelion (root and leaves), endive (Belgian), escarole, kale, lamb's quarter, mustard greens, okra, snow peas, scallions, Swiss chard, turnip tops, tomato

4) apricot, guava, kumquat, loquat, persimmon, raspberries, strawberries
5) apricot kernels, sesame, sunflower
6) hing (asafetida), hops
7) pistachios, bitter almonds
8) _____
9) shrimp
10) squab
11) heart (beef), lamb
12) beer, coffee (bitter), chocolate, ketchup, liquor, tobacco, wine
13) roasting, barbeque, grilling

EARTH

1) millet, sweet potato, yam, teff
2) chickpeas
3) artichoke (Jerusalem), bamboo shoot, calabash, corn on the cob (sweet), crookneck squash, eggplant, kuzu (kudzu), mallow, parsnip, pumpkin, rutabaga, spaghetti squash, winter squash (acorn, butternut, buttercup, hokkaido, Hubbard, etc.), tapioca
4) apple (sweet), banana, breadfruit, cantaloupe, cassava, coconut milk, currants (sweet), dates, figs, grapes (sweet), honeydew melon, mango, mulberries, muskmelon, orange (sweet), papaya, plantain, prunes, raisins, sweet cherries, tangelo, tangerine
5) pumpkin
6) allspice, achiote, anise, cardamom, cinnamon, licorice, turmeric, vanilla
7) almonds, beeches, filberts, pecans, pine nuts, macadamia nuts
8) fresh cheeses (cottage, farmer's, ricotta), ice cream, milk, yogurt (sweet)
9) anchovies (fresh), carp, salmon, sturgeon, swordfish, tuna (canned)
10) pheasant, quail
11) mutton, pancreas (beef), rabbit
12) carob, honey, barley malt, maple syrup, rice syrup, sherbet, sugar (brown and white), sweet chocolate
13) boiling

METAL

1) rice (brown and white), sweet rice, taro potato, white potato
2) great northern, navy, lima, soybean, tempeh, tofu
3) bok choy (white), cabbage, capers, cauliflower, celeriac, celery, chili, Chinese cabbage (Napa), cress, cucumber, daikon, garlic, ginger, iceberg lettuce, kohlrabi, leeks, lotus root, onion, radish, rape, shallots, spinach, turnips, watercress, water chestnuts
4) peach, pear
5) dill
6) basil, cayenne, coriander, fennel, fenugreek, mint, horseradish, black pepper, white pepper, thyme, sage
7) hickory, walnut

8) sharp aged cheeses, egg white
9) cod, flounder, haddock, halibut, herring, perch, scrod
10) turkey
11) beef
12) mochi (cooked molded sweet rice)
13) baking

WATER

1) buckwheat
2) aduki, black soybeans, black turtle, kidney, pinto
3) agar-agar, beets, beet greens, burdock, dulse, hijiki, Irish moss, kelp, kombu, mushrooms, nori, radicchio, red cabbage, salsify, wakame, water chestnuts
4) blackberries, black raspberries, blueberries, boysenberries, concord grapes, cranberries, watermelon
5) chia, black sesame
6) _____
7) chestnuts
8) _____
9) caviar, abalone, bluefish, catfish, clam, crab, cuttlefish, lobster, mussel, octopus, oyster, sardine, scallop, squid, turtle
10) duck
11) ham, kidney, pork
12) coffee (decaffeinated), sesame salt, miso, pickles (brine cured), salt, soy sauce, umeboshi plums, umeboshi vinegar, bancha tea
13) steaming, salt pickling

(Updated and reprinted by permission from The Natural Gourmet *by Annemarie Colbin; originally adapted from John Garvy,* The Five Phases of Food)

According to traditional Chinese medicine:

Wood corresponds to the spring, (when greens sprout), the color green, the eyes and the sense of seeing, the liver and gall bladder organ system, and the sour flavor. The emotions are frustration and irritability when Wood is out of balance, which may occur, if you have ingested excess fats, oils, hot spicy foods, and alcoholic drinks. When Wood is in balance, one is at ease with planning, decision making, and with the changes in life.

Fire corresponds to the summer, the color red, the tongue and the sense of touch, the heart and small intestines organ system, and the bitter flavor. The emotion is over excitability when Fire is out of balance, which may occur if you have ingested excess chocolate, coffee, liquor, or smoked to-bacco. When Fire is in balance, there is the ability to make things happen, and to exhibit and experience joy.

Earth corresponds to the Indian summer, deep yellow and orange colors, the lips and the sense of taste, the stomach and spleen organ system, and the sweet flavor. When Earth is out of balance, the emotion is worry, over-thinking so much one can't see the forest from the trees, which may occur if you have ingested excess icy cold foods and drinks, raw foods, sweets, and carbohydrates, especially those made with refined sugar. When Earth is in balance, one is sympathetic, imaginative, and able to transform life's experiences into wisdom.

Metal corresponds to the autumn (when the trees drop their leaves), the color white, the nose and the sense of smell, the lungs and large intes-tines' organ system, and the pungent or spicy flavor. When Metal is out of balance, the emotion is sadness, which may occur if you have ingested excess dairy, sugar, tart flavors, or smoked, or failed to drink enough water. When Metal is in balance, letting go of attachments is possible. We breathe in, take in life, and accept it. We breathe out and let go of the past.

Water corresponds to the winter, deep blue, purple, brown, black, and gray colors, the ears and hearing, the kidneys and bladder organ system, and the salty flavor. When Water is out of balance, the emotion is fear, and there are panic attacks, which may occur, if you have ingested excess salt, preservatives, or diuretics like coffee. When Water is in balance, one's perseverance, will, and vitality are strong.

Being calm while you eat heightens your senses and improves your diges-tion. Take your time. Forget your worries. Postpone your angry thoughts. In this moment, relax and enjoy the meal. Turn off the TV. Don't watch a violent newscast. Sit down with yourself or with family and friends. Eating on the run is stressful. Breathe deeply. With appreciation for the bounty on your plate, conscious eating enables you to nourish your entire being without overeating.

You may understand your food cravings by studying the "Nourishment and Control Cycles" of the five phases of food.

The Nourishment Cycle

Wood nourishes fire by providing its fuel. The ashes from fire decompose to make (nourish) earth. From the earth come mined metals. When melted, metal becomes (nourishes) water that nourishes (trees and plants) wood.

The "nourishment cycle" shows how one phase produces or increases the energy of the next one. If you found that you ate little from the Fire element, you may want to increase your intake of Fire foods as well as foods from Wood and Earth since Wood supports Fire and a deficient Fire could not nour-

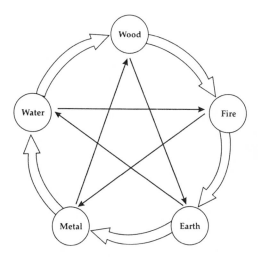

The five elements nourish (empty arrows) and control (dark-pointed arrows) each other according to the above pattern.

ish Earth. For food, look at the Five Phases of Food chart on pages 23-25. Look at the list of foods in the Fire, Wood and Earth phases. Try to include them in your diet and incorporate their cooking methods into your repertoire. Also, continue to eat from the Metal and Water phases, or you will create a deficiency in those phases.

In the "control cycle," one phase decreases the energy of the opposite phase. To balance meals and cravings, a look at the "control" cycle is illuminating, but not always true for everyone.

The Control Cycle

Metal cuts down Wood. If you eat too many pungent and spicy (Metal) foods, you may crave sour foods from the depleted Wood element.

Water puts out Fire. If you eat too many salty (Water) foods, you may crave bitter flavored (Fire) foods.

Wood penetrates Earth. If you eat too many sour foods (Wood), you may crave sweets (Earth).

Fire melts Metal. If you eat too many bitter foods (Fire), you may crave spicy foods (Metal).

Earth can dam up or interrupt the flow of Water. If you eat too many sweet foods (Earth), you may crave salty foods (Water).

Five Phase Substitutions

Use the Five Phases of Food chart on pages 23-25 for making substitutions. Sometimes a recipe calls for a particular ingredient that you are out of or do not like. Look at the chart for a substitute that either preserves the same flavor with another ingredient from the same phase, or find a different ingredient from another food phase to change the flavor. This is easy to illustrate with herbs and spices. For instance, caraway and cumin are both in the Wood phase. You could certainly make a tasty grain dish with either one. Substitute cinnamon from the Earth phase to sweeten the flavor and possibly your mood.

You can substitute green beans, green peppers, broccoli, or zucchini (vegetables from the Wood phase) for each other and achieve the same flavor with the same colored vegetables. You can change the taste and the color by substituting red bell pepper (Fire phase) for any one of the above vegetables.

Substituting similarly colored vegetables for one another preserves the color scheme, and in some instances changes the flavor. Exchange collard greens (Fire phase) for broccoli (Wood phase) in a soup, or chicory (Fire phase) for lettuce in a salad, for example. The same can be done with grains, beans, fruits, nuts, seeds, fish, and even the cooking techniques themselves.

Many authors have devised their own charts for the five phases of food. I have found that most charts are similar, but occasionally there are disagreements as to which phase a particular food belongs. Please use the chart on pages 23-25 as a guide. Use your intuition and your senses. As long as you rotate foods, cooking methods, and serve what looks to be a rainbow of colors on your plate, you are probably following the chart. If you begin to crave certain flavors, then you know you hunger for balance.

To cut down on using table salt, cook with foods from the Water phase: shiitake mushrooms, sea vegetables, red cabbage, beets, and burdock. Try seasoning black turtle beans, kidney beans, adukis, black soybeans, and pinto beans with herbs and spices from the other elements to complement their natural salty quality. See *Brazilian Black Bean Soup, Gypsy Bean Soup,* and *Autumn Minestrone* in chapter 7 for tasty examples.

Cooking Techniques

Note that each phase of the Five Phases of Food chart corresponds to a cooking technique. It is important to use a variety of cooking techniques to bring out all the flavors and textures available.

Cooking times also vary from phase to phase. Are you always eating raw foods or long-simmering soups and stews? Cooking time affects flavor. Flexibility is the key to creative cooking. It may mean that this is the time to invest in a pressure cooker or a wok. As you include all the possible cooking techniques with foods from each of the five phases, the choices and combinations are endless and self-generating.

To plan a balanced meal, select complementary proteins, such as grains with beans or fish. Decide on the cooking method and ingredients. Decide if you'd rather cook the vegetables alone in a side dish, or as part of the main dish. You can create simple, balanced meals by cooking the beans, grains, and vegetables separately and seasoning them differently. Add a dessert, too. Just be sure there is equal representation from each phase of food over a three-day period.

Eco Tip: If you are baking a squash, you could also use the oven heat to bake a pastry, beans, or fish, or roast nuts, grains, or potatoes. You could bake the whole meal, heat a leftover, or just use the available heat to roast some grains for another day.

Catch 22: It is enjoyable to sit down to a meal with several foods cooked in a variety of ways. A one-pot meal is easy to clean up, but a stew containing more than seven ingredients cancels out the unique flavor of each ingredient. Even if all five food phases are represented, instead of balance, there is chaos.

The five phase system goes well beyond the scope of food and into Chinese philosophy and medicine. For a more accurate diagnosis of one's health, moods and cravings using the five phase theory, consult a practitioner of Chinese herbal medicine or an acupuncturist.

Recipe First Aid

In cooking, it is vital to understand how to bring out the best flavor in each dish. Sometimes, however, improvisations don't work and we need to fix them. Here is an excerpt from Annemarie Colbin's Book, *The Natural Gourmet (p. 46):*

If you end up with seasoning problems, there are a few things you can do to repair the dish. If it is:

❖ too salty: add liquid (water, stock), or fat (oil, tahini, butter), or something bland (potatoes, grain, bread), or wash off the salt.

❖ too bitter: add fat, or something sweet (rice syrup, fruit juice), or something sour; avoid salt, which will intensify the bitter taste.

❖ too sweet: add liquid, fat, or salt.

- too spicy: add fat, or something sweet, or something bland, or something sour.
- too sour: add fat, salt, liquid, or something sweet.
- burnt: use only the upper unburnt part if grain, bean, or stew; if it's soup, however, discard it. Some things cannot be fixed.

Feel Free

In each of the following chapters, there are many variations on each recipe. Feel free to use the ingredient list as a guide, or make up your own proportions. I did. I selected fresh, seasonal, organic vegetables, rinsed and chopped them, and then measured them and wrote down the amounts. Have fun! Use the recipes as they are because they are really scrumptious, or create your own versions.

4

Quick Meals for Busy People

From start to finish, these quick meals and snacks take five to twenty minutes. Here are simple recipes and time-saving tips for quick cooking natural foods. *Also, check the list at the end of this chapter for more quick recipes with international flair that appear in other chapters.*

Time-saving Tips

* ❖ Have a well stocked refrigerator, freezer, and pantry. Keep on hand several choices of quick cooking ingredients, salad vegetables and dressings, fresh and dried fruits, and herbs and spices. Consult "Cornucopia of Quick Cooking Organic Ingredients" on page 34.

* ❖ Be aware of what you have in stock and where to find it.

* ❖ Are you ready to cook, but your kitchen isn't? Clear the sink and counter to be ready to rinse and chop vegetables.

* ❖ Give yourself sufficient lighting. Do you have a window, skylight, or light over the stove, counter, and sink?

* ❖ Place cooking oils, herbs, and spices an arm's distance away from the stove. Keep them close, but away from the heat, preferably in a cool, dark place.

* ❖ Leave a small jar of sea salt next to the stove. Many dishes require a pinch of sea salt.

* ❖ Is your vegetable knife sharp? A dull knife makes chopping a drag and slows you down. Steak knives are inappropriate and cumbersome. Sharpen stainless steel and carbon steel vegetable knives daily. Ceramic knives never dull, rust, or corrode. You won't waste time sharpening them. (To order ceramic knives, see appendix 4.)

* ❖ Presoak longer cooking grains and beans.

- Put cooking water on to boil first. Then, rinse and measure grains, chop vegetables for soup, or get the pasta.
- Rinse grains in the morning to cook in the evening.
- Make extra for busy days. Always starting from scratch can be challenging when you are on a tight schedule.
- Give yourself a break from cooking once and awhile, and stock some natural fast foods such as tofu hot dogs, ramen, tempeh burgers, bean dips, cookies, etc.
- Keep handy snack foods like popcorn, corn chips and salsa, nuts, seeds, fresh and dried fruit, salad vegetables, bread, etc.
- Be flexible.
- Be impulsive.

Common Improvisations For All Recipes

1. **For richer flavors**, sauté any vegetable before adding to soups, stews, and sauces.
2. **Change a vegetable dish to a quick one-pot meal.** Add a quick cooking complete protein — fish, tofu and noodles, or leftover cooked beans and grains — to any vegetable soup or stew.
3. **Substitute similar or different colored vegetables.**
4. **Substitute noodles for grains** or vice versa.
5. **Change the seasonings** of a dish by adding or changing the herbs, spices, or salty seasonings. See "Soups with International Themes" in this chapter for ethnic herb and spice combinations.
6. **Change the cooking techniques**; simmer instead of stir-fry, for example. Keep the ingredients the same, or change some.
7. **Alternate salty seasonings:** umeboshi vinegar, tamari, shoyu, sea salt, and Bragg Liquid Aminos.
8. **Substitute leeks, onions, shallots, and scallions** for each other.
9. **Make any ingredient larger or smaller in proportion.**
10. **Substitute leafy greens** for each other: bok choy for Chinese cabbage, etc.
11. **Substitute nuts and seeds** for each other: almonds for walnuts, etc.
12. **Season to taste.**
13. **Substitute to suit your mood,** likes, and what you have in stock.

≋ *Free Play* ≋

Create a soup with up to five quick cooking ingredients.

Choose between vegetables, noodles, and tofu. You can create different flavors with cooking liquids (see page 15), oils, herbs, and spices. See "International Themes" below. The combinations are endless. Use your imagination and what you have in stock.

Choose a combination of seasonal vegetables with different or similar colors, shapes, flavors, and textures.

Using more than five major ingredients (excluding sea vegetables, spices, and herbs) complicates the recipe, takes longer to prepare, and compromises the special contribution of each ingredient.

Keep it simple. For example, start with one vegetable and one herb, such as zucchini and basil, or two vegetables and one herb, such as zucchini, broccoli, and basil.

Soups With International Themes

Oriental:

Simmer vegetables in stock or water and then add seasonings or sauté vegetables before simmering in 1 teaspoon-tablespoon sesame, peanut or toasted sesame oil. Then add any of the following:

❖ Add 1-2 tablespoons of mirin or wine;

❖ One-inch piece of grated or sliced ginger;

❖ 1 tablespoon of tamari, Bragg Liquid Aminos, miso, or shoyu;

❖ Cilantro or chopped scallions, as garnish;

❖ For hotter Thai or Szechwan styles, hot pepper oil or crushed red pepper to taste;

❖ Tofu, sea vegetables, shrimp, or other fishes.

Italian:

Simmer vegetable(s) and then add seasonings, or sauté vegetables first in extra virgin olive oil and garlic and then simmer them in the soup stock.

❖ Add one or more of the following herbs: basil, oregano, marjoram, mint, thyme, rosemary, bay leaves, saffron, Italian parsley, sage, pepper. My favorite combination for Italian dishes is garlic, thyme, basil, and oregano. Try basil, black pepper, and garlic. Another classic combination is Italian parsley, bay leaf, thyme, garlic, and pepper.

❖ Italian soups frequently include beans and pasta. For quick meals, have leftover beans and pasta available.

Indian:

Simmer vegetables and then season with curry powder, or sauté vegetables with the following spices in sesame or extra virgin olive oil: cumin seeds, ginger, chilies, turmeric, coriander seed and powder, mustard seeds, cloves, cinnamon, cardamom, pepper, dill seed, and weed. Then simmer in water or stock.

❖ Season or garnish with fresh mint or cilantro.

❖ Include red lentils, mung beans, chick peas, and green peas in the recipe. Fresh peas and red lentils are best for quick meals.

Mexican:

Simmer vegetables and then add seasonings, or sauté vegetables in extra virgin olive oil, garlic, and cumin seeds. After the vegetables are tender, add oregano, pepper, basil, chili powder, or cilantro.

❖ Mexican soups also have beans. Be sure to have precooked: kidney, pinto, or anasazi beans on hands for quick Mexican soups or stews.

French:

Simmer vegetables and then add seasonings, or sauté vegetables in garlic, bay leaves, cloves, cumin seed, celery seed, or fennel seed, and then simmer in stock.

❖ Other herbal options are dill weed, marjoram, pepper, coriander, rosemary, mint, thyme, sage, mustard, basil, nutmeg, parsley, horseradish, paprika, savory, and tarragon.

❖ A simple soup may have one vegetable, such as zucchini, with garlic, parsley, and fresh ground pepper.

Cornucopia of Quick Cooking Ingredients

Grains

couscous	popping corn	kasha (buckwheat groats)
quinoa	spelt cous	bulgar
teff		

Couscous, quinoa, bulgar, spelt cous, and kasha (buckwheat groats) are quick cooking grains with a similar texture. Cook them in the following ratio: 1 part grain: 2 parts liquid, with the exception of spelt cous, which should be cooked in a ratio of 1 part grain: 1½ parts liquid. Cook teff with 3 times as much water as grain. Feel free to cook teff in combination with other grains, too. Feel free to substitute one grain for any other in any salad or pilaf recipe.

Pasta

Numerous kinds of pastas made from different grains, in many colors, shapes, and sizes, flavored with different vegetables, herbs, and spices are available.

GRAINS	COLORS	SHAPES	FLAVORS
wheat	brown	spirals	carrots
spelt	tan	elbows	tomatoes
kamut	beige	thin	spinach
corn	yellow	thick	wild yam
quinoa	red	wide	mugwort
buckwheat	green	cylinders	curry
rice	white	long	lemon
amaranth		short	pepper
soy			garlic, basil

Sea vegetables

dulse	arame	nori

Beans and Soy foods

red lentils	tempeh	tofu

Fish

For recipes, see chapter 10.

Cooking Vegetables

GREENS		REDS	YELLOWS
watercress	peas	tomatoes	corn on the cob
celery	snow peas	red peppers	Jerusalem artichokes
broccoli	peppers	red onions	yellow squash
mustard greens	escarole	red radishes	yellow peppers
greenbeans	spinach		patty pan squash
zucchini	asparagus		
bok choy	collards		
mizuna	tat soi		

REDS & GREENS	WHITES	GREENS & WHITES
beet greens	turnips	leeks
red chard	shallots	scallions
	mushrooms	Chinese cabbage
		green Swiss chard
		bok choy

Any root vegetable will cook quickly if sliced thinly.

Salty Seasonings

sea salt
gomasio (sesame salt)
tamari
vegetable salt
miso (mellow and aged varieties:
   barley, rice, chickpea, aduki bean,
   and black soy bean)

sauerkraut
pickles
Bragg Liquid Aminos
shoyu

umeboshi whole plum,
   paste, and vinegar
olives

Miscellaneous

prepared mustard
tofu mayonnaise
tahini
mochi
chips
salsa
whole wheat and corn tortillas
marinated sun-dried tomatoes

arrowroot
kudzu
nutritional yeast
relish
bagels
frozen vegetables

nut butters
jams
crackers
rice cakes
tomato sauce

Magical Transformations With Leftovers and Garnishes

1. Add one more ingredient, such as an herb, spice, or vegetable, to magically transform a leftover into something new.

2. Add a fresh garnish, such as a sprig of parsley, watercress, chopped scallions, toasted seeds, etc.

3. With extra beans, you can:

   ❖ add them to soups, stews, and salads;

   ❖ marinate them;

   ❖ serve them in tortillas with shredded lettuce, carrots, and chopped cilantro, topped off with salsa;

❖ refry beans with vegetables, herbs, and spices;

❖ puree beans with herbs, spices, vegetables, and nut and seed butters to transform them into dips, sauces, and spreads.

4. With extra noodles, you can:

❖ create a stir-fry with vegetables, tofu, tempeh, or fish;

❖ add them to soups and salads;

❖ top them with a sauce.

5. With extra grains, you can:

❖ add them to salads, soups and nori rolls;

❖ add more water, soy milk, or Rice Dream drink, cinnamon, vanilla, chopped dates, or other dried fruits to leftover cooked grains to make an excellent hot breakfast cereal. Also, you can add Indian spices, such as coriander and cinnamon, with raisins, currants and sucanat. Add some slivered almonds, too;

❖ briefly steam or pressure cook them in a ceramic pressure cooker in sert and garnish them with toasted seeds or nuts, gomasio, chopped scallions, chopped parsley, or roasted sea vegetables, such as nori or kelp powder;

❖ top them with a sauce;

❖ make a quick vegetable fried rice with leftover brown rice. Heat wok. Add sesame oil, tamari, mirin, ginger, garlic, and stir-fry *fast* cooking vegetables, such as bok choy, celery, and scallions. Then add and mix in rice. (Other leftover grains can also be refried. For example, you can sauté kasha with olive oil, mushrooms, and onions);

❖ leave leftovers out to sour. Use them as a starter to make sour dough bread.

6. With extra soup, you can:

❖ thicken it with kudzu or arrowroot to transform it into a stew or sauce;

❖ add a new garnish, vegetable, bean, grain, noodle, herb, or spice.

7. With extra stew, you can:

❖ add more cooking liquid and thin it out to a soup;

❖ add a thickener, like diluted kudzu or arrowroot, and transform it into a sauce.

8. With leftover cooked fish, you can:

❖ make a soup, salad, stew, dip, or sauce;

❖ make a sandwich or stuff it into a pita with sprouts and lettuce.

9. With leftover steamed vegetables you can:

❖ cut them up and add them to soups or stews;

❖ puree them into sauces, spreads, or dips.

10. With leftover stir-fry vegetables, you can:

❖ add them to a sauté with tofu, tempeh, seitan, noodles, or grains;

❖ add more water and turn them into a soup or sauce.

You can do many seemingly obvious things to magically transform leftovers, too:

❖ use a different serving bowl or platter;

❖ heat and serve with different garnishes or accompaniments, such as muffin or sandwiches.

Chinese Cabbage and Watercress Soup

1 quart of water
1 3-inch piece of dulse
1 bunch of watercress
2 large leaves of Chinese
(Napa) cabbage or bok choy
1 tablespoon miso, Bragg
Liquid Aminos, or tamari

OPTIONAL:

Garnish with scallions; add
deep fried or raw tofu

SERVES 4
TIME: 6 MINUTES

Simmer dulse and water for 5 minutes. Meanwhile, rinse and cut the watercress and cabbage leaves into bite-sized pieces. When you add them to the hot broth, they turn bright green. The soup is ready for seasoning. Stir in tamari or mash in miso. Taste it. Add more water if it is too salty or a bit more tamari or miso if it needs more salt. Serve immediately.

Improvisations

1. For color, add other colored vegetables, like sliced red tomatoes, grated carrots, yellow summer squash, or white mushrooms.

2. Italian style: change the vegetable combination to zucchini, tomatoes, and chives. Season with oregano or basil and sea salt. You can first sauté vegetables in garlic and olive oil, too.

Japanese Noodles in Tamari Broth

Here's another simple soup ready in 10 minutes.

1 package Japanese soba or udon noodles (7-8 ounces)
1 quart water
1 tablespoon tamari
3 scallions, thinly sliced

SERVES 4
TIME: 10 MINUTES

Boil noodles. Meanwhile, slice the scallions. After 8-10 minutes, taste the noodles to see if they are tender. If so, stir in the tamari, and taste the broth. Serve the soup garnished with the scallions.

Improvisations

1. You can add tofu or other quick cooking vegetables.

2. Even faster: If you have leftover cooked noodles, simply put them in water with tamari. Bring to a boil, taste, and serve.

3. Change the nationality of the dish by using American noodles, such as spelt or kamut angel hair varieties, parsley and garlic pasta, vegetable spirals.

4. Transform the water, tamari, and scallions into a quick sauce; serve over the noodles (see next recipe).

Quick and Easy Vegetable Sauce

Turn a noodle soup upside down. Transform a vegetable soup to a sauce and pour it over noodles.

SERVES 4
TIME: 5 MINUTES

Make ¼ of the previous recipe or any quick vegetable soup recipe. Bring the tamari and water to a boil. Dilute 1 tablespoon of arrowroot powder or kudzu in ¼ cup of cold water. Stir it into the tamari broth. Add chopped scallions. Taste it and adjust the seasonings. Serve over cooked grains, noodles, or fish.

Improvisation

You can add vegetables, spices and/or herbs.

Colorful Ginger Noodle Soup

Timing is the key in this recipe. Get the noodles started, and add the other ingredients as soon as they are washed and sliced.

8 ounces noodles, such as Japanese udon, or soba, or angel hair varieties
2 quarts of water
1 large carrot, sliced in match sticks
2 large collard greens, cut into thin, bite-sized pieces
1 small red onion, peeled and diced
4¼-inch slices of peeled ginger
1 3-inch piece of dulse
tamari or miso to taste

SERVES 4
TIME: 10 MINUTES

Boil noodles for 2 minutes. Add dulse and ginger. Peel, dice, and add the onion. Wash, slice, and add the other vegetables. Simmer all the ingredients together for about 5 minutes, or until the noodles are tender, the carrots are bright orange, and the collards are bright green. Taste the carrots. (Simmer soup longer if you want the carrots softer.) Add the tamari or mash in the miso. Stir, taste, and add more ginger juice or tamari, if desired.

Improvisations

1. Add grated ginger or ginger juice to the soup. (Grate fresh ginger in a ginger grater or onto a cutting board or piece of cheese cloth. Squeeze the grated ginger directly into the soup.) This will make the soup spicier.

2. Omit the onions; garnish with fresh chopped scallions and bean sprouts.

3. Simmer bay leaves or other herbs and/or spices with ginger.

4. Exclude noodles for a lighter version; include cooked beans for a heavier version.

Udon Noodle Soup

A piping hot ginger-noodle soup

1 quart of water
4 ounces udon noodles
⅛ cup arame or a 3-inch
piece of any sea vegetable
1 2-inch knob of ginger,
peeled and sliced
2 shiitake mushrooms,
fresh or dried
1 tablespoon shoyu,
tamari, ume vinegar, Bragg
Liquid Aminos, or miso
1 bunch scallions, chopped

OPTIONAL:
Add 1 teaspoon of mirin
to the broth

SERVES 4-6
TIME: 10 MINUTES

Boil water, add udon noodles, shiitake mushrooms, arame, and ginger. (Rinse arame and discard any shells prior to adding it.) Simmer for about 10 minutes or until noodles are done. Add tamari and taste. Serve in individual bowls, garnished with chopped scallions.

Improvisations

1. Sauté onions, carrots, celery, or other green leafy vegetables, such as mustard greens, broccoli, bok choy, or collards. Add them to piping hot ginger broth.

2. Use leftover noodles: divide them equally into separate soup bowls. Ladle hot ginger-tamari broth on top and garnish with scallions.

3. Presoak dried shiitake mushrooms. Slice them and then add them to the soup before serving so that everyone gets some.

4. Mushrooms are in. You can use shiitakes, as I have, or try regular mushrooms or exotic varieties, such as oyster, chanterelles, or porcini. Sauté mushrooms with garlic before adding them to hot broth, if you like.

Greens and Grains

A calcium-rich quick dish

1 teaspoon sesame oil
1 bunch kale, sliced
1 tablespoon umeboshi
vinegar*
1 cup kasha
2 cups boiling water

Heat pan. Add oil. Sauté kale for about 3 minutes or until it turns bright green. Add umeboshi vinegar* and stir-fry for 1 minute. Stir in kasha. Turn off heat before adding boiling water. Add boiling water. Simmer 10 minutes, or until water is absorbed.

SERVES 4-6
TIME: 15 MINUTES

Improvisation

For a delicious variation and one-pot meal, substitute cous cous for kasha and add ½ pound cubed tofu.

---

* If you don't have umeboshi vinegar, go ahead and make this dish anyway. You could substitute tamari, sea salt and fresh squeezed lemon, or wine or raspberry vinegar.

Quinoa Veggie Pilaf

Quinoa is the only grain that is a complete protein.
Cook it with vegetables for a quick, hearty, one-pot meal.

3 cups of water
1½ cups of quinoa,
thoroughly rinsed*
pinch of sea salt

OPTION #1
1 large carrot, sliced
in match sticks
1 stalk of celery, sliced
in thin diagonals
1 tablespoon of dill seeds
or cumin seeds

OPTION #2
1 clove of elephant garlic
or 2-3 regular garlic cloves
1 stalk of celery, sliced thin
1 large leek, sliced thin
in half moons

OPTION #3
Sauté vegetables first with 1
tablespoon of olive oil; stir
in the dry roasted quinoa
before adding the boiled
water.

SERVES 4-6
TIME: 15 MINUTES

Boil water. Rinse the quinoa thoroughly in a strainer. Dry roast wet quinoa, carrots, celery, dill seeds, and sea salt in a cast-iron skillet or stainless steel fry pan for 5 minutes, or until the quinoa begins to pop and smell like sesame seeds. Turn off the heat when you add the boiling water so it won't splatter.** Turn the heat back on. Cover and simmer for 10 minutes, or until the water is absorbed.

Improvisations

1. Quinoa is delicious in a salad. Cook the quinoa by itself and add mixed, fresh-chopped vegetables, oil, vinegar, and herbs (such as tomatoes, parsley, mint, red onion, cucumber, celery, olive oil, and ume vinegar.)

2. Cook quinoa with other quick cooking grains with or without vegetables. See next recipe.

---

* There is a naturally bitter residue on the outside coating of each grain of quinoa. Rinsing quinoa easily removes it. (If possible, rinse the quinoa in the morning. Leave it in a strainer in the sun. It may save you dry roasting time).

** Any time you add hot liquids to hot grain, turn off or remove the pot from the heat for safety's sake.

Quinoa Pepper Pilaf

1 cup quinoa, rinsed
1 large leek, sliced
1 clove elephant garlic or 2
cloves regular garlic, sliced
¼ teaspoon sea salt
1 cup couscous
2 peppers (same or different
colors), sliced
4 cups boiling water

SERVES 4-6
TIME: 10 MINUTES

Rinse and dry roast the quinoa with sea salt, garlic, and leeks for 2 minutes, or until it smells nutty. Add the couscous and peppers and dry roast for 2 minutes. Turn off the heat. Add boiling water. Simmer 5 minutes, or until the water is absorbed.

Improvisations

1. Use all couscous or quinoa.

2. Use celery instead of peppers.

Spanish Dancer

This recipe is a quick, delicious variation on the previous recipe, Quinoa Pepper Pilaf. With a little help from precooked beans, quickly steamed broccoli, and salsa, this recipe easily satisfies.

2 cups water, boiled
1 cup quinoa, rinsed
pinch of sea salt
1 tablespoon extra virgin
olive oil
3 cloves garlic, peeled
and sliced
1 red onion, diced or
sliced thin
1 cup cooked beans (anasazi,
pinto, kidney, or black)
pint of salsa

SERVES 4
TIME: 15 MINUTES

Boil water. Dry roast the quinoa and sea salt. Add oil. Stir in one at a time: garlic, red onion, and cooked beans. Turn off the heat. Add boiling water. Simmer 10 minutes. Serve topped with salsa, with bright green steamed broccoli on the side.

Improvisation

In summer, cook quinoa with tomatoes, green beans, zucchini, green pepper, onion, garlic, cilantro, and oregano, instead of adding salsa.

Hot or Cold Salad

This is another variation on the **Quinoa Veggie Pilaf** *from page 44. To change this into a salad, simply dice and add vegetables to the cooled cooked grain. Make a dressing with olive oil and vinegar or lemon juice.*

2 cups water
1 celery stalk, sliced thin
1 red onion, peeled and diced
1 carrot, sliced in match sticks
1 red pepper, cut into bite-sized squares
1 clove elephant garlic or 2-3 regular garlic cloves
1 cup whole wheat couscous
pinch of sea salt

OPTIONAL:
1 teaspoon-1 tablespoon extra virgin olive oil for sautéing the vegetables

SERVES 4
TIME: 12 MINUTES

Boil water. Meanwhile, slice the vegetables and garlic. Dry roast the couscous and sea salt. (Optional: you can add olive oil and sauté the vegetables and couscous before adding boiling water.) Stir the vegetables into the dry roasted grain. Turn off the heat when you add the boiling water so it won't splatter. Turn the heat back on after the water is added. Cover and simmer for 10 minutes or until the water is absorbed.

THE QUICK & EASY ORGANIC GOURMET

Juicy Ginger Vegetables

This dish is mildly spicy.
Use it as a topping for grains or noodles.

2 teaspoon dried (cut and
sifted) burdock*
1 teaspoon toasted sesame,
sesame, olive, peanut, or
safflower oil
2 teaspoons mirin
2 onions, sliced
3 cloves garlic, peeled and
sliced
2-inch piece of ginger, peeled
and grated
5 leaves bok choy, cut into
bite-sized pieces
²/₃ cup water, vegetable stock,
or noodle stock
2 tablespoons shoyu,
umeboshi vinegar, tamari,
or to taste

OPTION #1:
For a hotter, spicier taste, add
more grated ginger, ½ teaspoon or more of crushed red
pepper, or a pinch or more of
cayenne.

OPTION #2:
Garnish with bean sprouts or
scallions

OPTION #3:
Add celery and broccoli, too.
Stir-fry them for a couple of
minutes before adding bok
choy.

SERVES 4
TIME: 20 MINUTES

Heat a wok. Add oil, mirin, onions, garlic, ginger, and burdock. Cover and simmer for 5 minutes, or until burdock is tender. Taste burdock, and if it is as tender as you like it, add the bok choy. Stir-fry bok choy for a minute, until it turns bright green. Add tamari, stir, and taste. Adjust the seasonings, if necessary.

Improvisations

1. You could use fresh burdock; it just takes longer to cook.

2. Add tofu, tempeh, cooked grains, pasta, or fish.

3. Add cashews, other nuts, or seeds.

4. Add a little more water, thickening it with kudzu or arrowroot to make a sauce.

---

* Presoak burdock in water for 10 minutes while you slice the other vegetables. You can substitute another quicker cooking vegetable for burdock, such as Chinese cabbage, red pepper, or snow peas.

Ginger Tempeh

Mitoku's mirin is the key ingredient here.
It adds a sweet flavor that everyone loves.
This dish is fast, tasty, and versatile.

1 8- or 10-ounce
package tempeh*
2-inch knob of ginger, peeled
and sliced into 8 ¼-inch
pieces
1 teaspoon sesame oil or
extra virgin olive oil
(optional)
1 tablespoon mirin
1 tablespoon tamari or
shoyu
¾ cup of water
Garnish with a few sprigs of
chopped parsley or scallions

SERVES 3 AS A MAIN DISH
TIME: 10 MINUTES

Cut the tempeh in half and then cut each half again lengthwise to create 4 thin slabs. Spread the ginger slices out onto the bottom of a heavy-bottomed fry pan. Heat the skillet on medium high. Add the oil, mirin, and tamari.

Place the tempeh slabs on top of the ginger. Fry for a few minutes until almost all of the oil is absorbed. Flip the tempeh over and add water. Cook for a few minutes until tempeh absorbs the water and is brown on both sides.

Serve garnished with fresh chopped parsley or scallions. Serve in sandwiches with lettuce, tomatoes, sprouts, red onion, tofu mayonnaise, mustard greens and/or mustard.

Improvisations

1. You can use tofu instead of tempeh.

2. Cut cooked tempeh into cubes for a salad.

3. You can use the ginger, oil, mirin, and tamari mixture as a marinade or for a stir-fry for the tempeh, tofu, or fish.

4. Oil-free version: Omit the oil. Change the proportions of the other ingredients: 1 teaspoon mirin, 1-2 teaspoon's tamari, 2-3 slices of ginger, and ¼ cup of water. Simmer covered for 5 minutes.

---

* Tempeh comes in 8- and 10-ounce packages and in many flavors: soy, quinoa, sea vegetable, three-grain, garden vegetable. Use one with a grain for a quick dish with a complete protein.

Stir-fry Vegetables with Tofu

Serve over grains or noodles (any kind).

1 teaspoon-tablespoon toasted sesame oil
1 tablespoon mirin
1 tablespoon tamari or shoyu
1 large clove of elephant garlic or 3 regular garlic cloves
1 small turnip, sliced thin (match sticks)
1 large leek, rinsed and sliced
1 stalk celery, sliced
1 small pepper (any color), sliced
2 leaves Chinese cabbage, sliced in bite-sized pieces
1 pound firm or extra firm tofu, cut into bite-sized pieces

OPTIONAL:
Add fresh grated ginger

SERVES 4
TIME: 10 MINUTES

Heat wok. Add oil, tamari, mirin, garlic, and turnip. Stir-fry 2 minutes. Add leek and celery. Stir-fry for one minute. Add pepper, Chinese cabbage, and tofu. Stir-fry to coat all the ingredients with the seasonings of the pan. Taste and adjust the seasonings, if desired.

Improvisations

1. You can substitute tempeh, shrimp, or seitan for tofu.

2. If you are not in a hurry, you may marinate the tofu for 10 minutes in oil, mirin, tamari, garlic, ginger, and a fresh minced bunch of cilantro, before adding it to the stir-fry.

3. Go Italian: Sauté the tofu in olive oil with tomatoes, peppers, green beans, and zucchini, and season it with basil, thyme, oregano, and sea salt.

4. Add cooked brown rice or nuts.

Tofu Stroganoff

Very rich, cholesterol-free, and great for everyday and special occasions.

1 tablespoon sesame oil
2 onions (2 cups), sliced
2 cloves (2 teaspoons) minced garlic
8 ounces (2½ cups) sliced mushrooms, or 4-6 cups if you like lots of mushrooms
¼ cup finely chopped parsley, tightly packed
1 pound firm or extra firm tofu, or 2 cups seitan, cut into bite-sized pieces
½ cup almonds, ground
1½ cups water or noodle stock
2 tablespoons barley miso
2 teaspoons umeboshi paste, or to taste
2-3 cups cooked parsley garlic ribbons, fettuccini, or other pasta

OPTIONAL:
Reserve the pasta cooking water for making the almond milk and dissolving miso.

SERVES 4-6
TIME: 20 MINUTES

Heat a large stock pot. Add the oil. Add and sauté garlic and onions for 2 minutes. Add mushrooms and parsley. Sauté for about 5 minutes until the mushrooms are soft and juicy. Add tofu or seitan. Simmer vegetables. Grind the almonds in a food processor. Then add water or noodle stock, miso, and umeboshi paste. Blend well and add mixture to vegetables. Simmer for 5 minutes. Taste and adjust the seasonings. Serve over cooked noodles, or mix in cooked noodles.

Improvisation

Add a little more umeboshi paste and omit the miso.

Sweet-and-Sour Tofu

It's fabulous served over pasta or grains.

1 pound firm or extra firm tofu, sliced into bite-sized pieces
2 yellow summer squashes, sliced into half-moons (3 cups)
1 large onion (3 cups), sliced
3⅓ cups water
⅓ cup barley malt
4 tablespoons tamari or shoyu
2 tablespoons rice vinegar
2 tablespoons kudzu

Simmer onions, summer squash, tofu, and 3 cups of water for 15 minutes, or until vegetables are as tender as you like them. Stir in barley malt, rice vinegar, and tamari. Dilute kudzu in ⅓ cup of cold water. Stir it into the sweet-and-sour vegetables. Taste and adjust the seasonings, if desired, by adding more tamari for a saltier flavor, more barley malt for sweetness, or more rice vinegar for a more sour taste.

SERVES 4-6
TIME: 20 MINUTES

Cashew Carrot Curry Sauce

Rich cashew milk, sweet carrots, and flavorful curry
make a delicious sauce without dairy or salt.

2 ½ cups whole cashews*
3⅓ cups water
1 tablespoon sesame oil
1 large Spanish onion, sliced,
or 2 cups onions
2 pounds (6 cups) carrots, sliced
2 zucchinis, sliced
2 tablespoons curry powder
or to taste

SERVES 4-6
TIME: 5 MINUTES FOR
PRESSURE COOKING,
OR 15 MINUTES FOR SAUTE-
SIMMER

Grind the cashews into a meal in a food processor. Add 3 cups of water and blend until creamy to make cashew milk.

Heat a large stock pot. Add sesame oil and sauté the onions for 2-5 minutes. Add carrots, zucchini, cashew milk, and ⅓ cup water to the vegetables. Simmer for at least 5 minutes, or until the carrots are tender. Add curry powder to taste.

Or:

Heat sesame oil in a pressure cooker. Add the onions and sauté for 2 minutes. Add the carrots, zucchini, ⅓ cup of water, and about ½ cup of the cashew milk and pressure cook for 2 minutes, maintaining high pressure. Let the pressure come down naturally, or put the cooker inthe sink under cold running water to reduce pressure quickly. Open the lid. If the carrots are not tender, lock the lid back in place and allow them to steam in the residual heat for another minute or two. Stir in the rest of the cashew milk and curry powder. Taste and add more curry powder, if desired.

If you are serving this sauce on pasta or grains, it may need more curry powder. Also, try serving this sauce on fresh-sliced cucumbers or other vegetables.

---

* Avoid cashew pieces. They are often rancid.

Cashew Florentine Sauce

Here's a delicious variation on the Cashew Carrot Curry Sauce.

1½ cups whole cashews
3 cups water
1 large Spanish onion, sliced,
or 2 cups onions
1 tablespoon sesame oil
1 pound (3 cups) carrots, sliced
2 quarts spinach leaves,
rinsed
3 tablespoons curry powder,
or to taste

Follow the same directions as *Cashew Carrot Curry Sauce* on the previous page, with the following exceptions: grind the cashews into meal in a food processor. Add 2 cups of water and blend until creamy.

Heat sesame oil in a pressure cooker. Add the onions and sauté for 2 minutes. Add the carrots, spinach, 1 cup of water. Pressure cook for 2 minutes, maintaining high pressure.

SERVES 4-6
TIME: 5 MINUTES FOR
PRESSURE COOKING, OR
15 MINUTES FOR SAUTÉ-SIMMER

Almond Pesto

Wonderfully simple and dairy-free, this pesto is great on spaghetti.

²⁄₃ cups almonds
10 cloves garlic
½ cup water
⅓ cup umeboshi vinegar
¼ cup extra virgin olive oil
1 quart green or purple basil leaves, rinsed

Grind the nuts in a food processor. Add basil, olive oil, umeboshi vinegar, garlic, and water. Puree. Taste and adjust the seasonings, if desired.

MAKES 1 QUART
TIME: 5 MINUTES

Pasta Salada with Pesto

12 ounces pasta, such as dried
kamut, spelt, or whole wheat
spaghetti, elbows, or spirals.
¼ cup ground almonds
½ cup ground sunflower seeds
1 bunch (2 cups) tightly
packed fresh green or purple
basil leaves, rinsed
5 cloves garlic
¹/₈ cup extra virgin olive oil
¹/₈ cup umeboshi vinegar
¼ cup water

SERVES 4
TIME: 15 MINUTES

Boil 4 quarts of water. Add pasta and cook until tender (10-15 minutes, depending on the variety. Follow the instructions on the package or your intuition). Taste it to see if it is ready. When done, drain the pasta and save the cooking water for stock, if you like. Run cold water over the pasta to rinse it and prevent it from sticking.

In a food processor, grind the sunflower seeds and almonds into a meal. Add the garlic, basil, water, olive oil, and umeboshi vinegar to blend. Taste and adjust the seasonings, if desired.

Put the cooked pasta in a large serving bowl or individual serving bowls. Pour and mix the pesto into the pasta. Serve.

THE QUICK & EASY ORGANIC GOURMET

Another Great Pesto

Here is another version!

2 cups pignola nuts, ground
4 cups fresh basil leaves,
rinsed
3 cloves garlic
1 1/3 cups water
2 tablespoons and 2
teaspoons
sweet brown rice miso or
mellow miso

SERVES 4
TIME: 5 MINUTES

Follow instructions for boiling water and cooking pasta in previous recipe. Grind the nuts in a food processor. Add basil, miso, garlic, and water. Puree. Taste and adjust the seasonings, if desired.

Improvisations

1. Raw or roasted walnuts can replace pignola nuts.

2. Substitute raw sunflower seeds and walnuts for pignola nuts.

3. See the *Cilantro Pesto Pasta* on page 77.

Colorful and Crunchy

1/2 cup pumpkin seeds,
roasted
1 cup red cabbage, sliced thin
1 cup green cabbage, sliced
thin
2 teaspoons toasted
sesame oil
1/2 teaspoon rice vinegar
1 teaspoon tamari

SERVES 3-4
TIME: 5 MINUTES

Dry roast the pumpkin seeds in a dry skillet till they pop and are aromatic (about 2-3 minutes). Remove from heat, and mix all the ingredients together in a large bowl. Taste and adjust the seasonings.

Improvisations

1. Americanize (like coleslaw): Mix tofu mayonnaise (nayonnaise) and cabbage together.

2. Add red onion and parsley or carrot and peppers to either version.

There are more quick recipes in the following chapters:

Chapter 5: "The Art of the Stir-fry and Sauté"

Szechwan Broccoli
Japanese Fried Rice
Oriental Express
Green Noodle Sauté
Fat-free
Sauté of Garden Greens
Country-style Broccoli
Fragrant Indian Cabbage
Curried Tempeh with Tomatoes
Refried Beans

Chapter 6: "Around the World with Salads and Dressings"

Italiano Arugola Salad With Cauliflower
Cilantro Pesto Pasta
Spinach and Potato Salad With Capers
Easy Potato Salad
Japanese Rainbow Salad
Ruby Red Salad
Oriental Vegetable Salad
Mediterranean Tofu Dip
3-Bean Dill Salad
3-Bean Summer Salad with Cilantro and Capers
Lemony Carrot and Radish Salad

Chapter 7: "Secrets of Soups, Stews, and Sauces"

Quick Ginger Scallion Sauce
Mushroom Leek Sauce
Creamy Mushroom Basil Sauce
Vegetable Gravy

Chapter 8: "Calcium Without the Cow"

A Taste of Japan
Sautéed Kale with Leeks and Dill

Greens with Shiitake
Sweet Vegetable Lo Mein
Ginger Vegetables
The Works
Sunny Mushroom Pâté
Greens with Tahini Sauce
Tahini Parsley Sauce
Herb Pate

Chapter 9: "Cooking For and With Your Children"

French Toast
Emily's Strawberry Drink
Steamed Vegetables

Chapter 10: "Fish Cookery"

Smoked Fish Hors d'Oeuvres
Smoked Fish Salads
Chinese Stir-fry
Dorothy's Steamed Bay Scallops
Broiled Farm-raised Trout
Quick Fried Bass With Tartar Sauce

Chapter 11: "Grain Cookery"

Freckles
Millet Apple Raisin Cake
Kasha
Kasha Cous
Couscous and Teff
Bronze Delight

Chapter 12: "Teff: Gem of the Grains"

Basic Teff
Super Chocolate Chip Cookies
Chocolatey Pancakes

Chapter 13: "Guilt-free Desserts"

Chocolate Hazelnut Pudding/ Frosting
Apricot Compote
Hot Carob Fudge

The Art of the Stir-fry and Sauté

Stir-fry dishes are colorful and tasty. Here are some ways to create dishes with international flair.

Guidelines for Stir-fry

1. **Stir-frying is quick and decisive.**
   Select your ingredients. See "Who's in First" on the next page to decide in which order ingredients should be added. Make a list, if you need to. Rinse and slice produce before you heat a wok or heavy skillet. Remember that stir-fry vegetables are best when they are colorful and crunchy. Be careful not to overcook them.

2. **Heat wok or heavy-bottomed skillet to medium high heat.** A little oil goes a long way in a hot wok or pan. The heat quickly thins and spreads out the oil to cover the whole pan.

3. **Add oil, spices, leeks, and/or onions.**

   The following oils are best for sautéing: extra virgin olive oil, sesame, toasted sesame, peanut, walnut, almond, sunflower, and safflower.

4. **It is important to add the firm, root vegetables before the more tender, leafy ones.**

5. **When and if the wok or pan dries out, add water or vegetable stock.** Avoid adding extra fat (oil) and salt (tamari). Wait to the end of cooking to smell, taste, and see if the stir-fry needs more seasoning.

6. **Stir continuously,** or the top ingredients will only steam.

7. **Season to taste.**

8. **Serve with garnishes.** They add extra crunch, visual beauty, balance, and flavor:

   ❖ chopped scallions, chopped chives, bean sprouts;

❖ edible flowers: nasturtiums, mustard flowers, chive blossoms, etc.;

❖ raw or roasted nuts: cashews, almonds, peanuts, etc.;

❖ raw or roasted seeds: sesame, sunflower, pumpkin, etc.;

❖ sprigs of parsley, watercress, or any other herbs used in the stir-fry .

Every stir-fry is an opportunity to go wild with vegetables.

International Free Play

Here is a list of ingredients for stir-frying and a guideline for which ingredients should go in first, second, third, and last. Choose up to five vegetables from these lists and design your own stir-fry. You can give it an Oriental, Indian, French, or Italian flavor, as outlined later in the chapter.

Who's In First?

Oil, spices, onions, and then:

fresh or dried burdock;

dried shiitake mushrooms (presoaked in water and sliced);

rutabaga;

marinated eggplant (marinate sliced eggplant for an hour in either umeboshi
    vinegar, tamari, or salt and lemon juice);

tamari*;

umeboshi vinegar*

Stir-fry these vegetables for 3-5 minutes before adding others, or at least 10 minutes if they are the only ingredients being sautéed.

What's Next?

carrots	collards	turnips
broccoli	cauliflower	daikon
kale	tempeh	green cabbage
leeks	nuts	seeds
Brussels sprout tops (greens)		

Stir-fry 2-5 minutes (2-3 minutes for a crunchy, brightly colored stir-fry, and longer for softer textures). If you plan to add more ingredients, let these vegetables be a little undercooked.

Fish: Stir-fry fish 10 minutes for every inch of thickness measured at the thickest part. Add shrimp, bay scallops, cut up pieces of scrod or salmon, depending on its thickness. See page 192 for Chinese Stir-fry with scrod.

---

* You can add tamari and umeboshi vinegar to taste at the beginning or end of cooking.

THE QUICK & EASY ORGANIC GOURMET

Who's In Third?

celery	bok choy	Chinese cabbage (Napa)
tofu	string beans	snow peas
mustard greens	peppers	summer squash
mushrooms	spinach	watercress
Swiss chard	asparagus	mizuna
wild leeks	dandelion greens	seitan
tomatoes		

Stir-fry 1-2 minutes, until they turn their peak color, and are coated with the seasonings of the wok.

Home Run, Last But Not Least!

bean sprouts	cooked noodles	cooked grains
scallions	herbs	shoyu
Bragg Liquid Aminos		

Common Improvisations For All Recipes

You can substitute:

1. **Vegetables:** broccoli for carrots, etc. See page 17 "Making Substitutions," and page 29, "Five Phase Substitutions."
2. **Amounts** of each ingredient to suit what you like or what you have in stock: increase, decrease, or omit it.
3. **Leeks, onions, shallots, and scallions** for each other.
4. **Oils** for each other: sesame for extra virgin olive oil, etc.
5. **Alternate salty seasonings**: umeboshi vinegar, tamari, shoyu, sea salt, and Bragg Liquid Aminos.
6. **Fresh, dried, white, or wild mushrooms:** shiitake, chanterelle, white button, porcini, etc.
7. **Spices or herbs**: you can keep the vegetable combination the same and just change the seasonings.
8. **Add water or vegetable stock** for a juicier version. Add more water (4-6 cups) to transform the stir-fry into a soup.
9. **Add crunchy nuts or seeds for texture**.
10. **Season to taste.**

Designing an Oriental Stir-fry

When designing an Oriental stir-fry for about a quart of sliced vegetables, you can use:

1 teaspoon-tablespoon sesame, peanut, or toasted sesame oil
1 tablespoon Mitoku mirin
1-3 inches peeled, chopped, or grated ginger
2-3 cloves sliced or pressed garlic
1 teaspoon-tablespoon tamari, umeboshi vinegar, Bragg Liquid Aminos or shoyu (to taste)

OPTIONAL:
Add cilantro, mustard, or anise. For hotter Thai or Szechwan styles, use a hot pepper oil or add crushed red pepper (½ to 1 teaspoon), or to taste.

Szechwan Broccoli

Quick and easy

2 heads of broccoli (10 cups), sliced
3 tablespoons sesame oil
3 tablespoons umeboshi vinegar or tamari
10 cloves garlic, sliced
1 teaspoon crushed red pepper flakes

SERVES 6-8
TIME: 15 MINUTES

Cut the stems off the broccoli, slice them into ½-inch rounds, and put them into a large bowl. Discard any woody portions. Slice the heads of broccoli into bite-sized little (tree) tops and put them into a separate bowl. Heat a wok. Add oil, umeboshi vinegar, crushed red pepper, and garlic. Sauté one minute and add the broccoli stems. Stir continuously for about 5 minutes. Add the broccoli tops, and stir-fry for about 5 minutes, until broccoli is bright green or as crunchy as you like it.

THE QUICK & EASY ORGANIC GOURMET

Japanese Fried Rice

Great for a quick lunch.

1 tablespoon sesame oil
2 tablespoons mirin
4 cloves garlic, peeled, sliced, or pressed
1-inch piece of ginger, grated and squeezed
2 carrots (1½ cups), sliced thin or in match sticks
3 stalks celery (2 cups), sliced
3 cups cooked brown rice
2 tablespoons tamari
4 scallions, sliced

SERVES 4
TIME: 10 MINUTES

Heat a wok or heavy skillet. Add sesame oil, mirin, and garlic. Squeeze in ginger juice. Add and sauté carrots for 4-5 minutes. Add and sauté celery for 2-3 minutes. Stir in rice and tamari. Turn off heat and stir in scallions. Taste and adjust the seasonings, if desired.

Oriental Express

Here is a calcium-rich greens dish with plenty of flavor.

10 leaves (2 quarts) bok choy, sliced
10 leaves (2 quarts) Chinese cabbage (Napa), sliced
1 tablespoon sesame oil
1 tablespoon umeboshi vinegar or tamari
1 tablespoon mirin
5 cloves garlic, sliced or pressed
1 onion (1 cup), sliced

OPTIONAL:
Add 1 pound firm or extra firm tofu, cut into bite-sized pieces.

SERVES 4-6
TIME: 10 MINUTES

Slice bok choy and Napa, putting the stems and leaves in separate bowls. Heat a wok or heavy skillet. Add oil, umeboshi vinegar, mirin, garlic, and onions. Stir fry onions 4-5 minutes. Add bok choy and Napa stems. Stir fry 3 minutes. Add leaves. Stir fry 2 minutes.

Another option: Add tofu and stir-fry 1 minute. Taste and adjust the seasoning. You may want to add more umeboshi vinegar and mirin.

Green Noodle Sauté

1 tablespoon olive oil
1 clove of elephant garlic or
2-3 regular cloves
1 leek, rinsed and sliced
1 small rutabaga, sliced
thinly (match sticks)
1 small bunch of kale, 5-6
leaves, cut into bite-sized
pieces
4 ounces cooked mugwort, or
soba noodles or spinach
ribbons
2 tablespoons umeboshi
vinegar

SERVES 4
TIME: 15 MINUTES

Heat wok or heavy-bottomed skillet. Add olive oil, leeks, and garlic, and sauté 1 minute. Add rutabaga, and sauté for 5 minutes. Add kale, and sauté until tender. Add and sauté cooked noodles and umeboshi vinegar. Taste and adjust the seasonings, if needed.

Improvisations

1. You can add tofu for a complete protein.

2. You can add ¼ cup tahini for a creamier version.

3. You can substitute other colored noodles, or leave out the noodles.

Fat-free

You can make an oil-free sauté with any combination of vegetables. Feel free to substitute your favorite seasonal vegetables and create your own fat-free dish.

1 tablespoon mirin
1 tablespoon tamari or umeboshi vinegar
½ cup water
2 cloves garlic, sliced
1-2 inches ginger, peeled and grated
1 piece burdock root*, 8-12 inches, sliced thin in match sticks, or 1 tablespoon dried and sifted burdock
1 large leek, sliced
1 bunch kale sliced into bite-sized pieces
1 zucchini, sliced in half moons

SERVES 4
TIME: 12 MINUTES

Heat water, tamari, and mirin in a wok or heavy skillet. Add garlic, ginger, and burdock, and simmer 5 minutes. Add leeks and kale, and simmer 5 minutes. Add more water if wok dries out. Add zucchini. Simmer and stir continuously for about 2 minutes, or until vegetables turn bright green. Taste and adjust the seasonings.

Improvisations

1. Green leafy vegetables such as purple kale, Chinese cabbage, broccoli, Brussels sprout tops, and chard are great in an oil-free sauté. Add a sea vegetable, tempeh, or tofu, too.

2. Another great combination is onions, carrots, celery, bok choy, Chinese cabbage, and scallions.

3. You can change the vegetable, herb, and spice combination to onions, broccoli, and zucchini, with garlic, thyme, oregano, and basil for an Italian accent. Add a little balsamic vinegar, too.

---

* Dried burdock is available in the herb section of your natural foods store or through mail order (see appendix 4).

Designing an Italian Sauté

Extra virgin olive oil and garlic go with just about everything. Italian sautés use garlic with basil, oregano, marjoram, mint, thyme, rosemary, bay leaves, saffron, Italian parsley, sage, and pepper. My favorite combination is garlic, thyme, basil, and oregano.

Sauté of Garden Greens
Perfumed with herbs

1½ tablespoons extra virgin
olive oil
3 cloves garlic, sliced
or minced
2 onions, sliced
pinch sea salt or ½ teaspoon
umeboshi vinegar
1 large bunch kale (about 2
quarts), rinsed and sliced
into bite-sized pieces
2 teaspoons dried basil, or
2 tablespoons fresh, minced
2 teaspoons dried oregano, or
2 tablespoons fresh, minced
2 teaspoons dried thyme, or
2 tablespoons fresh, minced

SERVES 4-6
TIME: 15 MINUTES

Heat a wok or heavy skillet. Add oil, and sauté onions, pinch of salt, and garlic for 3 minutes. Add kale, and sauté until tender (5-10 minutes). Season with herbs. Stir-fry and taste. Adjust seasoning, if necessary. Serve immediately.

Improvisations

1. Omit the salt. Add 2 tablespoons of rinsed Gaeta capers, 1 pound sliced firm tofu, and 4 tablespoons white wine, such as Four Chimney's Cooking Wine with Garlic, before adding the herbs.

2. Add a cup of sliced white or wild mushrooms (fresh shiitake, oyster, cremini, or other).

3. Add fresh or marinated sun-dried tomatoes and peppers.

Country-style Broccoli

Garlic scapes, or the green tops of garlic, are a real delicacy. You can substitute garlic cloves for the garlic tops, too.

½ teaspoon extra virgin olive oil
1 head broccoli, sliced
3 garlic (tops) scapes, sliced, or 3 or more cloves regular garlic, sliced
1 bunch fresh basil, sliced or minced

OPTIONAL:
Add cooked pasta to the stir fry after the garlic tops and basil.

SERVES 4
TIME: 6 MINUTES

Heat a wok or heavy skillet. Add oil and heat for 15 seconds. Add broccoli and sauté for 3-5 minutes, depending on whether you want it to be crunchy or tender. Add and stir-fry garlic tops and fresh basil for 1 minute. Taste and add a salty seasoning, if desired. Serve on top of pasta garnished with olives, if you like.

Improvisation

You can add zucchini, string beans, tofu, onions (or leeks), tomatoes, or marinated sundried tomatoes.

Designing an Indian Stir-fry

Indian flavors come from cumin seed, ginger, chilies, turmeric, mustard seed, cloves, cinnamon, cardamom, pepper, coriander seed and powder, dill seed and weed, and of course curry powder, a blend of many of the spices and herbs listed above. If you are using whole cardamom pods and coriander seeds, grind them with a mortar and pestle or in a blender before cooking.

Fragrant Indian Cabbage

Exotic!

2 teaspoons brown mustard
seeds, dry roasted
2 tablespoons extra virgin
olive oil
1 large Savoy or green cabbage
or 2 small ones (10 cups),
sliced thin
3 inches peeled and grated
ginger
1 cup water
1 cup fresh peas
1 bunch (1 cup) cilantro,
sliced
1 teaspoon sea salt
¼ teaspoon black pepper
¼ teaspoon cardamom

Heat a wok or heavy skillet. Add the mustard seeds. Cover and dry roast them for about 1 minute, until you hear them pop and they turn gray. Add oil. Stir in the cabbage, water, and ginger. Sauté 5 minutes until the cabbage turns bright green and the texture is crisp and tender. Turn off heat. Mix in the other ingredients. Taste and adjust the seasonings. Serve warm.

SERVES 6
TIME: 20 MINUTES

THE QUICK & EASY ORGANIC GOURMET

Curried Tempeh with Tomatoes

***This is a colorful dish. If you don't have yellow
pepper, you can substitute green pepper; if you
don't have cauliflower, you can substitute onions.
Being flexible is the key.***

*1 teaspoon sesame oil
1 package (8-10 ounces)
soy or grain tempeh, cut into
bite-sized pieces
1 small cauliflower, cut into
florets and bite-sized pieces
5 plum tomatoes, sliced
1 yellow pepper, sliced
1 teaspoon curry powder,
or to taste*

OPTIONAL:
*Garnish, or add cashews
and coconut*

SERVES 3-4
TIME: 10 MINUTES

Heat wok or heavy skillet. Add sesame oil and
tempeh; sauté for a few minutes to coat the
tempeh. Add and sauté cauliflower for 3 minutes. Add sliced tomatoes, and sauté till juicy.
Add yellow pepper. Stir-fry all the ingredients till tender. Add curry. Taste and add more
curry for a spicier flavor.

Improvisation

You can substitute shrimp or cooked chick
peas for tempeh.

Designing a Mexican Stir-fry

Mexican combinations of herbs and spices include garlic, oregano, pepper, and basil, just like the Italians, plus cumin, chili powder, and cilantro.

High Energy

A cool-weather dish that never fails to please

1 cup quinoa, rinsed
1 tablespoon cumin seeds
2 tablespoons extra virgin
olive oil
1 onion (1-1½ cups), sliced
1 small cauliflower (2½
cups), sliced or 2 potatoes,
sliced ⅛-inch thin
1 yam (2 cups), sliced
⅛-inch thin
¾ cup dried sweet pepper*,
sliced
2½ cups water*
¼ teaspoon sea salt or
cumin powder

OPTIONAL:
*Garnish with fresh sprigs
of cilantro*

SERVES 4-6
TIME: 50 MINUTES

Rinse quinoa and set it aside in a strainer. Preheat the oven to 350 degrees. Heat a cast-iron or baking pot that has a cover. Add cumin seeds, then oil and onions. Sauté for 2 minutes and add yams and cauliflower. Sauté for a few minutes and add peppers. Sauté for a minute and add quinoa. Sauté for another minute and turn off the heat. Add water and bake covered for 30-40 minutes, until the water is absorbed and quinoa and vegetables are tender. Season to taste with sea salt or cumin powder. Garnish with cilantro, if you like.

---

* The amount of water may vary, especially if you substitute potatoes for cauliflower, or fresh pepper for dried. If you find that you are using a smaller quantity of vegetables, you can try 2-2½ cups of water. Add more water if after baking the vegetables are not soft and the water is absorbed. Also, you can substitute ¼-½ cup of wine for an equal amount of water.

Refried Beans

Garlic, cumin and cilantro team up with pinto beans to make a tasty dish.

1 quart cooked pinto, kidney,
or anasazi beans and their
bean juice (about ½ cup)
1 tablespoon olive oil
5 bay leaves
2 teaspoons cumin seeds
2-3 onions (about 2 cups),
sliced
6 cloves garlic, sliced
2 tablespoons dried
oregano, or fresh oregano
to taste
5 teaspoons mild Mexican
chili powder
3 teaspoons dried coriander,
or a fresh bunch cilantro,
sliced
½ teaspoon sea salt,
or to taste

OPTIONAL:
Garnish with salsa and/or
salad of chopped scallions,
olives, shredded lettuce,
carrots, and sliced avocado.

Sauté in oil the onions, carrots, cumin seeds, garlic, and bay leaves. (If you choose to cook this dish with fresh sliced pepper, add and sauté it with the onions.) Cook for about 5 minutes, or until carrots are tender and onions are translucent. Mix in cooked beans and their juice. Add oregano, chili powder, and coriander. Stir-fry and taste. Adjust the seasonings and add sea salt to taste. Serve with rice or cornbread and salad, or on tortillas, garnished with salad and salsa.

Improvisations

1. Use jalapeno pepper or a generous pinch of crushed red pepper flakes, or cayenne, and less chili powder.

2. Omit the chili powder and add more cumin seeds.

3. Add fresh green, red, or yellow peppers, or a combination.

4. Add 2 diced carrots.

SERVES 4-6
TIME: 10 MINUTES

Designing a French Sauté

French-style sautés include basil, garlic, bay leaves, cloves, dill weed, marjoram, pepper, cumin seed, coriander, rosemary, mint, thyme, sage, mustard, nutmeg, celery seed, fennel, parsley, horseradish, paprika, savory, and tarragon. A simple sauté uses garlic, parsley, and fresh ground pepper.

It Looks Like Meat Loaf

Tastes like a Thanksgiving stuffing.

3 cups boiling water
pinch of sea salt
2 cups spelt cous
1 tablespoon sesame oil
1 large leek or onion (2 cups),
sliced
4 cloves garlic, sliced
4 carrots (1½ cups), sliced
thin or diced
1-3 stalks celery and leaves
(1 cup), sliced thin or diced
2 teaspoons dried thyme,
or 2 tablespoons fresh
2 teaspoons dried sage, or
2 tablespoons fresh
6 tablespoons barley miso,
or 1-2 umeboshi apricots
or plums*
1 cup walnuts, finely ground
1 cup spelt flour

Preheat the oven to 350 degrees. Boil water and salt in a large stock pot. Add spelt cous. Simmer a few minutes, till water is absorbed. Transfer hot grain to a large bowl to cool.

Heat wok or heavy skillet. Add sesame oil. Sauté garlic and leeks for 2 minutes; add carrots and celery. Sauté for 2 minutes, or until the carrots are tender. Add thyme and sage, and mash in the miso.

Mix in ground walnuts. Mix the spelt flour into the cooked spelt cous. Then add the cooked vegetable mixture to the spelt cous. Mix well. Taste and adjust the seasonings, if desired.

Lightly oil a 1-quart loaf pan and press the mixture into the pan. Bake, covered, for 50-60 minutes. Let it cool for 30 minutes before slicing. Serve loaf with vegetable side dishes, such as *Sauté of Garden Greens* (see page 64), *Greens With Tahini Sauce* (see page 165), steamed vegetables, or a leafy green salad. Try the loaf topped with a vegetable sauce, such as *Mushroom Leek Sauce, Vegetable Gravy,* or *Quick GingerScallion Sauce* (see pages 144, 146, and 147).

Improvisations

1. Substitute bulgar for spelt cous and use 4 cups of water for 2 cups grain.

2. Substitue ½ cup sunflower seeds and ½ cup walnuts, finely ground, for 1 cup of finely ground walnuts.

3. Substitute a combination of nuts, nut flours, and seeds (1 cup), such as sunflower seeds, pistachios, and walnuts, for 1 cup of finely ground walnuts.

---

* Remove the pit before grinding the umeboshi plum up with the nuts.

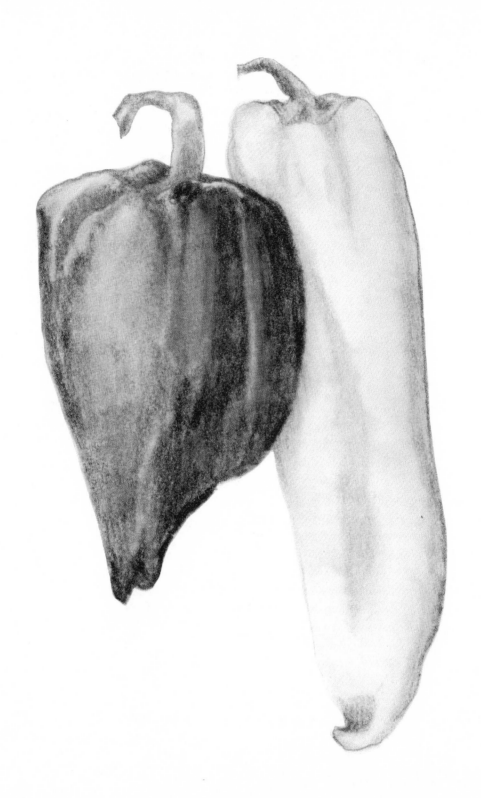

6

Around the World with Salads and Dressings

I improvise by going for colorful combinations of vegetables served on a bed of lettuce, pasta, or grains, mixed with seeds, nuts, beans, sea vegetables, or fish. For unlimited variety, change the base or the foreground of a salad. Choose and combine the freshest vegetables and fruits in season.

Add sharp contrast to the subtler flavors of lettuces and spinach with lively dressings with distinct character. Include olives, capers, sun-dried marinated tomatoes, unrefined cooking oils, vinegar, and herbs to awaken the spirit.

Common Improvisations For All Recipes

You can substitute:

1. **Vegetables**: purple cabbage for green cabbage or celery, etc. See page 17 for making substitutions.

2. **Red onions, scallions, wild leeks, and chives** for each other.

3. **Oils**: sesame for toasted sesame, etc.

4. **Beans**: chickpeas for pintos, etc.

5. **Pasta** with different colors and shapes, and even made from different ingredients: whole wheat macaroni for kamut spirals, etc.

6. **Grains**: basmati rice for brown rice, etc.

7. **Grains for pasta,** and vice versa.

8. **Spices or herbs**: Keep the other ingredients the same and just change the seasonings: cilantro for basil, etc.

9. **Alternate salty seasonings:** umeboshi vinegar, tamari, shoyu, sea salt and Bragg Liquid Aminos.

10. **Change amounts** of each ingredient to suit what you like or what you have in stock: increase, decrease, or omit.
11. **Umeboshi vinegar** for lemon juice and salt, and vice versa.
12. **Umeboshi vinegar** for umeboshi paste or plums.
13. **Nuts and seeds** for each other: walnuts for sunflower seeds, etc.
14. **Add more texture** to salads by adding nuts or seeds, like almonds or sunflower seeds.

Ancient Goddess Spring Tabouli

Spelt cous, cracked spelt grain, is similar to bulgar or cracked wheat. If you don't have spelt cous, you can substitute couscous, quinoa, or bulgar, using 6 cups of water for 3 cups grain.

4½ cups water
3 cups Spelt cous
½ teaspoon and a pinch of sea salt
1 small red onion, (¹/₃ cup), sliced, or bunch of scallions, sliced
1 large carrot, sliced in match sticks
1 bunch parsley (2 cups), chopped
juice of 2 lemons (½ cup), or to taste
½ cup extra virgin olive oil
1 tablespoon fresh chopped oregano
½ cup genuine Gaeta olives

Boil water with a pinch of salt, and add spelt cous. Simmer a few minutes until all the water is absorbed. Transfer hot grain to a large mixing bowl to cool. Then add carrots, onions, lemon juice, parsley, and olive oil. Stir and season with salt and oregano. Garnish with olives.

Improvisation

You can substitute other vegetables and herbs in season such as string beans, radishes, and fresh dill, or use a more traditional vegetable and herb combination, tomatoes, cucumber, parsley, scallions, and fresh mint.

SERVES 6
TIME: 30 MINUTES

THE QUICK & EASY ORGANIC GOURMET

Italiano Arugola Salad with Cauliflower

A refreshing salad, perfect as an appetizer

1 medium cauliflower, sliced
into bite-sized pieces
(1 quart)
1 large bunch arugola, cut or
torn into bite-sized pieces
(1 quart)
1 large carrot, sliced into
match sticks
juice of 1-2 lemons (½ cup,
or to taste)
salt and pepper to taste

OPTION #1:
Garnish with Gaeta olives

OPTION #2:
Garnish with pine nuts, roasted
pumpkin seeds, or almonds.

SERVES 6-8
TIME: 15 MINUTES

Put all the ingredients into a serving bowl and mix them together. Add a pinch of salt and about ¼ teaspoon black pepper or season to taste. Let mixture marinate for 10 minutes or more before serving.

Len's Sunny Macaroni Salad

Great for summer picnics, lunch, or dinner

4 cups cooked macaroni
1 cup roasted sunflower seeds
2-4 carrots (1 cup), diced
2-4 stalks celery, diced
1 small or medium red onion,
diced, or a bunch of scallions,
sliced
1 cup sliced red or green
cabbage, or 1 cup chopped
parsley
¼-⅓ cup extra virgin olive oil
(to taste)
2 tablespoons and 2 teaspoon
umeboshi vinegar

OPTION #1:
Add fresh or dried herbs, such
as oregano or lovage.
OPTION #2:
Add cooked beans or
fried tempeh.

SERVES 4-6
TIME: 30 MINUTES

Combine and mix all the ingredients in a large bowl. Taste and adjust the seasonings, if desired. Serve as is or on a bed of lettuce.

Improvisations

1. You can change the salad dressing. Try ½ cup soy mayonnaise and add pickles or pickle relish.

2. You can also dress this salad with a tahini parsley dressing, similar to the one on page 166.

Cilantro Pesto Pasta

4 quarts and ¼ cup water
½ pound dried pasta, such as
linguini, fettuccine, or
elbows
¼ cup ground walnuts
¼ ground sunflower seeds
1 large bunch (2 cups), tightly
packed fresh cilantro leaves,
rinsed
4-5 cloves garlic
1 tablespoon extra virgin
olive oil
1 tablespoon umeboshi vinegar

SERVES 4
TIME: 20 MINUTES

Boil 4 quarts of water. Add pasta and cook until tender (2-15 minutes, depending on the variety. Follow the instructions on the package or your intuition). Taste it to see if it is ready. When done, drain the pasta* in a colander. Rinse and drain the pasta in cold water to prevent it from sticking.

In a food processor, grind the sunflower seeds and walnuts into a meal. Add the garlic, cilantro, water, olive oil, and umeboshi vinegar. Blend them all together. Taste and adjust the seasonings, if desired.

Put the cooked pasta in a large serving bowl or individual serving bowls. Mix in the cilantro pesto and serve.

---

* Optional: Save the cooking water for stock.

Spinach and Potato Salad with Capers

A great change of pace for potato salad

11 small to medium potatoes (6 cups), scrubbed and cut into ⅛-inch slices
2-3 tablespoons garlic-herbal olive oil from sun-dried tomatoes (see recipe on page 84), or 2-3 tablespoons extra virgin olive oil
6 cloves garlic, sliced
1 medium onion (1 cup), sliced
2 stalks celery, sliced
¼ cup Gaeta capers, well rinsed
3 cups spinach, rinsed and sliced
⅓-½ cup water

SERVES 4-6
TIME: 20 MINUTES

Boil potatoes covered in water for 5-10 minutes, or until tender. Drain the water out. Save it for soup stock, if you like. Transfer potatoes to a large mixing bowl. Sauté onions and garlic for 2 minutes in olive oil and add them to the potatoes along with spinach, celery, and capers. Mix. Taste and adjust seasonings, if desired.

Or:

Heat up the oil in an open pressure cooker. Add onions and garlic. Fry for 1-2 minutes. Add potatoes and enough water to barely cover half the potatoes. Attach the lid to the pressure cooker. Lock it into place. Over high heat, bring the pressure cooker up to pressure. Cook for 2 minutes. Let the pressure come down naturally. Remove the lid. Taste a potato. If it's not done, lock the lid back in place and let potatoes cook in the residual heat. Stir in the spinach, celery, and capers. Taste and adjust the seasoning, if desired.

THE QUICK & EASY ORGANIC GOURMET

Easy Potato Salad

Kids love it!

2 quarts boiled potatoes
1 cup soy mayonaise,
or make your own
(see recipe on page 96)
1 large carrot, sliced into
match sticks
1 medium to large red onion,
or bunch of scallions, sliced
or diced
1 tablespoon dried dill weed,
or fresh bunch of dill

SERVES 6-8
TIME: 15 MINUTES

Scrub and boil potatoes in water to cover for about 10 minutes, or until they are firm and almost soft. Drain the potatoes and save the potato water for soup stock. Cut the potatoes into one-inch pieces, and put them into a large mixing bowl with the other ingredients. Stir together. Taste and adjust seasonings, if desired. Serve.

7.5 celery

Roasted Eggplant and Pepper Salad

Serve hot or cold, on a bed of pasta, rolled in tortillas
with lettuce, or stuffed inside pita bread.

1 medium eggplant
(2 cups), sliced
2 teaspoons sea salt
juice from 1 lemon
1 onion (1 cup), sliced
¼ cup extra virgin olive oil
2 peppers (2 cups)
(any color), sliced
3 cloves of garlic, sliced
2 zucchinis, sliced in quarters
1½ cups cooked beans, such as
anasazi or chickpeas
1 handful or bunch of fresh
basil, torn or cut into bite-
sized pieces

SERVES 4-6
TIME: 2-3 HOURS

Slice eggplant into ½-inch rounds and then into quarters. Place sliced eggplant into a large mixing bowl. Marinate eggplant in lemon juice and 1 teaspoon of sea salt for 1-2 hours. (The salt draws out liquid from the eggplant.)

Preheat the oven to 400 degrees. Discard the excess liquid from the eggplant.

Place eggplant in a covered crock or baking dish with the sliced peppers, onions, garlic, olive oil, and 1 teaspoon sea salt. Mix them all together and bake for 50-60 minutes, until the eggplant is tender.

Put the roasted vegetables in a large bowl. Add the cooked beans, zucchini, and basil. Mix together.

Improvisation

Let the roasted vegetables cool off before adding the other ingredients. Mix together.

Babaghanoush

Serve as a dip on top of a bed of lettuce, surrounded by
pita bread, olives, sliced tomatoes, carrots, and celery.

1 large eggplant
(2 quarts), sliced
1 teaspoon sea salt
1 tablespoon extra virgin
olive oil
4-5 cloves garlic, sliced
½ cup tahini
1 teaspoon umeboshi paste*

SERVES 6-8
TIME: 2 HOURS, 15 MINUTES

Slice eggplant into ½-inch rounds, and then into quarters. Place sliced eggplant into a large mixing bowl. Add salt and marinate eggplant for 2 hours. Discard the excess liquid from eggplant (2 quarts of marinated eggplant shrinks down to about 1 quart). Sauté eggplant and garlic in olive oil for about 5 minutes, or until eggplant is tender. Taste. Add tahini. Mix and sauté eggplant and tahini for 2 minutes. Puree sautéed eggplant, umeboshi paste, and tahini in a food processor.

Improvisation

Add parsley. Taste and add more umeboshi paste or tahini, if you like.

---

* If you do not have umeboshi paste, make this recipe with the more traditional combination of fresh lemon juice and sea salt.

Japanese Rainbow Salad

Black and delicate, with a mild, semi-sweet flavor, arame has a pleasing texture like a very thin noodle. Use your imagination to create endless variations of this salad.

½ cup dry arame
2 cups water
1 cup or a small bunch of parsley, chopped
1 quart of chopped red or green cabbage
1 large carrot, sliced
2 stalks celery, sliced
1 tablespoon toasted sesame oil or sesame oil
2 tablespoons umeboshi vinegar, shoyu, or tamari
2 tablespoons rice vinegar

SERVES 4-6
TIME: 10 MINUTES

First, look arame over and remove any tiny seashells. Cover the arame in 1 cup of water. Rub together and whirl to release any sand. Next, lift out the arame and discard the water. Soak arame in 1 cup of cold water for 5 minutes. Drain out the water. Put arame in a mixing bowl. Add the chopped vegetables, oil, umeboshi, and rice vinegar. Stir all the ingredients together, taste, and adjust the seasonings, if necessary.

Marinated arame salads keep well in the refrigerator for several days.

Improvisations

1. Steamed beets are wonderful in arame salads. See *Ruby Red Salad* on the next page.

2. Combine organic vegetables in season. Try fresh garden peas, mustard greens, and radishes in arame salads. Fresh chopped scallions and red onions are also great in arame salads. Check the salad vegetable list on page 89 for other suggestions.

3. You can add mirin for a sweeter dressing.

Ruby Red Salad

A delicious variation on the Japanese Rainbow Salad

*3 beets, grated or sliced
and steamed
½ cup dry arame
1 cup water to soak arame
4 cabbage leaves, sliced thin
into bite-sized pieces
1 red onion (medium),
sliced or diced
1 bunch of radishes, sliced
1 tablespoon extra virgin olive,
sesame, or toasted sesame oil
1 tablespoon rice vinegar
1 tablespoon tamari or
umeboshi vinegar*

SERVES 4
TIME: 15 MINUTES

Slice beets into thin (⅛-¼-inch) rounds and steam until tender, about 5 minutes. Rinse and soak arame in 1 cup of water for 5 minutes. Drain out the soaking water. Dice steamed beets. Put them in a large mixing bowl with all the other ingredients. Stir and taste. Adjust the seasonings to your taste (add more vinegar or tamari), if desired.

Improvisations

1. Add cooked brown rice, or udon or spiral noodles.

2. You can try fresh or steamed beets with arame, scallions, parsley, daikon, and red cabbage, or with green cabbage, red onion, and parsley.

Oriental Vegetable Salad

*1-2 quart(s) of assorted fresh-
cut vegetables in season
1 tablespoon sesame or toasted
sesame oil
1 tablespoon umeboshi vinegar
1 tablespoon rice vinegar*

SERVES 4
TIME: 5 MINUTES

Mix vegetables and seasonings in a large bowl. Toss and serve.

Improvisations

1. Japanese Cole Slaw: Try green and red cabbage, parsley, and scallions.

2. For a sweet variation, add mirin.

Marinated Sun-dried Tomatoes

So simple, and of course there are many ways to make them.

❖ Put dried tomatoes in a bowl or jar with olive oil for 10 minutes. Add your favorite Italian herbs, garlic, and sea salt to taste. Store them in a cool place, or serve them.

❖ Add dried tomatoes directly to a salad or a pasta dish, and let them soak up the dressing.

❖ Layer dried tomatoes in a jar with garlic cloves and fresh herbs, such as oregano and mint, or basil, oregano, and thyme. Add enough extra virgin olive oil to cover.

Special Marinade for Sun-dried Tomatoes

1½ cups dried tomatoes
1¾ cups wine, such as **Four Chimneys Organic Cooking Wine with Garlic**
¾ cup extra virgin olive oil
4 peeled garlic cloves
½ teaspoon dried oregano, or a couple of fresh sprigs, or 2 teaspoons fresh leaves
1½ teaspoons dried basil, or 1½-2 tablespoons fresh leaves
1½ teaspoons dried thyme, a couple of fresh sprigs, or 1½-2 tablespoons fresh leaves

OPTION #1:
Add sea salt, wine, wine vinegar, or balsamic vinegar to taste

Soak dried tomatoes in enough wine to cover them (about 1¾ cups). You can also marinate them in balsamic or wine vinegar. Drain and save the cooking wine (for other cooking) after 2 hours. Marinate tomatoes in olive oil (enough oil to cover them to preserve their moisture). Stir in garlic and herbs. Put the lid on the jar and shake it. Taste the tomatoes.

Improvisations

1. You can dress salads with the garlic-herbal olive oil, too.

2. For a quick and tasty dinner, fry tempeh in olive oil or in the garlic-herbal olive oil. Add it to a salad of parsley, red onions, cabbage, and sun-dried marinated tomatoes.

OPTION #2:
Add rosemary, too.

3. Add sun-dried marinated tomatoes to the *Roasted Eggplant and Pepper Salad* on page 80.

MAKES 1 PINT
TIME: 2 HOURS, 5 MINUTES

Keep it Going

When I ran out of these marinated (in wine) sun-dried tomatoes, I marinated some more (2 cups) sun-dried tomatoes in 1½ cups *Four Chimneys Organic Red Wine Vinegar* for 2 hours. Then I strained the wine vinegar (which only came to ¾ cup) and put the tomatoes in the same jar with the garlic-herbal olive oil mixture (that the other sun-dried tomatoes marinated in). I added 3 cloves of garlic and more basil, oregano, and thyme. I put the cover back on and shook the jar. They were ready to use.

Mediterranean Tofu Dip

Serve with vegetables and chips,
or as a spread for bread or crackers.

1 pound firm tofu
1 bunch parsley (2 cups parsley tops), rinsed
3 cloves garlic
10 marinated sun-dried tomatoes (see previous recipe)
SERVES 4
TIME: 10 MINUTES

Blend all the ingredients in a food processor.

Festive Rice Salad

1 quart cooked, long-grain
brown rice, or brown basmati
rice or a combination of the
two (see page 204 for cooking
instructions)
½ cup fresh mint leaves
½ cup fresh oregano leaves
1 medium red onion
(1 cup), sliced
juice from 1 lemon
5 marinated sun-dried
tomatoes*, sliced
⅛ cup of garlic-herbal olive
oil**, or ⅛ cup olive oil with
some fresh minced basil and
pressed garlic
¼ cup Gaeta olives
¼ cup Gaeta capers,
rinsed under cold water to
remove salt
1 zucchini, sliced in quarters

Put the rice in a bowl and let it cool. When the rice is room temperature, stir in the other ingredients. Taste and adjust the seasonings, if desired.

---

* See *Special Marinade for Sun-dried Tomatoes* recipe on page 84.

** See page 84.

SERVES 4-6
TIME: 1 HOUR

The Ultimate Pasta and Bean Salad

Feel free to cut this extra-large salad in half.
It is a delicious variation on the
Festive Mediterranean Rice Salad.

12 ounces kamut pasta spirals,
or other pasta
2 cups chickpeas,
cooked with a piece
of sea vegetable
4 small carrots, or 1 large one
(1 cup) sliced
1 handful (1 cup), raw string
beans, sliced
1 medium red onion
(1 cup) sliced,
1 bunch (1 cup) fresh dill,
minced
1 cup lemon juice (from 2-4
lemons, depending on the
size)
1/3 cup extra virgin olive oil
1/4 cup Gaeta capers, well rinsed
1 teaspoon sea salt, or
umeboshi vinegar to taste

Boil kamut spirals 12-15 minutes. Strain the water. Rinse and drain pasta in cold water. Put all the ingredients in a large bowl. Mix them all together. Taste it and adjust the seasonings, if desired.

Improvisation

You can substitute another bean, such as navy beans, for the pasta.

SERVES 8
TIME: 1 HOUR

3-Bean Dill Salad

Quick and classy

2 cups cooked chickpeas
2 cups cooked navy beans
2 cups raw string beans, sliced
1 bunch (6-8) radishes, sliced
1 bunch of sweet, small sum-
mer carrots (1½ cups), sliced
1 red onion (1 cup), sliced
⅛ cup extra virgin olive oil
⅛ cup apple cider vinegar
1 bunch (½ cup) fresh dill,
minced
¼ teaspoon sea salt, or to taste

SERVES 4-6
TIME: 15 MINUTES

Combine all the ingredients in a large bowl. Mix. Taste, and adjust the seasoning, if desired.

Improvisations

1. **3-Bean Summer Salad with Cilantro and Capers:** Substitute the juice of 1-2 lemons for the apple cider vinegar. Substitute an equal amount of cilantro for dill. Omit the radishes. Substitute 1 package (3.5 ounces) Gaeta capers (well rinsed) for the sea salt. Mix up all the ingredients. Taste and adjust the seasonings, if desired.

2. You can substitute yellow, green, and purple string beans for cooked beans.

Composed Green Salads

You can create endless variations of composed green salads.

Choose from a variety of lettuces:

bibb	romaine	iceberg	hydroponic
green leaf	red leaf	Boston	

Lettuce leaves are delicate and range in color from pale to bright green, from chartreuse to pink, red, and russet. Growing in clusters, they come in a variety of forms and textures: ruffled, soft, irregular, even, and slender. You can select buttery or crisp varieties. Add other spicier greens or vegetables with different colors for a simple or complex design.

Succulent greens add different shades of color, plus bitter and pungent flavors:

chicory	watercress	arugola	spinach
endive	frisee	mizuna	tat soi
celery leaves	escarole	parsley	corn salad (mache)
fennel	red mustard	green mustard	young radish greens
red, purple, or	tender green kale		

Add a wild or semi-wild green:

lamb's quarter	sorrel	purslane	nettles
grape leaves	violet greens	violet flowers	dandelion greens

≈ *Free Play* ≈

Choose a total of 5-7 ingredients from the lists above. Remove any wilted or yellow leaves. Pull off the leaves you want to use. Rinse them in cool water. Dry them. Gently shake them, air dry them on a dish rack, pat with a towel, or spin them dry in a salad spinner. Tear them into bite-sized pieces. Put them into a beautiful large bowl or into individual salad bowls.

Now that you have created your green salad, use your imagination and add one of many colorful garnishes. Fresh sprigs of herbs or colorful edible flowers sprinkled on top of a salad are exquisitely beautiful and festive.

Fresh Herbs

thyme	oregano	mints	sorrel
arugola	basil	chives	cilantro

dill	fennel	rosemary	sage
lemon thyme	marjoram	parsley	tarragon
summer savory			

Edible Flowers

nasturtium	marigold	rose petal	squash flower
wild mustard	pansy	gladiolus	red clover
chive flower	bee balm	fuchsia	daylily flowers and pods
borage	calendula	chrysanthemum	johnny jump-ups
violet *			

* Mix fresh violet flowers with thin rounds of onion, olive oil, and vinegar to complement cold salmon.

Caution: Many common varieties of flowers are poisonous. The list includes iris, rhododendron, sweet pea, lily of the valley, and daffodil. Positively identify any flower you are thinking of eating.

Eat only organically grown flowers, preferably from your own garden. Flowers picked along the road or bought from the florist may have been sprayed with insecticides.

Sprouts

alfalfa	red clover	radish	mung bean
green pea	sunflower	dill	red and brown lentil
wheat			

Sprouts are crisp and nutritious. Even apartment dwellers can grow their own fresh sprouts all year round. Although there are special kits available for sprouting, a wide-mouth-quart jar, a gauze pad, and a rubber band are all you need. For a fraction of what it costs to buy sprouts at the store, you can grow your own.

Here's how:

To make a quart of sprouts, put ½ cup of any seed or one cup of any bean mentioned above in an empty, clean, wide-mouthed quart jar. Soak them in water overnight. Attach a gauze pad to the top of the jar with a rubber band. Drain the water. Rinse the seeds twice daily for 2-4 days (give the rinse water to house or garden plants). Keep the jar in a dark place, such as underneath the sink or in a kitchen cabinet. Red lentils sprout tails ⅛-½ inch long. Other seed and bean sprouts have longer tails ½-1½ inches long.

Alfalfa, radish, clover, and wheat sprouts will turn green if you leave them in the sunlight for an hour after sprouting. Store sprouts in the refrigerate for a few days in their sprouting jars with the gauze pad on top. Sprouts are delicious in sandwiches. Use them as a garnish or mix them into any salad.

Alfalfa and clover sprouts are mild flavored and popular. Ready in 3-4 days they can be served in salads and sandwiches.

Radish sprouts taste like radishes. They also take 3-4 days to harvest.

Red and brown lentils have a peppery flavor that can spice up any salad. Brown lentil sprouts need 3-4 days of rinsing, but red lentils are quicker. They are ready in 1-2 days. These crispy sprouts are also great as a garnish for soups.

Mung bean sprouts sometimes lose their green covers when sprouted. In 3-4 days, they are ready to go into Chinese stir fries, soups, salads, and sandwiches. They taste a little like string beans.

Sprouted whole peas taste like peas. They are ready to harvest in 3 days. Add them to salads or stir fries.

Wheat berries become sweet and chewy when sprouted. They also take 3-4 days to harvest and are a welcome addition to salads, sandwiches, and breads.

Sprout **sunflower seeds** with their shells on. After 3-4 days, they break out of their shells and are ready to be eaten or baked into muffins. They taste a little like a crunchy artichoke heart.

Nuts and Nuts — and Seeds, Too

Raw and roasted nuts and seeds are great sources of protein, calcium, and B vitamins. They make a nutritious garnish for salads. Their crunchy texture is a great contrast to soft lettuce leaves, pasta, beans, juicy vegetables, and sprouts. Nuts and seeds are high in fat and calories. About 80% of their calories come from fat (even if it is good fat-unsaturated vegetable oil). Nut and seed oils make wonderful salad dressings, so enjoy, but in moderation.

Remember pickles, sauerkraut, olives, or colorful vegetables, such as tomatoes and red onions are also great additions.

Dress composed green salads with a little extra virgin olive oil and umeboshi vinegar or any one of the dressings in this chapter.

Improvisation

Combine a lettuce or succulent green with a red, purple, white, and orange vegetable, such as red cabbage, carrots, cucumber, and red pepper. You could also add cooked beans, pasta, cooked grains, fish, marinated tofu, or deep-fried tempeh. Combine them in any proportion, but keep the number of ingredients to 7. More than 7 confuses the palate, especially if you are planning to dress the salad.

Salad Dressings

These are quick, easy, and delicious!

Creamy Garlic

The tantalizing flavor of garlic and chili powder complement the refreshing taste of parsley. This lively dressing is equally good on cooked grains and pasta. I love it on green salads.

1 pound extra firm tofu
¼ cup water
⅓ cup sesame oil or peanut oil
⅓ cup apple cider vinegar
¼ cup tamari
6 cloves garlic, peeled
1 bunch parsley, or 2 cups parsley tops, rinsed
2 tablespoons chili powder
½ cup fresh oregano
½ teaspoon black pepper

Blend all the ingredients in a blender or food processor.

SERVES 8 OR MORE
TIME: 5 MINUTES

Green Queen

The marriage of basil and cilantro creates a sensational dressing for fresh green vegetable salads, cooked grains, and pasta.

1 bunch (2 cups), fresh basil, rinsed
1 small bunch (1 cup), cilantro, rinsed
juice of 1 lemon (about ⅓ cup, or to taste)
⅓ cup extra virgin olive oil
1 teaspoon sea salt
½ teaspoon black pepper

Blend all the ingredients in a blender or food processor.

Improvisation

Substitute parsley for cilantro, omit the black pepper, and add fresh garlic cloves or garlic tops.

SERVES 8 OR MORE
TIME: 5 MINUTES

Golden Goddess

Perfect for a quick, colorful, cabbage salad

⅛ cup extra virgin olive, sesame, or canola oil
3 tablespoons fresh minced dill, or a handful of Gaeta capers, rinsed
juice of 1 lemon (¼ cup)
1¼ teaspoon wet mustard

Combine these ingredients. Pour dressing over 1 quart of chopped veggies, such as a colorful blend of carrots, celery, red cabbage, and parsley. Another fine vegetable combination is watercress, cauliflower, carrots, and parsley.

SERVES 4
TIME: 5 MINUTES

Will's Dressing

This dressing is superb on fresh lettuce or cooked beans.

*1 cup extra virgin olive oil,
peanut, sesame, or canola oil
3 cloves garlic, peeled
¼ cup apple cider vinegar
½ cup water
4 tablespoons tamari
1½-2 tablespoons powdered
roasted kelp
juice of ½ lemon or lime,
or to taste
Choose one: 2 tablespoons
chopped chives, chive flowers,
fresh dill, red onion, or
scallions*

SERVES 8 OR MORE
TIME: 5 MINUTES

Blend all the ingredients in a blender. (You can make your own powdered kelp by roasting kelp in a 400-degree oven for 10 minutes and then grinding the kelp in a nut and seed mill or suribachi.)

Improvisations

1. You can substitute balsamic vinegar, rice vinegar, or barley vinegar for apple cider vinegar.

2. You can substitute a bunch of scallions or a red onion for garlic.

3. Substitute mellow, white, sweet brown rice, or chickpea miso for tamari. Miso is slightly sweeter in flavor.

4. You can add 2 tablespoons of rice syrup for a sweeter dressing.

Pinto Parsley Salad

SERVES 4-6
TIME: 1 HOUR

When I first made *Will's Dressing* (previous recipe), I made it without measuring and without water. I just put some lime juice, garlic, apple cider vinegar, chives, chive flowers, tamari, and olive oil into a food processor and blended them together. When I first tasted it, I discovered that I put in too much apple cider vinegar. Then I added more garlic and chive flowers. I tasted it again. It still needed some olive oil and tamari. I added some, blended it, and tasted. It was wonderful—the perfect complement to a bean salad. Cook pinto beans with a piece of digitata or other sea vegetable (see page 119 for recipe). Pour cooked beans into a large bowl to cool. Then add a bunch of chopped parsley. Mix in *Will's Dressing* or make up your own variation on it.

Lemon Fire

Oil-free and flavorful

Juice of 2 lemons (¹/₃ cup)
1-2 tablespoons ginger juice,
or 1-2 inches grated and
squeezed ginger
½ cup water
drop of tamari

Grate the ginger onto a cutting board. Gather the grated ginger in your hand and squeeze the juice out into a mug or measuring cup. Combine and stir all the ingredients together. Serve over boiled salads, salads, and steamed vegetables.

MAKES 1 CUP
TIME: 5 MINUTES

Tofu Mayo

A soy mayonaise that's creamy and delicious on potato and macaroni salads

mustard
cider vinegar
garlic
parsley
dill

1 pound of soft tofu
juice of 1 squeezed lemon
1 handful of parsley or dill,
rinsed
1 teaspoon tamari or shoyu, or
¼ teaspoon sea salt

OPTION #1:
Add 1 tablespoon of mustard.

OPTION #2:
Add a fresh chopped (small or medium) red onion, or a bunch of scallions, and 2 cloves of garlic.

OPTION #3:
Add chopped olives, and/or chopped pickles and their juice.

SERVES 8 OR MORE
TIME: 5 MINUTES

Blend all the ingredients together in a food processor or blender.

Improvisation

You can substitute 1 tablespoon umeboshi vinegar or umeboshi plum paste for the lemon and tamari or sea salt.

THE QUICK & EASY ORGANIC GOURMET

Winds of Japan

Light and tasty

*2-inch piece of ginger, grated
and squeezed (1½ table-
spoons fresh-squeezed
ginger juice)
3 tablespoons tamari
2 tablespoons sesame seeds
1 tablespoon mirin
¼ cup water*

Grate the ginger onto a cutting board. Gather the grated ginger in your hand and squeeze the juice out into a mug or measuring cup. Stir the other ingredients into the ginger juice. Serve over boiled salad, noodles, or fish salad.

**MAKES ABOUT ½ CUP
TIME: 5 MINUTES**

Exciting Oil-free Salads

Add zing to your salads without adding oil in dressings. Numerous styles, techniques, and garnishes add pizzazz.

Key Ingredients

- ❖ Lemons, pickles, salsa, mustard, sauerkraut, sea salt, olives.
- ❖ Vinegars: apple cider, brown rice, umeboshi, balsamic, wine, and herbal.
- ❖ Fresh red and green peppers, parsley, hot scallions, mustard greens, pungent watercress, and fresh herbs. Best of all: during peak harvest time, fresh vegetables taste great without any dressing.

Grated Salads

It's simple! Grate one or more vegetables, such as carrots, beets, or radishes. Add chopped parsley. Squeeze on fresh lemon juice and sprinkle sea salt, or top it off with a little rice vinegar. Mix it up and serve. Remember that beets turn a salad red.

Improvisations

1. A simple grated salad of horseradish, beets, and carrots is also divine.
2. Substitute other leafy greens, such as mustard greens or watercress, for parsley.
3. You can add other fresh herbs, such as sorrel, arugola, or chives.

Lemony Carrot and Radish Salad

This salad is refreshing and light.

1 lemon, juiced (¼ cup)
2 large carrots, grated
1 small daikon, or a 6-7-inch
piece, grated
½ teaspoon sea salt

OPTIONAL:
Add fresh chopped parsley,
watercress, or mustard
greens.

SERVES 4
TIME: 5 MINUTES

Combine and mix all the ingredients together.

Improvisations

1. Try different combinations: beet and daikon; carrot, beet, and daikon; carrot, beet, daikon, and parsley; carrot, daikon, and mustard greens; carrot, daikon, mustard greens, and parsley; carrot, daikon, and watercress.

2. You can dress the salad with just rice vinegar.

3. You can dress the salad with tamari and rice vinegar.

4. You can add a little flax seed oil.

Boiled Salads

Dip up to 5 vegetables into boiling water separately and then mix them together in a salad bowl. Dip the delicate flavored vegetables first to protect their mild flavors. Save stronger flavored vegetables, such as turnips, celery, and watercress, for last. Dip greens for 20-30 seconds, and root and other vegetables for 1-2 minutes. Vegetables become brighter. Pungent and bitter green vegetables, such as mustard greens, lose their bite. Broccoli, cauliflower, snow peas, string beans, and asparagus stay crunchy. You can boil just about any vegetable except lettuce. One of my favorite combinations is daikon, carrots, celery, and parsley. Another great combination is collards, celery, parsley and green cabbage. Save the boiling water for soup stock.

Serve a boiled salad immediately or, to preserve their bright colors, rinse boiled vegetables in cold water. Serve boiled salads with a lemon ginger, tofu, or umeboshi dressing.

Marinated Salads

Marinated vegetable salads are sweet and crisp. Put shredded or thinly sliced vegetables in a bowl. Sprinkle a little sea salt or tamari, shoyu, or umeboshi vinegar on them. (The salt draws out liquid from the vegetables to make a delicious dressing.) Add a little mirin to the marinade for sweetness, or a little rice vinegar or fresh lemon juice for a more sour taste.

Marinated Tofu

A wonderful side dish or salad centerpiece

1 pound extra firm tofu
3 cloves garlic, sliced
2 inches of ginger, peeled and grated
2 tablespoons tamari
1 tablespoon mirin

SERVES 6
TIME: 30 MINUTES

Press tofu for 10-15 minutes to remove excess water by putting it between two cutting boards with a heavy book on top. Cut tofu into ¼-inch-by-1-inch pieces. Put tofu in a mixing bowl with all the other ingredients. Mix them together. Marinate for at least 15 minutes. Serve as a side dish, or as part of a salad.

Pressed Salads

Pressed salads are a cross between a pickle and a raw vegetable. Popular in Europe and the Orient, they are stronger in flavor than marinated salads.

Slice one or more vegetables thin and layer them in a large bowl, pickle press, or crock. Sprinkle a small amount of sea salt (use 1 teaspoon of sea salt for each quart of chopped vegetables). Mix the vegetables and sea salt by hand. If you are not using a pickle press, place a plate that fits inside the bowl or crock over the vegetables. Put a weight, such as a rock or a gallon jar of beans or grains, on top of the plate.

Check pressed salads after 15 minutes. If the vegetables are still dry, add more pressure or salt. If the vegetables are drowning in their own water, reduce the pressure. The water should not rise above the pressure plate, or the vegetables will become stringy instead of juicy.

Most pressed salads are ready in 30-60 minutes. The longer the time of pressing, the more like a pickle they become. Sauerkraut is a good example. Thinly slice 5 pounds of red and/or green cabbage. Mix in 3 tablespoons of sea salt. Press for two weeks to make sauerkraut.

My favorite vegetables to press are crisp, firm, and bright in color: cucumbers, red cabbage, green cabbage, Chinese cabbage, round red radishes, long white daikon radishes, turnips, scallions, red onions, carrots, mustard greens, and watercress. Fresh chopped herbs, such as cilantro, summer savory, or dill, and spicy seeds, like caraway, anise, or dill, add zest to pressed salads; cayenne does, too.

First Aid: If your pressed salad turns out too salty, rinse the vegetables in cool water.

Optional: Add wine vinegar to the finished salad, if desired.

Pressed Cucumber Salad

Easy and delicious

2 cucumbers, rinsed,
thinly sliced
2 teaspoons caraway
or dill seeds
½ teaspoon sea salt

Put sliced cucumber, caraway seeds, and sea salt in a pickle press or improvised pickle press (bowl with a plate on top and a weight on top of the plate). Press the salad for 45 minutes. Stir and serve.

Improvisation

SERVES 4-6
TIME: 50 MINUTES

You can substitute 1 bunch of radishes for cucumbers, or add it to them.

Pressed Cabbage Salad

6 cups sliced green and/or
red cabbage
1 tablespoon sea salt
1 red onion, sliced
1 cucumber, sliced

OPTION #1:
Add 1 teaspoon caraway or
dill seeds.

OPTION #2:
Add shredded or thinly sliced
carrots for color.

OPTION #3:
Add a small bunch of chopped
cilantro.

Put all the ingredients in a pickle press or large mixing bowl. Mix them up with your hands or a large mixing spoon. Put a plate that fits inside the bowl on top of the salad. Put a heavy weight on top of the plate, such as a gallon jar filled with grains or a rock. Press the salad for an hour.

Improvisation

Substitute 1 bunch of mustard greens, radishes, or a small daikon radish for the cucumber.

SERVES 4-6
TIME: 1 HOUR, 10 MINUTES

Homemade Sauerkraut

Like a fine wine, naturally fermented sauerkraut is rich in digestive enzymes. Traditionally, sauerkraut is green cabbage and sea salt, but you can use red cabbage, or a combination of the two. Also, you can add onions, carrots, shredded rutabaga, turnips, daikon, apples, juniper berries, nasturtium flowers, and dill or caraway seeds.

Sauerkraut with Carrots and Onions

1 large green cabbage, sliced thin
1 red cabbage, about the size of a grapefruit, sliced thin
4 carrots, sliced
1 medium to large red onion, sliced
3 tablespoons sea salt

MAKES 2-3 QUARTS
TIME: 2 WEEKS

Put the vegetables and sea salt in a large mixing bowl. Use your hands to mix them up and distribute the salt. Transfer the salted vegetables to a clean crock or pickle press. If using a pickle press, cover with a dish towel, cheesecloth or gauze. If using a crock, use a small plate that fits inside the crock to function like a press. Place a heavy rock or a brick on top. It may take 12-24 hours until the weight of the rock creates a tight closure and the crock's lid fits. In the meantime, cover the crock with a clean dish towel, gauze, or bamboo mats. Put the crock or the pickle press in the pantry, dry basement, or a dark, cool corner counter of the kitchen.

Check the next day to make sure that the cabbage is covered by its own juice—if not, add more weight. Check again the next day, and if the cabbage is not covered by its own juice, add a little bit more salt. Check the sauerkraut daily. Skim off any mold that forms on top. After 10 days, taste. If the cabbage is sufficiently fermented, refrigerate it in clean jars for up to a year. If not, taste again the next day. Sauerkraut is ready in 10-14 days.

First Aid: If your sauerkraut turns out too salty, rinse or soak in cool water for a day.

Pickles

OPTIONAL:
*Add ½ teaspoonful of
peppercorns.*

MAKES 1 GALLON
TIME: 3-4 DAYS

Long Brine Pickling Method: Food is submerged in salt water in the classic pickle barrel. Instead of the ever popular cucumber, try carrots, string beans, red onions, cauliflower, or broccoli.

Wash 2-3 pounds of vegetables, such as cucumbers, carrots and string beans. Put them in a large sterile gallon jar or crock. Add two dill blossoms or one tablespoon dill seed, 2-4 cloves of garlic, one large quartered red onion, and 2 bay leaves.

Make a brine solution with ⅓ cup sea salt and 10 cups of water. Bring the mixture to a boil and simmer it until the salt dissolves, 2-3 minutes. When cool, pour the mixture over the vegetables (some will float).

Put the lid on the crock, close the lid on the jar (but not tightly), or cover the container with a plate or cheesecloth. Then, if you used a jar, cover it with a clean dish towel to keep it in the dark. Put the crock or jar in the pantry, dry basement, or a dark, cool corner counter of the kitchen for three to four days. Taste the pickles. If they are not as you like them, let them sit for another day. If they are as sour as you like, they are ready to eat. Store pickles in the refrigerator for up to a month.

First Aid: If your pickles turn out too salty, rinse or soak them in cool water for a day.

7

Secrets of Soups, Stews, and Sauces

Homemade soups, stews, and sauces are delicious and easy to prepare. Changing the amount of water in the recipe determines whether you get a soup, a stew, or a sauce. Thicken a leftover soup to create a sauce or stew. Add more water to a stew; voilà, it's a soup.

With the bounty of autumn's harvest or with winter's stored root vegetables, you can create colorful, flavorful soups, stews, and sauces to woo any palate. Thick, thin, smooth, or chunky styles—it's all up to you! Vary presentation and seasonings and go around the world without leaving your kitchen.

There is more than one way to cook a soup, stew, or sauce. Pressure cook, bake, boil or simmer. Puree raw vegetables, and fruits, too. Sometimes add beans and sea vegetables. Other times add pasta, fish, or grains. Season with salty seasonings, herbs, and spices for infinite variations all year round.

A simply delicious soup can be made from one vegetable. See *Fancy French Onion Soup* on page 110, for example. *Sweet Borscht* on page 111 is a beautiful red color, simple to prepare, and has only two vegetables. Of course, you can make a colorful soup with five to seven vegetables. More vegetables and ingredients complicate the flavor and compromise the distinct character of each vegetable. See *Invent Your Own Miso Soup* on page 113 and "Who's In First?" on page 116, for more guidance and improvisational techniques.

Rich flavors come from sautéing vegetables, spices, and cooked beans in extra virgin olive oil or sesame oil before adding them to a soup, stew, or sauce. See *Paradise of India* on page 123 and *It Must Be Chili* on page 133 for examples.

Creamy style soups are thick and satisfying. There are a number of ways to achieve a luscious, creamy texture without using milk or cream. Puree cooked vegetables and beans, add nut and seed milks, soy milk, Rice Dream drink, leftover cooked grains, or cooked grains, such as rolled oats, brown rice, or barley, in 6 times more water. For savory examples, see *Shiitake Barley Mushroom Soup* on page 112, *Heavenly Potato Leek Soup* on page 126, and *Creamy Cauliflower Soup* on page 127.

Stocks: The Basis of Soup, Stew, and Sauce Making

Vegetable Stocks

Add minerals and subtle favors. Save the water used from steaming vegetables, boiling pasta, or simmering beans, or make a stock from scratch by boiling one or a combination of the following: sea vegetables, shiitake mushrooms, vegetables, stinging nettles, herbs, spices. Making vegetable stocks is an excellent way to make use of vegetable scraps, such as onion skins, parsley stems, celery leaves, carrot tops and ends, roots of scallions and leeks, outer leaves and cores of cabbage. Cook the vegetables in a covered pot in twice as much water—if you have a pint of vegetables, use two pints of water. Boil for 20-30 minutes. Strain liquid through a colander and discard (compost) the residue. Use the stock immediately, save it in the refrigerator for up to a week, or freeze it for later use. Vegetable stocks work well in all cooking techniques.

Secrets

To make stew: Reduce the water in soup recipes by 50%. Add juicy chunks of vegetables, seitan, fish, or beans to the stock. Bean stews are great served over grains and noodles.

To thicken soups and stews: Add about a cup of cooked grains, such as oatmeal, barley, or brown rice.

To make a cholesterol-free creamy soup: Add flaked or cooked grains. Overcook the grains. They will become very creamy.

To thicken or extend the quantity of soups: Add quick cooking couscous or kasha. Add one-half cup grain and one cup of water, plus seasonings.

To make the flavor richer: Sauté the vegetables in extra virgin olive or sesame oil before you add them.

To use less salt: Add herbs, such as thyme, oregano, and basil, instead of salt. Use vegetables with salty flavors, like shiitake mushrooms and burdock.

To thicken leftover vegetable soup: Add diluted kudzu or arrowroot to make a sauce.

To make delicate soups and sauces: Add more water or stock; using fewer beans, vegetables, or grains.

To make a one-pot meal: Add either fish, tofu and noodles, or beans and grains to a vegetable soup or stew.

To make a quicker version of a soup, stew, or sauce made with beans: Start with precooked beans.

Common Improvisations for All Recipes

Substitutions

1. **Vegetables, herbs, and spices.** Invent your own combinations from what is fresh in your garden or refrigerator.

2. **Same-colored vegetables** for each other: carrots for winter squash and yams, etc.

3. **Leafy greens** for each other: bok choy for collards, etc.

4. **Foods from the same phases**. See charts on the Five Phases of Food on pages 22.

5. **Fresh herbs** for dried herbs and vice versa; use 3 times more fresh herbs than dried herbs, or to taste.

6. **Leeks,** onions, shallots, and scallions for each other.

7. **Beans** for each other: pinto beans for chickpeas, etc.

8. **Faster version of any recipe with dry beans**, you can substitute twice the amount of precooked beans.

9. **Sea vegetables** for each other: wakame for ocean ribbons, etc.

10. **Nut and seed milks** for each other: almond for cashew milk, etc.

11. **Salty seasonings** for each other: miso, tamari, shoyu, umeboshi vinegar, sea salt and Bragg Liquid Aminos.

12. **Flaked grains** for each other: rolled oats for kamut flakes, etc.

13. **Cloves of elephant garlic** for regular garlic.

14. **Amounts** of each ingredient according to what you like or what you have in stock: increase, decrease, or omit it.

15. **Cut the water in half** and pressure cook a simmered soup or stew in an insert.

16. **Puree** any bean or vegetable soup.

Fancy French Onion Soup

**Really quite simple and elegant, this soup is a
Thanksgiving tradition at my house.**

4 onions (1 quart),
sliced
2 quarts water
5 bay leaves
1 strip wakame
shoyu, tamari, or miso to taste

SERVES 6-8
TIME: 1-2 HOURS

Simmer onions, water, and bay leaves together for 1-2 hours. The soup just keeps getting sweeter, the longer it simmers. Season with miso, shoyu, or tamari. Garnish with lots of herb croutons (see recipe below).

Improvisation

Onion Sauce: Simmer 1-2 onions and 2 bay leaves in water to cover for 5-10 minutes, or until the onions are as soft as you like them. Season to taste with 1-2 tablespoons of either fresh dill, thyme, basil, or tarragon and a salty seasoning, such as Bragg Liquid Amino Acids or tamari. To make a spicy onion sauce, add ½ teaspoon of curry powder and 2 pressed cloves of garlic.

Herb Croutons

Be sure to make extra for salads and snacking.

6 slices of bread (1 quart),
cut into ½-inch cubes,
2 teaspoons dried oregano
2 teaspoons dried basil
2 teaspoons dried thyme
2 cloves garlic,
pressed or minced
5 tablespoons extra
virgin olive oil
¼ teaspoon sea salt

SERVES 6-8
TIME: 30 MINUTES

Preheat the oven to 350 degrees. Mix up the ingredients in a 9x13x2-inch baking dish. Bake for 20 minutes. Let croutons cool before serving.

Sweet Borscht

2 bunches of beets (about 2
quarts), without the greens,
sliced small, almost diced
5-inch strip of kelp or dulse
2 cups sliced potatoes
2½ quarts water

Put all the ingredients in a large soup pot. Simmer 15-25 minutes, till the beets are tender. Take the seaweed out and slice into tiny pieces. Stir it back into the soup. Taste and add a salty seasoning, if desired.

SERVES 6-8
TIME: 30 MINUTES

Chinese Hot and Spicy Soup

8 cups water
6 dried shiitake mushrooms
1-inch piece ginger, peeled
and sliced into 8
1/8-inch slices
2 carrots (1 cup),
sliced
1-2 stalks celery (1 cup),
sliced
1 small red bell pepper
(¼- 1/3 cup), sliced
½ pound firm tofu, sliced
into small bite-sized pieces
1 tablespoon tamari
½ teaspoon hot pepper
oil, or to taste

OPTIONAL:
1 package (5 ounces)
cooked clear noodles (bifun)

Simmer shiitake mushrooms in water for 15 minutes. Add slices of ginger and simmer for 10 minutes. Add carrots, celery, and red pepper. Simmer for 10 minutes. Add tofu and simmer 5 minutes. Add tamari and hot pepper oil to taste. If adding noodles or other cooked grains, you may want to add more hot pepper oil and/or tamari.

Improvisations

1. Add sliced snow peas as garnish.

2. For a one-pot meal, add a cooked grain, such as quinoa or rice.

3. Substitute fresh shiitake mushrooms for dried. Add them with the other vegetables.

SERVES 4-6
TIME: 45 MINUTES

Shiitake Barley Mushroom Soup

*1 cup barley, rinsed and
soaked overnight—expands to
2 cups
10 cups water
10 dried shiitake
mushrooms
1 strip wakame
2 onions, sliced
½ pound mushrooms,
sliced
3 carrots, sliced
2 stalks celery, sliced*

OPTIONAL:
*Add a salty seasoning,
such as miso or tamari,
to taste.*

**SERVES 4-6
TIME: 1 HOUR, 45 MINUTES**

In a large stock pot bring to a boil and simmer the barley, wakame, and shiitake mushrooms for an hour. Take out the wakame and shiitake mushrooms. Slice them into bite-sized pieces. Discard the mushroom stems. Return the shiitake and wakame to the soup. Add onions, and simmer for 10-20 minutes. Add sliced mushrooms, and simmer 5-10 minutes. Add carrots and celery. Simmer 10 minutes. Taste and add a salty seasoning, if desired.

Invent Your Own Miso Soup

OPTIONAL:
Add slices of ginger and/or shiitake mushrooms.

Choose either a 3-inch piece of dulse, wakame, alaria, ocean ribbons, kombu, digitata, kelp, or a small handful of sea palm, arame, or hiziki. Simmer in 4-6 cups of water.

Add 1-5 sliced raw or sautéed vegetables (see page 116 for sequencing guide). Simmer a short time for crunchy textures or longer for soft melt-in-your-mouth veggies. Turn off the heat. Mash a tablespoon of miso* into the soup pot or, if you prefer, ladle out some broth into a soup bowl. Dilute the miso** and add it back to the soup pot. Taste the soup and add more miso for a saltier flavor, if you like. Optional: garnish with chopped scallions.

---

* South River Miso is my personal preference. It has a chunky texture because it isn't pureed by a machine.

**Do not boil miso. Instead, add it to soups or stews after cooking to preserve its enzymes and beneficial living cultures that aid digestion.

Miso Vegetable Soup

Noodles are everyone's favorite. Save their cooking water and use it for soup stock. While this soup takes a while to simmer, it is not labor-intensive.

12 cups water
1 strip of wakame or any other variety of sea vegetable
10 shiitake mushrooms dried
3 onions, sliced
1 giant carrot (1½ cups), sliced
6 collard greens
1-2 tablespoons miso, or to taste
1 bunch of scallions, sliced

SERVES 4-6
TIME: 1 HOUR, 40 MINUTES

Simmer the water, shiitakes, wakame, and noodle water 1 hour. Strain out the mushrooms and wakame. Slice them. Discard the stems, or return them to the soup. Some people, especially children, like to eat the stems. Others find them too tough to chew. Add the onions and carrots and simmer for 30 minutes. Add collard greens and turn off the heat. Mash in miso, or take out a ladle of broth, dissolve the miso in it, and pour it back into the soup. Taste and add more for a saltier flavor. Serve, garnished with scallions.

Improvisations

1. In a hurry? Just simmer 1 quart of water or noodle stock with quicker cooking vegetables, such as watercress, bok choy, or scallions. Omit the dried shiitake mushrooms and use fresh shiitake or white button mushrooms. (Or, if you happen to have just made pasta, you can strain the water and use it. If you have pasta stock in reserve in the refrigerator, you can use that, too, adding water to make up the balance of the twelve cups.)

THE QUICK & EASY ORGANIC GOURMET

2. Try other combinations of vegetables: onions, carrots, tofu, and celery; delicata squash, leeks, celery; onions, parsnips, and carrots; scallions and tofu; onions, shiitake mushrooms, broccoli, string beans, Chinese cabbage, and tofu.

3. **Macro Mushroom Sauce:** Use this vegetable combination, or use the base of this soup, the shiitake mushrooms, to make a sauce. You can add sliced ginger and burdock, or make up your own vegetable combination. Use only 2-3 cups of water. Simmer twenty minutes. Thicken with ¼ cup of kudzu diluted in ½ cup water. Season to taste with tamari or shoyu. Serve on top of grains or noodles. Garnish with toasted sesame seeds, fresh chopped parsley, or scallions.

Invent Your Own Soups, Stews, or Sauce

Who's In First?

Red and brown lentils	presoaked beans
sea vegetables	long cooking grains,
split peas	such as barley
dried shiitake mushrooms	bay leaves

If you are not starting with a stock, you may want to add a few herbs and/or spices to flavor the water, such as: rosemary, thyme, peppercorns, cumin seeds, celery seeds, basil, oregano, marjoram, sage, garlic, coriander seeds, cilantro, cloves, ginger, parsley. You can sauté vegetables in herbs or spices before adding them to the soup. Also, you can season the soup to taste with herbs or spices after cooking.

Followed soon (10-15 minutes) by: onions, leeks, potatoes, fresh or dried burdock

What's Next?

Firm, root, round and cylindrical vegetables. Add these after the beans have cooked 20-30 minutes, or, if you want the beans to be creamy and the stock rich, after the beans have cooked about 45-60 minutes. If you are not making a bean soup, slice and add some of these vegetables after the onions and sea vegetables have cooked 10-20 minutes:

carrots	turnips	green cabbage
winter squash	parsnips	beets
daikon	cauliflower	kale
red cabbage	spices	celery
"quick" cooking grains,		
such as kasha, and uncooked pasta		

For a creamy soup, add cooked grains or other flaked grains, such as rolled oats, spelt flakes, or kamut flakes.

Fish: Shrimp, cut up pieces of scrod, cusk, monkfish, or salmon. Add vegetables before or after the fish, depending on the thickness of the fish. Simmer fish 10 minutes for every inch of thickness.

Who's In Third?

Quick cooking vegetables require little or no cooking. Simply add them to hot stock or water and turn off the heat immediately. The heat stimulates their fibers to reach a brilliant, peak color:

bok choy	collards	Napa cabbage
string beans	snow peas	summer squash
mushrooms	watercress	tofu
mustard greens	mizuna	Swiss chard
asparagus	broccoli	bean sprouts
wild leeks		
precooked beans, noodles, and grains		

Let tofu, precooked grains, and noodles coming straight from the refrigerator simmer about 3 minutes, till hot. Thin cod fish, cusk, or monkfish (the chowder fishes) can be added at this stage as well.

Home Run: Last But Not Least!

herbs	mirin	tamari
vinegar	shoyu	salt
miso	spices	Bragg Liquid Aminos
diluted arrowroot or kudzu		

Bean Cookery

Beans are versatile and often a favorite with children. Some beans cook faster if presoaked. Some beans can be cooked on a whim.

Split peas, mung beans, and red and brown lentils cook relatively quickly, without presoaking. They offer you the most spontaneity. Soak black beans, pintos, kidneys, navies, limas, adukis, anasazi , and other medium-sized beans at least 2-4 hours before cooking. Chickpeas and black, yellow, and white soybeans need 6-8 hours or overnight soaking.

Pick through a measured amount of beans and discard any stones. Rinse beans at least three times. If they need presoaking, put beans in a large bowl or large jar with triple the volume of water. Crowded presoaking beans do not expand and take longer to cook.

Quick Bean-Soaking Method: Boil 3 cups of water for each cup of beans. Put the beans in a bowl and pour boiling water on top. Let beans stand for at least one hour. (Soaking beans in hot water cuts the soaking time by 25%.) Drain and rinse beans before simmering, baking, or pressure cooking.

Overnight Soaking: While not as spontaneous as the quick method, it works. Rinse beans at least three times and soak them in twice their amount of water until the next morning. Then rinse the beans until the water runs clear.

Bean skins can get caught in the vent, lid, or rubber gasket of a pressure cooker. Use a ceramic pressure cooker insert, or simmer bean soups in a stock pot.

Cook's Tips: Beans double in size with soaking. Plan accordingly. If you want to cook 1 cup of beans, soak ½ cup. Always discard beans' soaking water, as it is gas producing.

Whether I am going to make a spicy Mexican bean dish, a Mediterranean marinated bean salad, a hot Indian curry, or just plain beans, I always cook the beans with a sea vegetable. Almost any one will do.

Using a Ceramic Pressure Cooker Insert (Rice Crock)

The proportion of beans to liquid depends on whether you want the beans to be whole, soft, or creamy. Are you in the mood for a bean soup? Stew? Or just plain beans? Will the beans cook alone, or with grains, vegetables, or spices?

For whole beans suitable for a salad or side dish and pressure cooked inside a ceramic pressure cooker insert, cook an equal amount of beans to water. Presoak one cup of pinto or other beans that need presoaking. Drain out the soaking water. Cook beans with a 3-inch piece of a sea vegetable and only one cup of water.

If you want to make a stew, cook 1 cup of dry or presoaked beans with 2 cups of water. Add vegetables, spices, and a sea vegetable. You can also sauté spices and vegetables before pressure cooking them with beans. Add herbs like dill, basil, or thyme, and a salty seasoning to taste after pressure cooking.

If you want to make a soup, cook 1 cup dry or presoaked beans with 3 cups of water, along with vegetables and spices. Add herbs and salty seasonings to taste after pressure cooking.

For specific instructions on "How to Use a Rice Crock in a Pressure Cooker," see page 202.

Basic Beans

Once cooked, add beans to a stew, a soup, or a salad,
or mash and season them for a dip.

1 cup dry chick peas, kidney, pinto, anasazi, navy, lima, or black beans, presoaked overnight and drained
2 cups water if simmering or 1 cup water if pressure cooking beans inside a ceramic pressure cooker insert
3 inches kelp, ocean ribbons, or dulse
Chopped parsley or scallions for garnish

SERVES 4-6
TIME: 1-2 HOURS

Rinse beans. Boil and simmer beans and water with the sea vegetable for 1½–2 hours.

Or:

Pressure cook rinsed beans, water, and sea vegetable inside the insert for 45 minutes—1 hour.

Improvisations

1. Pressure cook red and brown lentils in the insert for only 10-20 minutes, without prior soaking.

2. **Creamy Beans:** Puree half of the cooked beans. Mix them together with cooked whole beans for a saucy consistency. See *Brazilian Style Black Bean Soup* on page 130.

3. Use cooked beans to make chili or refried beans (see page 69).

4. **Ginger Mustard Beans:** Cook beans with slices of ginger. Season cooked beans to taste with mustard and barley malt or molasses.

Autumn Minestrone

Inspired by the colorful New England fall foliage

1 cup dry kidney beans, presoaked and rinsed
5 bay leaves
5 cups water
3-4-inch strip digitata, or other sea vegetable
1 tablespoon extra virgin olive oil
8 cloves garlic, sliced or pressed
1 onion (large or medium), sliced
11-12 plum tomatoes, sliced
2-3 carrots (1½ cups), sliced
1-2 stalks celery (1 cup), sliced (use leaves, too)
1 cup or 1 bunch fresh basil
1½ teaspoons dried summer savory, or a fresh bunch
1 teaspoon sea salt, or to taste

Simmer kidney beans and bay leaves in water for about 15 minutes. Add seaweed. Simmer till beans are done, about another 30-40 minutes. Add more water, if needed. Sauté onions and garlic in olive oil for 2 minutes, and add them to cooking (almost soft) kidney beans. Rinse and slice tomatoes. Add them to kidney beans. Simmer 1 hour, or until they turn into a sauce. Add carrots and celery. Simmer an hour, or until tender. Add basil and savory. Simmer 5 minutes. Season to taste with sea salt.

Improvisations

1. Add cooked macaroni or shells to the finished soup. Adjust the seasonings, if desired.

2. Season the soup with oregano and thyme.

SERVES 6-8
TIME: 2 HOURS

THE QUICK & EASY ORGANIC GOURMET

Thanks, Grandma

I will always remember my Grandma Ethel's Lima Bean and Barley Soup. *Here is a delicious variation on it without meat.*

*1 cup presoaked and rinsed
lima or navy beans
6 cups water
1 strip of a sea vegetable, such
as wakame or ocean ribbons
1 onion, sliced
1 carrot, sliced
2 stalks celery, sliced
1 small bunch of dill,
minced, or at least
1 teaspoon dried
miso, or salt and pepper
to taste*

OPTIONAL:
*Add bay leaves
or other herbs and spices,
such as garlic, black pepper,
and coriander.*

SERVES 4-6
TIME: 40 MINUTES

Simmer beans in water with wakame and onions for 20-30 minutes until beans are soft. Add carrots and celery. Simmer for 5 minutes, or until these vegetables are as soft as you like them. Taste a carrot. Add dill. Taste and add a salty seasoning and pepper, if desired.

Or:

Pressure cook all the ingredients except the dill in an insert for 30 minutes. Use only 3 cups of water.

Improvisations

1. Add some more greens: 1 or 2 leaves of sliced collards or a stem of broccoli.

2. Enhance the color of the soup by adding sliced red pepper.

3. Substitute barley for lima beans.

Red Lentil Asparagus Soup

Rich in flavor and salt-free

2 cups red lentils, rinsed
8 cups water
1 red or yellow
onion, sliced
5-inch piece of dulse
2 dozen asparagus
spears, sliced

OPTIONAL:
1 teaspoon
curry powder

Simmer water with red lentils for 30 minutes. Add dulse and onions, and simmer 20 minutes. Add asparagus, and simmer 10 minutes.

Improvisation

Instead of asparagus, substitute 1 bunch of broccoli, or mustard greens, or a head of cauliflower.

SERVES 4-6
TIME: 1 HOUR, 5 MINUTES

THE QUICK & EASY ORGANIC GOURMET

Paradise of India

Everyone loves this soup.

1 teaspoon mustard seeds
1 teaspoon cumin seeds
1 tablespoon extra
virgin olive oil
2-3 large cloves garlic,
peeled and sliced
2-3-inch piece of ginger,
peeled and grated
1 large onion, sliced
1 medium cauliflower,
(1 quart), sliced into bite-
sized pieces for a smooth
texture, or florets for a
chunky-style soup.
3-inch piece of dulse
1½ cups red lentils or
mung beans, rinsed
5 cups water or stock if
simmering, (noodle stock is
particularly delicious), or 3
cups water if pressure cooking
in an insert

OPTION #1:
Add a stalk of celery and a
carrot, sliced, when you add
cauliflower.

OPTION #2:
Add ½-1 teaspoon of curry
powder, or to taste.

SERVES 4-6
TIME : 60 MINUTES FOR
SIMMERING OR 20 MINUTES
FOR PRESSURE COOKING
IN AN INSERT

Dry roast the mustard seeds and cumin seeds till the mustard seeds pop. Add olive oil, garlic, ginger, and onions. Sauté for about 5 minutes till the onions and spices blend together and are coated with the oil. Add cauliflower, dulse, water, and lentils and simmer for an hour or pressure cook in the insert for 20 minutes. Season with curry, miso, or salt and pepper.

Improvisation

Substitute carrots and celery or potatoes for cauliflower.

Lentil Soup

This is a great cold weather, warming entree.
Serve with peasant bread and salad.

1 cup brown lentils*, rinsed
3 shiitake mushrooms, or ¼-½
pound white mushrooms
1 onion, sliced
1 large carrot, yam, or small
butternut or delicata squash,
sliced
2 stalks celery, sliced
3-inch piece of dulse,
wakame, or ocean ribbon
3 cups water for pressure
cooking in an insert, or 6 cups
water for simmering
miso, Bragg Liquid Aminos,
shoyu, or salt and pepper
to taste

OPTION #1:
Omit the shiitake mushrooms.
Add any one or all of the
following: 3 cloves of garlic,
some wine, a bay leaf or two.

OPTION #2:
Omit the shiitake mushrooms.
Add tomato sauce and
season to taste with fresh or
dried basil, oregano, and
thyme after pressure cooking,
or when lentils and veg-
etables are cooked. For a
spicy version, add a pinch of
red pepper flakes, or sauté
vegetables in hot pepper
sesame oil.

SERVES 4-8
TIME: 20 MINUTES PRESSURE
COOKING IN AN INSERT
OR 50 MINUTES FOR SIMMERING

Boil and simmer lentils for about 15 minutes. Add a sea vegetable, shiitake mushrooms, and onions. Simmer for 15-20 minutes. Add celery, carrots, and garlic. Simmer for 10-15 minutes, or until lentils and vegetables are soft and even creamy. Season to taste with herbs and/or a salty seasoning.

Or:

Put all the ingredients in the pressure cooker insert. Place the lentils on the bottom and the sea vegetable on top . Pour 1 quart of hot tap water in the pressure cooker. Put the insert into the pressure cooker. (Hot water should reach halfway up the insert.) Lock the lid into place. Bring the pressure cooker up to pressure and cook for 20 minutes for the brown lentils, 10 for the red. Allow the pressure cooker to come down naturally, or put the pressure cooker under cold water to quickly release pressure. Take off the lid. Stir and taste the lentils. Season to taste with herbs, and/or a salty seasoning.

Improvisation

Other great vegetable combinations are butternut squash, onion, and parsnip or burdock.

---

* You could use red lentils, or a combination of the two.

THE QUICK & EASY ORGANIC GOURMET

Sweet Split Pea Soup

1 cup rinsed yellow or green
split peas
6 cups water for simmering,
or 3 cups water for pressure
cooking in a rice crock
3-inch strip of wakame or
other sea vegetable
1 onion, sliced
1 yam, sliced, or 1 small
winter squash (such as a
delicata or butternut), peeled
and cut into
bite-sized pieces
1 celery stalk, sliced

OPTIONAL:
Add 1 teaspoon of your favorite
dried herb, or a small bunch
of minced fresh herbs. You can
try dill for an Eastern Euro-
pean flavor, rosemary for a
French accent, curry for
Indian fire, etc.
Season to taste with salt and
pepper, Bragg Liquid Aminos,
or miso.

SERVES 6-8
TIME: 55 MINUTES FOR PRESSURE
COOKING IN AN INSERT, OR 1
HOUR, 15 MINUTES FOR
SIMMERING

Boil and simmer the split peas and water for 30 minutes, or until the split peas soften. Skim off foam. Add sea vegetable and onions. Simmer for 15-20 minutes. Add yam and celery. Simmer until these vegetables are soft, about 10-15 minutes. Season with herbs, spices, or salty seasoning.

To pressure cook the soup in an insert, place all the ingredients in insert. Mix them up now, or after cooking. Pour 1 quart of tap water in the pressure cooker. Put the insert into the pressure cooker. (Hot water should reach halfway up the insert.) Lock the lid into place. Bring the pressure cooker up to pressure and cook for 45 minutes. Add herbs or curries, and season to taste with a salty seasoning.

Improvisations

1. Try ¾ cup split peas with one of the following combinations:

   a. 1 yam, 1 carrot, 2 stalks of celery, and onion.

   b. 1 large Jerusalem artichoke or potato, 2 carrots, 1 stalk of celery, and 1 onion.

   c. 1 small cauliflower cut into small florets, 1 yam, 2 onions, 2 stalks of celery.

2. **Split Pea Barley Soup:** Add cooked barley, or cook barley in with the soup.

Blender Soups

Heavenly Potato Leek Soup

5 1/3 *cups water*
1 strip wakame
6 potatoes (4 1/2 cups), sliced
2 leeks (1 1/2 cups), sliced
1/3 cup almonds
2 teaspoons savory or thyme

SERVES 6
TIME: 30 MINUTES

Boil and simmer 4 cups of water and wakame. Slice and add potatoes. Clean and slice leeks. Add them to the soup. Simmer 15-20 minutes, until potatoes are soft. Stir in savory. Turn off the soup. Grind the almonds into a fine meal in a food processor. Add 1-1 1/3 cups of water. Blend the water and almonds to make almond milk. Strain the almond milk and mix it into the soup. Taste and adjust the seasonings, if desired.

Improvisations

1. **Creamy Squash Soup:** Substitute butternut squash and onions for the potatoes and leeks. Season to taste with cinnamon, nutmeg, and cloves.

2. You can make a scrumptious pureed squash soup by just simmering butternut squash with onions and ocean ribbons (kombu) till tender. Puree in a blender and season to taste with either tamari or basil, dried celery leaves, and sea salt.

Creamy Cauliflower Soup

It's smooth, creamy, and simple to make. You can use it as a sauce, too. It thickens as it stands, but don't add water, just heat and serve.

8 cups noodle stock
or water
1 onion (1 cup), sliced
1 medium cauliflower
(1 quart), cut into
bite-sized pieces
1½ cup kamut flakes
tamari, shoyu, Bragg
Liquid Aminos, or salt and
pepper to taste

OPTIONAL:
Add a fresh bunch of herbs, such
as dill, thyme, or oregano, to
the blender.

Simmer all the ingredients for about 30 minutes. Blend soup in a blender or food processor.

SERVES 6-8
TIME: 40 MINUTES

Creamy Broccoli Soup

This basic recipe is versatile and simple to prepare.
Spelt flakes require 25% less water than oatmeal or
kamut flakes. I decided to add more spelt flakes,
rather than decrease the water.

2 cups spelt flakes
8 cups water
1 teaspoon sea salt
1 head of broccoli (about 1
quart), sliced into
bite-sized pieces
1 onion, sliced
1 carrot, sliced
2 stalks celery, sliced
½ pound mushrooms, sliced
miso or umeboshi vinegar,
to taste
fresh dill, chives, or other
herb for garnish

Simmer spelt flakes, water, and salt for 20 minutes. Add vegetables and simmer for 10 minutes, or simmer all the ingredients for 30 minutes. Puree soup in a blender. Season to taste with miso or umeboshi vinegar, and garnish with herbs.

Improvisation

Add a sea vegetable.

SERVES 6-8
TIME: 40 MINUTES

Gypsy Bean Soup

A delightful dinner soup for a cold winter's day or any time of year. Scoop it up with crusty peasant bread.

1 cup dry aduki bean, rinsed and soaked overnight in 3-4 cups water
8 cups water
3-inch strip of a sea vegetable, such as kelp or ocean ribbon
1 pound of carrots, sliced
1 onion (1 cup), sliced
1 teaspoon extra virgin olive oil
2 cloves garlic, sliced
1 teaspoon basil
½ teaspoon oregano
½ teaspoon thyme
2 tablespoons umeboshi vinegar

OPTIONAL:
You can substitute lemon juice and sea salt for the umeboshi vinegar.

SERVES 4-6
TIME: 1 HOUR, 10 MINUTES

Discard soaking water and rinse adukis several more times till the water runs clear. Put beans in a large soup pot with kelp and 8 cups water. Simmer for 45 minutes, until beans are soft. Add carrots and simmer 10 more minutes, or until carrots are tender. Sauté the onions, garlic, umeboshi vinegar, and herbs in olive oil for about 5 minutes, or until the onions are soft. Add to the simmering soup. When the carrots are tender, puree the soup in a food processor or blender.

Improvisations

1. Since aduki beans taste like potatoes, substitute potatoes for all or some of the aduki beans.

2. Another tasty herbal combination to try is thyme and rosemary.

3. Do not purée the soup.

Brazilian Black Bean Soup

1 cup dry black beans, soaked
overnight or for at least 2
hours (expands to 2½ cups)
4 bay leaves
3-inch strip of kelp, dulse,
alaria, or any other sea
vegetable
4 cups water for simmering
or 2¹/₃ cups water for
pressure cooking
in a rice crock
1 small cauliflower,
or green cabbage
(1¹/₃ cups), sliced
1 teaspoon-1 tablespoon
sesame or extra virgin
olive oil
1 Spanish or large onion (1¼
cups), sliced
3 cloves garlic, sliced
or whole
1-2 teaspoons cumin seed
2-inch piece ginger,
peeled and grated
bunch of cilantro
(at least ¹/₃ cup)

OPTIONAL:
Season to taste with sea salt or
umeboshi vinegar.
Serve with fresh wedges of
lime or salsa.

SERVES 4-6
TIME: 1½ HOUR FOR SIMMER-
ING, OR 50 MINUTES FOR PRES-
SURE COOKING IN AN INSERT

Boil and simmer black beans with bay leaves, 4 cups water, and the sea vegetable for about an hour, until black beans are soft. Add cauliflower. Sauté the onions, cumin seeds, and garlic in olive oil. Add them to the cooked beans. Simmer soup till cauliflower is soft, about 15-20 minutes. Squeeze the grated ginger juice into the pot. Puree half or all of the soup in a blender or food processor with the cilantro. Return pureed soup to the pot. Mix with remaining soup, if any. Season to taste with salsa, sea salt, or miso.

Or:

Sauté olive oil, garlic, ginger, cumin seeds, bay leaves, and onions for a couple of minutes in a large skillet. Rinse beans. Put beans, water, kelp, cauliflower, sautéed spices, and onions in a medium insert. Put its lid on. Pour 1 quart of tap water in the pressure cooker. Put the insert into the pressure cooker. (Hot water should reach halfway up the insert.) Lock the lid into place. Bring the pressure cooker up to pressure and cook for 40 minutes. Season to taste with salsa, sea salt, or umeboshi vinegar.

French Patty Pan Stew . . . and Soup

Transform this scrumptious stew to a soup
by adding 1 pint of water.

3 tablespoons extra virgin olive oil
2 large onions (4 cups), sliced
9 cloves garlic, sliced
6 bay leaves
7 patty pan squashes (21 cups), sliced
2 bunches of celery and their leaves (about 13 stalks or 7 cups), sliced
1 bunch parsley tops (2 cups), (use the stems, too if they are tender) sliced
2 tablespoons fresh thyme leaves, or 2 teaspoons dried, or to taste
1 teaspoon sea salt, or to taste

OPTIONAL:
Season to taste with pepper.

SERVES 6-8
MAKES 3½ QUARTS OF STEW. ADD
1 PINT OF WATER
TO MAKE 4 QUARTS OF SOUP.
TIME: 25 MINUTES

Heat a stock pot. Add and sauté olive oil, onions, bay leaves, and garlic for 3 minutes. Add squash. Cover the pot and stew for 5 minutes. Add celery. Cover the pot and stew for 10 minutes, while you take the leaves off the stems of thyme. Stir up the vegetables. They are very juicy from keeping the cover on the pot. Add and stir in the parsley, when the vegetables are tender and juicy. Then add and stir in the thyme. Taste it and add the salt, if you like. Season to taste with salt and pepper.

To create a soup add a pint of water, and a bit more salt and thyme.

Sweet Bean Stew

For a faster version of this recipe, you can start with 2-3 cups of cooked beans.

1 cup of beans, such as pintos,
kidneys, navies, adukis, or
chick peas, presoaked
3-3½ cups water
1 strip of wakame, dulse,
kelp, or ocean ribbon
3 bay leaves
2 leeks, or 1 large onion
(at least a cup), sliced
1 rutabaga or large carrot,
sliced into chunks (roll or
triangular cut)
Choose either 1 delicata
squash, 1 butternut squash,
2 sweet potatoes,
or 1 large yam
miso or tamari to taste

OPTIONAL:
Season with 1 teaspoon dried
thyme, oregano, or marjoram
and 1 tablespoon basil,
or with fresh herbs, such as a
bunch of dill

SERVES 4-6
TIME: 45 MINUTES

Soak beans overnight. Drain and rinse beans until the water runs clear. Cover beans with 3-3½ cups of water, simmer beans, water, bay leaves, and sea vegetable for about 20 minutes, or until beans begin to soften. Add sliced onions. Scrub and slice squash or yams into 1-inch squares. Add to stew. Wash, slice, and add carrots. Simmer 20 minutes, or until beans are tender and squash is soft. Taste and season with miso or tamari, if desired.

Improvisation

You can add any one of these vegetables: parsnip, cabbage, celery, burdock, daikon, or shiitake mushroom.

---

* If you are starting with precooked beans, you don't need to use 3-3½ cups of water. Start with about ½-1 cup of water before adding the onions and other vegetables. Add more water if the pot dries out.

It Must Be Chili

1¼ cup pinto or kidney
beans, presoaked and rinsed
3 cups of water
3-inch piece ocean ribbon
1 tablespoon extra virgin
olive oil
1 Spanish onion or 2 onions
(2 cups), sliced
5 cloves garlic, sliced
5 bay leaves
1 tablespoon cumin seeds
3 cups unseasoned tomato
sauce, or can of crushed
tomatoes
1 large carrot, or fresh
corn, steamed and cut off
2 large cobs, or 2 cups
canned or frozen corn
1 large green pepper (1 cup),
sliced or celery
2 tablespoons dried oregano,
or small bunch of fresh
oregano
or marjoram, chopped
2 tablespoons dried basil, or
a fresh bunch of basil,
chopped
2 tablespoons chili powder
½-1 teaspoon sea salt,
or to taste

OPTIONAL:
Add ¼ teaspoon cayenne pepper.

SERVES 4-6
TIME: 1 HOUR, 20 MINUTES

Simmer pinto beans, ocean ribbon, and water for an hour. Sauté olive oil, garlic, cumin seeds, bay leaves, and onions for 5 minutes in a large skillet or stock pot. Add cooked beans, and sauté for 5 minutes. Add tomato sauce, corn, and pepper. Simmer for 5 minutes to blend flavors. Stir in basil, oregano, chili powder, and cayenne. Season to taste with sea salt and more cayenne for a spicier chili.

Improvisations

1. For a faster version of this recipe, you can start with 3 cups cooked pinto beans.

2. Use fresh tomatoes instead of canned.

3. Use a fresh hot chili pepper or crushed chili peppers instead of cayenne.

4. In the winter, when fresh organic peppers and tomatoes are hard to find, use a can of seasoned tomato sauce. Add fresh carrots and celery. Season to taste with chili powder, oregano, and sea salt.

French Peasant Stew

Wow!

1¼ cups chickpeas, presoaked
overnight
3½ cups water
4 bay leaves
1 strip dulse
1 tablespoon extra virgin
olive oil
6 cloves garlic, sliced
1 large onion
(at least 1 cup), sliced
2 carrots (1½ cups)
1 small cauliflower (3 cups),
cut into bite-sized pieces
1 tablespoon dried basil
½ teaspoon black pepper
½ teaspoon cardamom
¼ teaspoon dried cloves
¼ teaspoon sea salt

SERVES 4-6
TIME: 1 HOUR

Drain and rinse beans well. Simmer beans, water, dulse, and bay leaves for about 30 minutes, until the beans begin to soften. Sauté garlic, onions, cauliflower, and carrots in olive oil for 5 minutes. Add them to the beans. Simmer for 15 minutes. Season with basil, cardamom, cloves, salt, and pepper.

Improvisations

1. Change the nationality of the stew by changing the seasoning. For instance, add curry powder, garam marsala, cinnamon, and cardamom for an Indian accent.

2. Leave out the cauliflower, or otherwise vary the vegetables. Try some potatoes and peppers.

3. Change the beans to kidney or pinto. Switch the herbs and spices to garlic, oregano, pepper, basil, cumin, and chili powder for a Mexican chili.

THE QUICK & EASY ORGANIC GOURMET

Sunset Casserole

1 recipe **Mushroom Leek Sauce**
(see page 146).
1½ cups string beans
¼ cup almonds
2 cups butternut or delicata
squash, sliced ½-inch thick
into bite-sized pieces
1 large carrot (1 cup), sliced
into match sticks or 3-4 cups
squash and no carrots

SERVES 4-6
TIME: 1 HOUR

Preheat the oven to 350 degrees. Make the *Mushroom Leek Sauce*. In a 9x13x2-inch baking dish, place the string beans. Then spread the almonds throughout the pan. Add the squash, and then place the carrots on top. Pour the mushroom leek sauce over the vegetables. Bake the casserole covered for 30-45 minutes, or until the vegetables are tender.

Improvisation

Substitute 1 stalk (2 cups) of sliced broccoli for string beans, leave out the carrots, and use more butternut squash (4 cups).

Seitan-making Party and Pot Roast

5½ cups whole wheat
bread flour
6¼ cups water
a few strips (2 oz)
ocean ribbon
4 bay leaves
4 dried shiitake mushrooms
6 cloves garlic, peeled
2-inch piece ginger,
peeled and sliced
1 large onion or leek,
cut in chunks
2 carrots, or a winter squash,
or large yam,
sliced in chunks
1 parsnip or summer squash,
sliced in chunks
½ cup tamari

OPTION #1:
Add mirin, wine, or sherry.

OPTION #2:
Add sage during the last 5
minutes of cooking.

SERVES 6-8
TIME: 2 HOURS

Mix together the flour and 3¼ cups of water. Knead the mixture into a ball for 5-10 minutes, or until it has the consistency of an earlobe. Cover with cold water for at least 10 minutes. If you have room, put it in the refrigerator; otherwise, add ice cubes to the bowl. You can leave it in cold water for several hours.

Spill out the cold water. Rinse the dough in a colander with warm water, squeezing and kneading it until the water runs clear (15 minutes), and it resembles a brownish-tan sponge. In the final rinses, use cold water to make the dough firm like a rubber ball. To check if you have rinsed it enough, lift the dough up and squeeze it. The liquid released should be clear. If not, continue rinsing and kneading. (After rinsing, the dough shrinks, but it does expand back to its original size after cooking.) You can put the rinsed seitan (dough) in a large stew pot and let it rise for 10 minutes.

Place the ocean ribbons on the bottom of a large stew pot. Add the garlic, ginger, bay leaves, onions, shiitake mushrooms, carrots, and parsnips. Place the seitan on top. Pour tamari and 3 cups of water to come up to the level of the seitan, or to barely cover it.

Cover and simmer or bake (325 degrees) for about an hour, or until the seitan is tender.

THE QUICK & EASY ORGANIC GOURMET

Improvisations

1. **Tamari-ginger Gravy:** Transform the tamari-ginger broth into a gravy. Dilute 1 tablespoon of arrowroot or kudzu in ¼ cup of cold water for each cup of liquid you want to thicken. Simmer gravy and add diluted kudzu. Stir. Serve over noodles, grilled or fried tofu, or seitan.

2. **Cutlets:** You can also deep fry slices of seitan. Bread it first in arrowroot powder. Deep fry it in sesame oil. Serve deep-fried seitan with mustard and sauerkraut as an appetizer or main dish.

3. You can also make the seitan without vegetables. Simmer it in just the ginger, tamari, water, and ocean ribbon for an hour, or until tender. Enjoy it as is, or add it to chili, stir fries, bean stews, kabobs, or sweet-and-sour sauces.

Holiday Tempeh

Try it for Thanksgiving or any fall or winter day.

2 tablespoons extra virgin
olive oil or sesame oil
2 10-ounce packages
of tempeh, cut into
bite-sized cubes
1 delicata squash or yam
(2½ cups), cut into
bite-sized pieces
15 Brussels sprouts,
cut in half
3 cups water*
1½ tablespoons mustard
1½ tablespoons barley miso
2 teaspoons dried sage
2 teaspoons dried oregano
2 teaspoons dried rosemary
2 teaspoons dried thyme
1 tablespoon kudzu
or arrowroot diluted in 2
tablespoons of water

SERVES 6
TIME: 50 MINUTES

Heat a heavy pot. Add olive oil. Sauté tempeh in olive oil for 5 minutes, till tempeh is golden. Add squash, Brussels sprouts, herbs, mustard, miso, and water. Simmer for 30-40 minutes, until tempeh and vegetables are tender. Dissolve kudzu in 2 tablespoons of cold water. Stir it into the pot for about a minute, till sauce thickens. Taste and adjust the seasonings. Serve as a stew or sauce. It is delicious accompanied by *Roasted Potatoes* (see page 177).

Improvisation

Add onions, leeks, cauliflower, potatoes, or mushrooms.

---

* You can substitute one cup of white wine such as *Four Chimneys Cooking Wine with Garlic*, for one cup of water.

THE QUICK & EASY ORGANIC GOURMET

Emperor's Sweet-and-Sour Tempeh

A great way to introduce newcomers to tempeh.

*1 8- or 10-ounce package
of tempeh, cubed
¼ cup tamari
⅓ cup barley malt
1½ tablespoons rice vinegar
½ cup water
3-4 carrots (½ pound), sliced
1 large onion, sliced
10 red radishes,
or 1 small daikon, sliced*

SERVES 3-4
TIME: 1 HOUR, 5 MINUTES

Simmer everything 1 hour, or until tempeh is tender.

Sweet-and-Sour Tempeh and Vegetables

No salt added!

*1 8- or 10-ounce package
tempeh (soy or grain), cubed
1½ cups water
1 large onion, sliced
15 Brussels sprouts, or 2 carrots
and 1 zucchini, sliced in
small chunks (roll cut)
½ cup barley malt
1½ tablespoons rice vinegar
2 tablespoons kudzu*

SERVES 3-4
TIME: 40 MINUTES

Simmer tempeh in 1 cup of water for 5 minutes while you slice vegetables. Add the onions, carrots, and then the zucchini. Add barley malt and rice vinegar. Simmer 30 minutes, until the tempeh and carrots are tender. Dilute kudzu in ½ cup cold water. Stir it into the stew or sauce. Simmer 2 minutes, until thick. Add more diluted kudzu for a thicker stew. Taste it and adjust the sweet or sour flavors, if necessary.

Improvisation

Substitute tofu or fish for tempeh. Fish will not need to be simmered as long. Cook fish 10 minutes for each inch of thickness. Most fish are less than an inch thick.

Sweet-and-Sour Everything

*Serve sweet and sour vegetable sauces on top of baked
fish, deep-fried tofu, fried fish, cooked grains, and pasta.*

Improvisations

1. You can make a sweet-and-sour sauce with just rice vinegar and barley malt. Thicken it with diluted kudzu. Serve it over vegetables, noodles, grains, fish, tofu, or tempeh.

2. Make a sweet-and-sour sauce with just one vegetable, like string beans, or two, such as string beans and peppers.

Curried Vegetables

Curried vegetables are delicious as a side dish or as a topping for grains or pasta. You can add beans, tofu, and nuts, too. There are endless satisfying combinations. These savory recipes are mildly spicy and salt-free.

Vegetables in Indian Spices

*1 tablespoon sesame oil or
extra virgin olive oil
1 large onion, sliced
5-6 red, yellow, or white
potatoes (1 quart), sliced
1 cup water
3 large carrots, sliced
3 peppers, sliced, or
2 cups peas
1 tablespoon curry powder
1 teaspoon garam marsala
1 teaspoon dried coriander
1 teaspoon cinnamon*

Sauté onions and potatoes in oil in a 4-quart stock pot for 5-10 minutes; add water when the pot dries out. Add carrots and sauté-simmer till they turn bright orange. Add peppers. Sauté till all the vegetables are tender. Stir in spices. Taste and adjust seasonings, if desired.

SERVES 4-6
TIME: 25 MINUTES

Curried Summer Vegetables

1 teaspoon sesame
or extra virgin olive oil
1 large onion, sliced
2 medium potatoes, sliced
1 large carrot, sliced
1 zucchini, sliced
20 string beans, sliced
½ cup water
1 teaspoon curry powder

OPTIONAL:
Add garlic.

SERVES 4-6
TIME: 25 MINUTES

Sauté potatoes and onions in oil for 5-10 minutes; add carrots and sauté for a few minutes, till they turn bright orange. Add zucchini and string beans and sauté a couple of minutes, till tender. Add water whenever the pot dries out. Add more water for a thinner sauce, and less for a stew. Season to taste with curry.

Curried Vegetables with Cashews

1 tablespoon extra virgin
olive oil
1 onion, sliced
2 potatoes, sliced
1 cup water
1 cauliflower, cut into florets
2 carrots, sliced
1 cup cashews
1 tablespoon curry powder
1 teaspoon garam marsala
1 teaspoon dried coriander
1 teaspoon cinnamon

SERVES 4-6
TIME: 25 MINUTES

Sauté onions and potatoes in oil in a 4-quart stock pot for 5-10 minutes; add water when the pot dries out. Add carrots and cauliflower; sauté-simmer till carrots turn bright orange. Add cashews. Sauté till all the vegetables are tender. Stir in spices. Taste and adjust seasonings, if desired.

THE QUICK & EASY ORGANIC GOURMET

Indian Red Bean Sauce

¾ cup of red lentils, rinsed
2½ cups water
3 bay leaves
4-inch piece of dulse
3-5 mustard leaves (depending
on the size), washed
and finely chopped
1 teaspoon curry powder,
or to taste
1 teaspoon tamari or shoyu,
or to taste

SERVES 4-6
TIME: 25 MINUTES

Boil and simmer lentils and bay leaves for 10 minutes. Add dulse and simmer 5-10 more minutes, until lentils are creamy. Mix in mustard greens. Simmer for 2-5 minutes, or until the mustard greens are bright green. Stir and add tamari and curry powder to taste. Serve the sauce over rice or noodles, with a salad or *Quinoa Veggie Pilaf* (see page 44 for recipe).

Improvisations

1. You can add more water for a soup, or more vegetables for a stew. (Cook lentils with water in a ratio of 1:2 for a stew and 1:3 for a thick soup or sauce.)

2. Add fresh or dried pepper.

3. If time is not critical, add longer cooking vegetables, such as potatoes, sweet potatoes, and onions, when you add the dulse.

Quick Ginger Scallion Sauce

***Extra cooking liquid from chick peas creates
a tantalizing sauce, but you can also use water.***

*4 scallions, sliced
2-inch piece of ginger,
peeled and grated
2 cups chick pea cooking
water, or any other reserved
bean broth, noodle cooking
water, or plain water
2 tablespoons kudzu or
arrowroot, diluted in ¼ cup
cold water*

OPTIONAL:
*Add umeboshi vinegar
or shoyu, to taste.*

Simmer scallions and ginger in chick pea broth or water for 2 minutes. Dilute kudzu in ¼ cup of cold water, and stir in into the simmering ginger and scallions. If you are not using the extra bean cooking liquid, you may need to add a salty seasoning such as umeboshi vinegar or shoyu. Serve sauce over grains or noodles.

**SERVES 4
TIME: 5 MINUTES**

Tahini Cream Sauce

*1 cup rolled oats
4 cups water or stock
pinch of sea salt
¼ cup tahini
⅛ cup tamari*

Simmer the rolled oats, water, and salt for about an hour, or until the oatmeal is creamy. Stir in the tahini and tamari. Taste and adjust the seasoning, if desired. Serve over steamed vegetables or noodles.

**SERVES 4-8
TIME: 1 HOUR AND 5 MINUTES**

Ginger Burdock Sauce

A good way to cut down on salt is to use vegetables, herbs and spices, like shiitake mushrooms and burdock, with salty flavors.

1 large onion (2 cups), sliced
1 carrot (²/₃ cup), sliced thin
or in match sticks
1 tablespoon dried
burdock or a small fresh
burdock, sliced
2 cups water or stock
2-inch piece peeled, grated,
or sliced ginger
1-2 tablespoons kudzu,
diluted in ¼ cup cold water*
1-2 tablespoons
tamari or shoyu, or to taste

OPTIONAL:
Add 2-6 dried or fresh shiitake
mushrooms, decrease or omit
the tamari.

Put all the ingredients except the kudzu and ¼ cup of water in a pot. Simmer for 15-20 minutes, or until the burdock and vegetables are as tender as you like. Stir in diluted kudzu. Taste and season with a salty seasoning, if desired. Serve over noodles or grains such as *Barley Rice* (see recipe on page 205).

Improvisations

1. Omit the kudzu and add more water for a soup.

2. Use fewer vegetables for a thinner sauce.

---

* One tablespoon of kudzu makes a silky sauce. Two tablespoons of kudzu makes a thick and chunky style sauce.

SERVES 4
TIME: 25 MINUTES

Mushroom Leek Sauce

You can change this basic recipe with your choice of herbs.

*8 ounces mushrooms
(2 cups), sliced
1 large leek (1 cup), sliced or
a small onion (⅓ cup), sliced
1 cup water
¾ teaspoon dried rosemary
½ teaspoon dried thyme or
summer savory
1 tablespoon kudzu, diluted
in ¼ cup water
salt to taste,
or 1-2 tablespoons tamari
or shoyu, to taste*

SERVES 4
TIME: 10 MINUTES

Simmer mushrooms and leeks in water for about 5 minutes, until the aroma of mushrooms fills the air. Add herbs, diluted kudzu and shoyu or salt to taste. Serve over *Millet Croquettes* (see page 211) , noodles, baked fish, or a baked vegetable casserole.

THE QUICK & EASY ORGANIC GOURMET

Creamy Mushroom Basil Sauce

This heavenly sauce is salt-free.

1 tablespoon extra virgin
olive oil
1 onion, sliced
4 garlic cloves, sliced
½ pound mushrooms, sliced
1 cup water or stock
2 cups fresh basil leaves

OPTION:
Add 1 teaspoon balsamic
vinegar.

Sauté garlic and onions in olive oil for 2 minutes; add mushrooms and sauté for 2 minutes. Add 1 cup of water and simmer for 2 minutes. Puree the cooked mushrooms and onions with fresh basil in a blender. Taste it. If desired, add balsamic vinegar or salt to taste. Serve over pasta or steamed greens.

SERVES 4
TIME: 10 MINUTES

Vegetable Gravy

1 teaspoon-tablespoon extra
virgin olive oil
1 lb. mushrooms or onions, or
1 lb. combined celery, leeks,
and carrots
3¼ cups water
1-2 tablespoons arrowroot or
kudzu
sea salt and fresh herbs,
to taste

Sauté about 1 pound of mushrooms or onions, or a combination of aromatic vegetables such as celery, leeks, and carrots in 1 teaspoon to 1 tablespoon of extra virgin olive oil, for 3-5 minutes. Add 3 cups of water. Simmer 5 minutes. Dissolve 1-2 tablespoons arrowroot or kudzu in ¼ cup cold water. Stir arrowroot slurry into the vegetable stock to thicken. Season to taste with sea salt, dill, thyme, and other herbs.

SERVES 6
TIME: 15 MINUTES

8

Calcium Without the Cow

Controversy reigns supreme. Debate continues as to how much calcium is enough. However, it is not quantity that counts, because there are foods that drain the body's calcium, too.

Concentrated sugars, high protein foods, refined flours, and grains can produce acids that inhibit or even reverse calcium absorption. Dairy, often thought of as an ideal form of calcium, contains high concentrations of phosphorus, which can combine with calcium in the digestive tract and prevent its absorption.

Tomatoes, peppers, eggplant, potatoes, and tobacco (the nightshades) can dissolve calcium from the bones and deposit it in the joints, kidneys, arteries, and soft tissues. Salty foods, processed foods, caffeine, alcohol, vinegar, and citrus can also drain calcium from the body. These foods, unless consumed at a minimum, will increase our calcium needs.

Vitamin D helps the body to absorb calcium. Get at least fifteen minutes of sunlight a day to help your body synthesize this essential vitamin. Regular exercise also stimulates the body to retain calcium.

What to Eat

A wide variety of simple and delicious foods can provide the body with much needed calcium:

Hardy Green Leafy Vegetables: collards, kale, broccoli, parsley, bok choy, watercress, chard, dandelion greens, mustard greens, beet greens, carrot greens, turnips and their green tops. These have the highest ratio of calcium to calories.

Grains: It is unusual for grains to have a significant amount of calcium, but teff has 387 milligrams of calcium per cup, 40% of the US RDA, almost equal to that of kale. Buckwheat groats (kasha) is an alkalizing grain with some calcium. Too much grain (over 40%), unless accompanied by appropriate amounts (40%- 45%) of vegetables, sea vegetables, or fruits can make the body acidic. (See chapter 12, "Teff: Gem of the Grains," for other calcium-rich recipes using teff and for wheat-free baking with teff flour.)

Nuts and Seeds: The concentration of calcium in sesame seeds is 10 times higher than in milk. Hulled sesame seeds (white in color) have more available calcium than the unhulled. Also good: almonds, brazil nuts, roasted walnuts, roasted peanuts, and sunflower seeds.

Nut and Seed Milks: These are excellent sources of calcium, particularly almond, sunflower, and sesame milks. Add molasses for a tasty calcium-rich drink. (See chapter 2, "Improvisation: Creating Your Own Themes and Variations," for recipes for nut and seed milks.)

Beans and Bean Products: These traditionally complement grains to make complete proteins. Garbanzo beans (chickpeas), pinto, kidney, and navy beans, tofu, tempeh, soybeans, and other soy foods are alkalizing and good sources of calcium.

Fish: Bony fish, such as salmon and sardines, carp, haddock, little neck clams, and farm-raised oysters, are other non-dairy sources of calcium.

Umeboshi Plums, Umeboshi Paste, and Umeboshi Vinegar: These all have an alkalizing effect on digestion and a tangy, salty flavor, similar to lemons and salt. Serve an umeboshi plum as a garnish on grain. Substitute umeboshi plums, vinegar, or paste for tamari, miso, shoyu, or lemons and salt. Umeboshi is delicious in sauces, spreads, dips, and salad dressings.

Sprouts: These are also good sources of calcium. (See chapter 6, "Around the World with Salads and Dressings," for how to make your own sprouts.)

Vegetables From The Sea

Sea vegetables are getting more attention now that sushi is so popular. For thousands of years, cooks on every continent have made flavorful meals from sea vegetables—soup, stews, garnishes, condiments, and even desserts. Sea vegetables are rich in minerals and vitamins and low in calories. You may also find that eating sea vegetables satisfies your need for salt. (Rinse sea vegetables before cooking them to reduce their sodium content.)

Sea vegetables particularly, hijiki, arame, alaria, kelp, and wakame, are extremely rich in calcium. A 3½-ounce serving of hijiki has 1400 milligrams of calcium. Sea vegetables are also rich in iron, phosphorous, potassium, manganese, sodium, zinc, iodine, vitamins A, C, and B-complex. One tablespoon daily cooked in a variety of ways supplies plenty of vitamins and minerals, including calcium.

Most people eat Irish moss, a sea vegetable, without even knowing it. Irish moss is boiled down to make carrageenan, an important stabilizer in ice cream, puddings, pies, fruit syrups, cheeses, and instant soups. You can use it at home to thicken vegetable dishes or to gel desserts. Irish moss is high in vitamin A, iodine, and trace minerals. Gelatins made with Irish moss are soothing remedies for ulcers. Irish moss also relieves respiratory ailments.

Other Popular Sea Vegetables

Agar agar can be used to make jams, jellied salads, aspics, kanten (gelatin), and non-dairy custard. Simmer 1 tablespoon agar agar flakes per cup of liquid into your dessert stock, such as juice, add spices and fruits, chill, and serve. Unlike other sea vegetables, agar agar is odorless.

Nori (sea lettuce) is a delicate purplish-black sheet that turns green when lightly toasted. Wrap it around rice, cooked and raw vegetables, noodles, tofu, seitan, tempeh, or fish to make sushi, a great lunch, appetizer, or traveling snack. Toasted and crumbled nori is a tasty garnish and condiment. Of all the seaweeds, it is the highest in protein, iron, vitamins A and B2, and is the only one without sodium.

Kombu looks like a narrow, olive-brown lasagna noodle. It enhances flavors and is a tenderizer, too. Sodium glutamate is extracted and concentrated by long simmering of kombu and then added to foods to enhance their natural flavors. Monosodium glutamate (MSG) is a synthetic version. To tenderize and to blend kombu into other foods, cook it a long time. It reduces flatulence when cooked with dried beans. You can use it in soup stocks, stuffings, fish and vegetable stews, or you can pickle or deep fry it. Kombu is high in iron, calcium, and iodine.

Kelp and Ocean Ribbons are quicker cooking, sweeter, delicate, thinner, leafy varieties of kombu. Digitata's (horsetail kelp's) tough texture softens with longer cooking. Kelp and kombu isolate radioactive substances in the body for elimination. They cleanse the circulatory system, and reduce hypertension and reduce high blood pressure.

Wakame is a dark green sea leaf. It is the seaweed highest in alginic acid, which cleanses heavy metals, such as lead, mercury, and cadmium, from the intestines. Fermented foods, such as miso, facilitate this function. Use wakame in miso soup, in salads, with fresh or marinated vegetables, or in tender root vegetable and bean dishes. Roast it lightly. Add roasted sesame seeds. Grind the two together in a suribachi or food processor and use the mixture as table salt. Wakame is high in calcium and B12.

Alaria is similar to wakame. Its mild flavor is delicious when simmered for a long time in stews and soups. Before drying, some wakame is blanched in boiling water, but alaria is not.

Arame has a mild, sweet flavor. It looks like black threads. To cook, rinse and soak for 5 minutes. Add it to soup, stews, sautés, or marinate it for salads.

Hijiki, an erect black sea grass, is popular as a side, or in soups, salads, and sandwiches. Hijiki and arame are good camping foods. Soak them for 5 minutes and eat them without cooking. Hijiki has the most calcium of all the sea vegetables. It is very rich in iron and vitamin A, too. Oriental folk medicine recommends it for pregnant women.

Dulse is a soft, leafy, deep red, purple, and brown sea vegetable, perfect for a snack. It melts in your mouth. Kids love it. Add it to oatmeal, soup, stews, bean dishes, or rinse it and add it to a salad in place of spinach. Dulse is high in potassium, phosphorus, iron, protein, vitamin C, and fat (3.2 grams per 100, high in fat compared to the other sea vegetables). The fat in combination with protein yields a nutty flavor.

Sea palm, the fettuccine of sea vegetables, is dark green, versatile, and sweet. With all its salt water minerals and trace elements intact, it is my children's favorite in soup. It is also delicious in salads, sautés, stews, and noodle dishes.

In macrobiotic cooking, sea vegetables are considered tasty preventive medicine for high blood pressure, arteriosclerosis, rheumatism, allergies, arthritis, and nervous disorders. Because they contain vitamin B12 and iron, sea vegetables are good blood builders.

Sea vegetables contain the trace elements barium, boron, chromium, lithium, nickel, silicon, silver, strontium, titanium, vanadium, and zinc, which are sometimes lacking in our soil and vegetables.

These wild, wonderful foods are harvested from rocky surfaces deep in the ocean at appropriate times of the year. Superior quality sea vegetables are wild crafted from pristine waters. Then they are sun-dried, packaged, and stored. They can keep for years in a cool, dry, dark, place.

Common Improvisations For All Recipes

You can substitute:

1. **Sea vegetables** for each other: wakame for ocean ribbons, etc.
2. **Leafy greens** for each other: kale for collards, etc.
3. **Nuts and seeds** for each other: sunflower seeds for almonds, etc.
4. **Nut and seed milks** for each other: almond for cashew milk, etc.
5. **Beans** for each other: pinto beans for chickpeas, etc.
6. **Leeks, onions, shallots, and scallions** for each other.
7. **Amounts** of each ingredient to suit what you like or what you have in stock: increase, decrease or omit it.
8. **Spices or herbs** for each other.
9. **Same- or different-colored vegetables.**
10. **For variety, alternate umeboshi vinegar, tamari, shoyu, and Bragg Liquid Aminos.**
11. **Fresh white or wild mushrooms,** such as shiitake, chanterelles, or porcini, for dried shiitake mushrooms.
12. **Sauté vegetables** before simmering in a soup stock.

Children's Special Soup

My kids love the fetticini noodle-like texture of sea palm. They also love shiitake mushrooms.

10 cups water
½ cup dried sea palm
10 dried shiitake mushrooms
1-2 onions (1 cup), chopped
2-5 carrots (1 cup), sliced
1 large or 3 small stalks
broccoli (1 quart), sliced
1 pound firm or extra firm
tofu, cubed
2 tablespoons miso or tamari,
or to taste

SERVES 6
TIME: 30 MINUTES

Simmer sea palm and shiitake mushrooms in the water for at least 10 minutes. Add onions. Simmer 10 minutes, at least. (I have often simmered the onions, shiitake mushrooms, and sea palm for an hour. The stock boils down and becomes very flavorful.) Add carrots and simmer 5 minutes. Add broccoli and tofu. Simmer for a minute, or when broccoli turns bright green, turn off the heat. (Simmer longer if you prefer the broccoli soft.) Add miso or tamari to taste.

Improvisations

1. Add celery.

2. Substitute yams for carrots.

A Taste of Japan

6 cups water
1 3-inch strip wakame or
other sea vegetable
4 dried shiitake mushrooms
1 teaspoon toasted sesame
oil or sesame oil
1 medium onion, sliced
1 carrot, sliced in
match sticks
1 stalk celery, sliced
2 stalks of bok choy, sliced

OPTIONAL:
Add ginger or tofu.

SERVES: 4-6
TIME: 20 MINUTES

Simmer shiitake mushrooms, wakame, ginger, and water for 10-30 minutes. While this is simmering, stir-fry the other vegetables. First, heat a wok. Add oil. Then stir-fry onions for 2 minutes. Add carrots. Stir-fry till they are bright orange, about 2 minutes. Add celery, tofu, and bok choy. Stir-fry for about a minute, until they are bright green. Fish out the wakame and shiitake mushrooms from the soup stock. Slice them into bite-sized pieces and discard the stems. Add the sliced shiitake, wakame, and stir-fried veggies to the simmering soup stock. Simmer for 2 minutes.

Improvisations

1. Vary the vegetables.

2. Stir-fry all the ingredients before adding the water, in which case soak the shiitake mushrooms for 30 minutes, soak the wakame for 5 minutes, (and slice both) before adding them to the stir-fry.

3. Add water to any stir-fry to create a soup.

4. Leave the shiitake mushrooms whole.

Sautéed Kale with Leeks and Dill

1 tablespoon sesame oil
4 leeks (5 cups), sliced
2 tablespoons
umeboshi vinegar
2 large bunches purple or
green kale (3 quarts), sliced
1 large bunch dill (2 cups),
minced

OPTIONAL:
Add cooked kasha to the
finished sauté.

SERVES 4-6
TIME: 10 MINUTES

Heat a large skillet or stock pot. Add oil and leeks, and sauté for 3 minutes. Add umeboshi vinegar, and kale, and cover the pot. Let kale simmer in its own juices for 5 minutes, or until tender. Mix in dill. Taste and adjust the seasonings.

Italiano Green Sauté

OPTIONAL:
Add walnuts and capers.

Sauté one or more varieties of green leafy vegetables, such as chard, broccoli, beet greens, dandelion greens, or kale, in extra virgin olive oil and umeboshi vinegar, with lots of sliced garlic and leeks. Add a little water to the natural juices produced by the greens for juicy sauté.

THE QUICK & EASY ORGANIC GOURMET

Greens with Shiitake

3 fresh or dried shiitake
mushrooms
1-inch piece of dulse
(soak 10 seconds before you
start to cook)
1 teaspoon-1 tablespoon
mirin
6 large leaves of kale, cut
into bite-sized pieces

If you use dried shiitake mushrooms, presoak in enough water to cover them for 5-10 minutes, until they soften. Hand squeeze the excess liquid from the mushrooms into the wok. Slice the caps and discard the stems. Heat wok. Add the muhrooms and soaking water*, mirin, and dulse. Simmer 3 minutes. Add kale. Simmer until bright green, or longer if you want the kale more tender.

SERVES 3-4
TIME: 20 MINUTES

* Add enough water so the wok does not dry out, if you are using fresh mushrooms.

Sweet Vegetables Lo Mein

8 ounces soba or udon
noodles, cooked (my favorite
is jinejo soba)
1 tablespoon sesame oil
2 tablespoons mirin
2 cloves garlic, sliced
1-inch piece ginger,
peeled and grated
1 onion, sliced
1 large carrot, or 3 small,
sliced into match sticks
3 stalks celery, sliced
6 leaves of collards, sliced
into bite-sized pieces
½ cup noodle cooking
water, or water
1 tablespoon umeboshi
vinegar

Cook noodles, drain, save the noodle cooking water, and set noodles aside. Heat wok. Add oil, mirin, garlic, ginger, and onion. Stir-fry for 2-3 minutes. Add carrots. Stir-fry for 2 minutes, or until they turn bright orange. Add ½ cup of water. Stir. Add celery and collards. Stir-fry 2-3 minutes, until they are bright green or as tender or crunchy as you like them. Stir in umeboshi vinegar. Add cooked noodles and stir everything together. Taste and add more umeboshi, if desired.

Improvisations

1. **Vegetable Fried Rice:** Stir-fry cooked brown rice instead of noodles.

2. Add tofu, tempeh, seitan, or shrimp.

SERVES 4-6
TIME: 20 MINUTES

Ginger Vegetables

1 tablespoon mirin
1 teaspoon tamari or
umeboshi vinegar
1 teaspoon sesame oil or
toasted sesame oil
½ cup water
2-inch piece ginger,
peeled and grated
1 carrot, sliced into
match sticks
6-8-inch daikon or
piece, sliced
2 celery stalks, sliced
5 cabbage leaves, sliced
into thin bite-sized pieces
5 kale leaves, cut
into bite-sized pieces

Heat wok. Add mirin, oil, water, and tamari. Then add ginger, daikon, and carrot. Stir and simmer for 2 minutes. Add celery, kale, and cabbage. Cover and cook for 5 minutes. Taste and adjust the seasonings or cook longer if you want the vegetables, more tender.

Improvisations

1. You can change the vegetable combination to leeks, carrots, celery, turnip, and Chinese cabbage.

2. Make up your own vegetable combinations. Choose at least 1 green leafy vegetable or sea vegetable.

SERVES 4-6
TIME: 12 MINUTES

The Works

1 teaspoon sesame oil
3 cloves garlic,
sliced or minced
1 inch ginger,
peeled and grated
1 tablespoon mirin
2 onions, sliced
4 dried shiitake
mushrooms, soaked in
water to cover
3-inch strip of dulse,
cleaned and soaked in
¼ cup water
¼ cup of water
1 bunch kale, sliced
3-4 carrots, sliced
1 stalk celery, sliced
1 teaspoon umeboshi
vinegar or tamari

SERVES 4-6
TIME: 12 MINUTES

Heat wok. Add oil, mirin, ginger, garlic, and onions. Slice shiitakes and discard their stems. Add sliced shiitake mushrooms and their soaking water to wok. Sauté-simmer for 5 minutes; add dulse plus its soaking water, carrots, and kale. Stir-fry-simmer 5 minutes. Add ¼ cup of water when the wok dries out. Add celery. Stir-fry for 2 minutes. Add umeboshi vinegar or tamari to taste.

Black, White, and Greens

½ cup hijiki
1 cup water
1 cauliflower (6 cups),
cut into florets
2 tablespoons mirin
4 collard leaves, cut
into bite-sized pieces
3 stalks celery (2 cups),
sliced
2 tablespoons tamari,
shoyu, or umeboshi vinegar
1 teaspoon sesame oil

OPTIONAL:
Garnish with sesame seeds.

SERVES 4-6
TIME: 40 MINUTES

Rinse hijiki and soak it in water. After 5 minutes, put hijiki and soaking water in a hot wok. Simmer for 15-20 minutes. Add cauliflower and mirin. Simmer until cauliflower is tender (5-10 minutes) and add collards and celery. Stir-fry for 1-2 minutes. Stir in tamari and sesame oil.

Improvisations

1. Vary the vegetables cooked with hijiki.

2. Drain and reserve hijiki's soaking water. Stir-fry hijiki in oil instead of simmering it. Add the soaking water later when the wok dries out, or save it for soup stock.

3. You can cook hijiki with 1, 2, or 3 vegetables. Try hijiki with onions and carrots; or onions, carrots, and cabbage; or onions, burdock, sweet dumpling squash, or other varieties of sweet winter squash, like delicata or buttercup.

Vegetarian Sushi

Nori rolls with mustard greens, carrots, ginger pickles, and umeboshi paste—this is one of my favorite combinations.

2½ cups short-grain brown rice, or 2 cups short-grain brown rice and
½ cup sweet brown rice
5 cups water if simmering, or 3 cups water if pressure cooking in a rice crock
pinch of sea salt
6 mustard leaves
3 large carrots
6 sheets toasted sushi nori
umeboshi paste
ginger pickles
wasabi (Japanese horseradish)
1-3 bamboo sushi mats

MAKES 48 SLICES
(6 NORI RICE ROLLS CUT
INTO 8 SLICES)
SERVES 8
TIME: 15 MINUTES,
IF YOUR RICE IS PRECOOKED

Cook brown rice, water, and sea salt see page 204 . Rinse the mustard leaves and put them in a colander or dish rack to air dry. Scrub and cut the carrots into long quarters. Steam carrots for a couple of minutes, until they turn peak orange. Remove cooked rice from the pot or insert and place it in a large bowl, if you want it to cool fast.

Roll the nori rolls when the rice is cool enough to handle but still warm. Lay bamboo mat down with its strings running vertically. Lay one sheet of nori on the bamboo mat. Take about ½ cup of cooked rice and put it on the bottom ½ of the nori (closest to you). Lay 2 long strips of carrots horizontally on top of the rice. Press them gently into the rice. Lay ginger pickles and/or pickled shiso leaves (which come in the same package with the ginger pickles) on top and across the length of the carrots. Place a mustard green on top of ginger pickles. Spread umeboshi paste across the top inch of the nori. Roll. Starting at the end closest to you, roll up the sushi mat around the nori and rice. Slowly pull the leading edge of the mat back so it does not roll into the nori roll. Roll, pressing the ends inward, using even pressure. Replace any of the filling that might fall out. Give the mat a gentle squeeze to insure a tight roll. Leave the sushi in the mat for about a minute. Unroll the mat.

Slice nori roll into 8 slices. If you are not using a ceramic knife, wipe the knife clean after each slice. Put 1 tablespoon of wasabi powder in a condiment tray or small bowl. Add enough water to cover it and stir it into a paste. Use more water for a less hot, thinner dip. Prepare the other nori rolls. Put the little bowl of wasabi in the middle of a serving dish. Slice and arrange slices of nori around the bowl of wasabi.

Dip slices of nori into wasabi. Wasabi is very hot. It will clear your sinuses instantly. A little bit goes a long way.

Improvisations

1. Instead of steamed carrots, use fresh grated carrots or other fresh grated vegetables, such as beets or daikon. Optional: Season grated vegetables with a little rice vinegar.

2. Add long strips of deep-fried tofu, tempeh, or seitan instead of or in addition to carrots.

3. You can mix a little rice vinegar into the rice.

4. Instead of mustard leaves, add fresh, whole scallions, long strips of raw celery, watercress, or naturally prepared mustard.

5. Instead of ginger pickles, try long strips of cucumber pickles, green or red sauerkraut, or homemade string bean or carrot pickles (see page 105 for recipe).

6. Other great fillings include: chopped watercress, sliced avocado, and toasted sesame seeds.

THE QUICK & EASY ORGANIC GOURMET

7. Substitute cooked udon or soba noodles for brown rice. Noodles must be well drained and dry.

8. Children really enjoy rolling and eating nori rolls. Mustard greens and wasabi may be too spicy for them. Find out what they want in their nori rice rolls. Let them roll their own with their favorite fillings. My kids love cucumber pickles and brown rice in their nori rolls.

Chickpea Vegetable Pâté
Super hummus!

1 cup chickpeas, rinsed and soaked overnight
1-2 strips ocean ribbons, or 3-inch piece of alaria, kelp, or wakame
1-1¼ cups water if pressure cooking in an insert, or 2-3 cups water simmering

ALTERNATIVE:
Use 2 cups chickpeas cooked with a sea vegetable
1 bunch of parsley, or 2 cups of parsley tops
1 red onion, cut into 6 or 8 chunks
2-3 cloves garlic or 1 clove elephant garlic
½ cup tahini
2 teaspoons umeboshi vinegar

SERVES 4-6
TIME: 1 HOUR, 10 MINUTES

If you are not starting with cooked chickpeas, drain the soaking water from the chickpeas and rinse them several more times. Boil and simmer chickpeas for at least an hour, or pressure cook chickpeas, ocean ribbons, and water for 40 minutes in an insert. Put the hot chickpeas, seaweed, and cooking liquid in a food processor. Add all the other ingredients. Blend until smooth.

Improvisations

1. **2-Bean Vegetable Pâté:** Substitute 1 cup of cooked pinto or kidney beans for 1 cup of cooked chickpeas. Then follow above recipe.

2. **Any Bean Pâté:** Mash 2 cups of just about any cooked bean—lentils, split peas, navy beans, etc. Season to taste with garlic, parsley, thyme or dill, and sea salt or tamari. You can also add roasted sunflower seeds, miso, fresh or sautéed onions, and celery.

Sunny Mushroom Pâté

¾ *cup sunflower seeds,*
dry roasted
1 bunch asparagus
(½-¾ pound), steamed
2½ cups mushrooms
(6-8 ounces), sliced
2 onions (2 cups), sliced
1 tablespoon extra
virgin olive oil
½ teaspoon dried sage
½ teaspoon dried oregano

Dry roast the sunflower seeds briefly in a dry skillet, till they pop. Set them aside to cool. Steam the asparagus for about 5 minutes, till tender. Sauté onions and mushrooms in olive oil for 3-5 minutes.

In a food processor or blender, grind the sunflower seeds. Add sautéed and steamed vegetables and herbs. Blend till smooth.

SERVES 4-6
TIME: 15 MINUTES

Chickpeas in Garlic Sauce

Cooking beans with sea vegetables creates a delicious,
thick gravy.

1 cup dry chickpeas, rinsed
and soaked overnight
3 cups water
3-inch piece of kelp
4 bay leaves
2 onions, sliced
5 cloves garlic, sliced
1 bunch kale, sliced into
bite-sized pieces
1 tablespoon umeboshi
vinegar

Drain and rinse chickpeas. Simmer chickpeas, water, bay leaves, and kelp 20-30 minutes, or until beans soften. Add onions and garlic. Simmer 10 minutes. Add kale and simmer until tender, at least 5 minutes. Add umeboshi vinegar. Stir and simmer briefly to blend flavors. Taste and add more umeboshi vinegar for more salty and tangy flavor.

Improvisation

You can add some tahini or almond butter for a creamy texture.

SERVES 4-6
TIME: 50 MINUTES

THE QUICK & EASY ORGANIC GOURMET

Greens With Tahini Sauce

Garlic and umeboshi are a natural pair.
Tender, sautéed kale is delicious with creamy tahini.

1 teaspoon extra virgin olive oil
6 cloves of garlic or garlic tops, or 2 cloves elephant garlic, peeled, sliced, or pressed
2 large, long leeks or 4 small leeks, or a bunch of wild leeks, sliced*
2-3 tablespoons of umeboshi vinegar, or to taste
1 large bunch of kale (2 quarts), cut into bite-sized pieces or use collards, chard, beet greens and/or broccoli instead or in combination with kale
1 cup of water
⅓ cup of tahini

OPTIONAL:
Add 1 pound firm or extra firm tofu, cut into bite-sized cubes, and/or cooked pasta, such as macaroni, after you stir in tahini.

SERVES 4-6
TIME: 10 MINUTES

Heat a wok. Sauté oil, leeks*, umeboshi vinegar, and garlic for about a minute; then add kale and water. Stir until kale is bright green, or as soft as you like it. Taste it. Then add tahini. Stir in the tahini until the sauce is creamy. Add more umeboshi vinegar for a tangy, saltier flavor. For a creamier consistency, add more tahini and water. Serve as a side dish or on top of grains or pasta.

Improvisations

1. Add some zucchini.

2. Add more leeks and garlic.

3. Use more water and less vegetables to make a thinner sauce.

---

* If you use wild leeks, add them with the tahini.

Tahini Parsley Sauce

This sauce is great on grains or noodles.

1/4 cup tahini
2 cloves garlic, minced,
pressed, or sliced
1/2 cup water
1 tablespoon umeboshi
vinegar, or juice of half
a lemon and 1 teaspoon
of tamari
7 large sprigs parsley,
rinsed and chopped fine

OPTIONAL:
*Add chopped red
onion or scallions.*

SERVES 3-4
TIME: 4 MINUTES

Simmer tahini, garlic, and water for 2 minutes. Add umeboshi vinegar. Simmer for 1 minute. Add and stir in the parsley. Taste and adjust seasoning if necessary. Serve it hot or cold over noodles, grains, steamed vegetables, or salad.

Improvisations

1. Substitute scallions for the parsley.
2. Add more water for a salad dressing.
3. Use less water for a spread.
4. Do not cook the ingredients.

Tempting Tempeh Casserole

1 package tempeh (8 or
10 ounces), sliced into
bite-sized pieces
2 dried shiitake
mushrooms, whole
2 bay leaves
1 large carrot,
sliced thick
2 turnips, sliced
1 large onion, sliced
1/4 cup kudzu, diluted
in 2 1/2 cups of cold water
1/2 cup tamari

SERVES 4
TIME: 50 MINUTES

Preheat the oven to 350 degrees. Place all the ingredients in a large baking dish (9x13x2-inch). Bake for 45 minutes. Serve over noodles.

THE QUICK & EASY ORGANIC GOURMET

Versatile Tofu

Whip tofu into a salad dressing, dip, spread, pie filling, or topping. You can add cubed tofu to soups, stews, salads, and stir fries. Deep-fry it plain or breaded with cornmeal, herbs, and spices. See *Tofu Stroganoff* on page 50, *Sweet-and-Sour Tofu* on page 51, and *Elegant Vegetable Quiche* on page 227, too.

Shiitake In the Wok

When I cook with shiitake mushrooms, I hardly use salt.

5 fresh or dried shiitake mushrooms
2 teaspoons extra virgin olive oil
2 cloves of elephant garlic or 3 cloves regular garlic
1 onion, sliced
1 bunch broccoli, sliced
1 pound tofu, cut into bite-sized cubes

OPTION #1:
Season to taste with umeboshi vinegar.

OPTION #2:
Garnish with fresh sprigs of cilantro.

SERVES 4-6
TIME: 25 MINUTES

If you are using dried shiitake mushrooms, soak them in water to cover until they soften, about 5-10 minutes. Remove and squeeze out the excess liquid from the mushrooms into the wok. Slice the caps and discard the stems. Heat wok. Add oil, garlic, shiitake mushrooms, and onions; sauté 5 minutes. Add sliced broccoli; stir-fry 5 minutes. Stir in tofu. Add umeboshi vinegar or cilantro, if desired.

Herb Pâté

1 pound extra firm tofu
2 teaspoons umeboshi
paste, or 1 umeboshi plum,
pit removed
1 4-inch slice ginger, peeled,
grated, and squeezed (1
tablespoon juice), or 2-3
cloves garlic
1 small bunch dill, basil, or
parsley (½ cup of
parsley tops)
1 bunch of scallions,
chives, or garlic chives, or
1 red onion, sliced

SERVES 4-6
TIME: 5 MINUTES

Blend the tofu and all the other ingredients in a food processor until smooth.

Improvisations

1. You can create a salad dressing by adding more water and/or using a soft or silky tofu.

2. Blend tofu with a vegetable stir-fry.

3. Blend steamed vegetables with tofu. Add almond butter, tahini, or toasted ground nuts or seeds.

4. Blend tofu with other seasonings: mustard, curry powder, shiso leaves, or rice syrup.

9

Cooking For and With Your Children

Children love to play with food. They roll, mold, shape, and arrange anything they can get their hands on. Odds are if they helped make it they will eat it. Instead of sending your children off to watch TV while you prepare supper, include them. Here are tips and recipes for appetizers, soups, main dishes, salads, snacks, and desserts that you can cook for and with your children.

Kids love noodles, all shapes, all kinds, and particularly colorful ones.

Put noodles in soups, salads, casseroles, and stir-fries. Serve them plain, with kasha, topped with vegetable sauces, tomato sauce, or ketchup.

Stock an assortment of noodles. There are many types of whole grain noodles: whole wheat, kamut, spelt, quinoa, corn, rice, amaranth, buckwheat (soba), vegetable, and herb and spice varieties. They are available in many colors, shapes and sizes: red, yellow, green, brown, elbows, spirals, shells, ribbons, trumpets, confetti, bowties, corkscrews, zitti, thin, thick, long, wide, short, flat, somen, angel hair, udon, spaghetti, fettuccine, lasagna.

Let children test taste cooking noodles. Their opinion is important.

Kids like beans simply cooked with a small piece of a sea vegetable. Garbanzo, lima, pinto, and anasazi beans are my kids' favorites. Add a few beans to a vegetable soup. Tofu is another favorite.

Kids like plain cooked grains. They like the exotic ancient grains like teff, spelt, quinoa, and kamut, too. Cook grains in combination with other grains, such as brown rice and spelt, brown rice and barley, millet and teff, etc. Serve cooked grains with a little tamari or garnished with chopped parsley. Kids like to make grain balls. They are easy to make with pressure cooked sweet or regular brown rice, and millet. Put a few scoops of grain in a large bowl to cool. Roll warm grains into balls. Roll the grain balls onto a plate of roasted and ground nuts or seeds, such as walnuts or sesame seeds. These make delicious appetizers for dinner and parties. Children enjoy arranging them, too.

Children enjoy sea vegetables. Dulse and toasted nori are great snacks. Kantens, made with agar agar, are light and refreshing. Kids like them for desserts and after-school snacks. Sweet-tasting sea palm is noodle-like and delicious in vegetable soups. Ocean ribbons kombu is a favorite with cooked beans.

Children like to eat most vegetables raw, baked, or steamed.

Children usually do not like very spicy, bitter, or sour foods. There are always exceptions, like pickles and salsa.

Generally, kids do not like their foods mixed together. Sometimes they may even want a separate bowl for each food item, so that different foods do not touch each other.

Be a good role model. We also feed our children our attitudes towards food.

Buy premium quality. Feed your kids the best quality organic foods you can find.

Add your love, patience, humor and flexibility. They are very nutritious ingredients.

Support your children's greatest health. I feel very fortunate not to spend time or money going to the doctor with sick children. My kids stay healthy on an organic diet. Their rare colds are mild compared to their friends, who eat lots of sugar, highly processed dairy, and conventionally grown foods.

Keep the fruit bowl full to lessen the temptation for candy. As the seasons change, the fruit in my fruit bowl does, too.

Children eat more often than adults. Have mini-meals or leftovers on hand for quick snacks, such as noodles, cooked beans, soups, cooked grains, as well as an assortment of their favorite fruits and raw vegetables, dried fruits, popcorn, puffed cereals, mochi, nuts, chips, whole grain breads, bagels, and crackers.

Make it easy for children to help in the kitchen. Get a stool or a chair for little ones to stand on to reach the sink and to see and share in the action of meal preparation. Make sure the kitchen counters are clear. That way you can spread out and work together without getting in each other's way. Let them measure, stir, mix, and pour whenever possible. Kids love these tasks.

Engage their senses. Let them see how and what you are doing. Demonstrate what you want them to do. Observe the different colors, shapes, textures, and sizes. Show them how foods change when chopped, blended, and cooked.

Shop and cook with your nose. Select fruits, fish, and herbs with your sense of smell. (Fresh fish should not have a smell.) Rub a fresh herb between your fingers. Use your sense of smell when deciding how much seasoning to add or whether to add an herb or spice.

Listen to the sounds of foods cooking: waters boiling, frying foods sizzling, the hissing of the pressure cooker, the sounds of a knife chopping vegetables.

Touch and feel the different textures of green leafy vegetables compared to round root vegetables. Touch and smell a melon to see if it is ripe. Touch the cookie dough and shape it into a cookie, etc.

Taste the different flavors of the different colored foods. Taste the batter, soup, salad dressing. Does it need more salt, more sweetener, or is it just right? Bring out two spoons for both you and your child to taste it together.

It is fun cooking together. Many hands make light work. I have never heard a child say they don't want to get their hands dirty.

Children like to cook what they like to eat, but helping you create a new dish or one that they have never tried before may be an inducement to try it.

Be realistic. Don't expect preschoolers to prepare their own snacks or chop vegetables. Have them rinse and scrub vegetables, tear lettuce, shell peas, shape cookies, or suggest ingredients for a soup, stew, or sauce. With supervision, they can pour and measure, turn on blenders and food processors, sift dry ingredients for a cake, and stir batters. Elementary-aged children can design serving platters, frost cakes, knead bread, and roll nori rolls.

Patience, encouragement, and kindness are the best teachers. If you are hypercritical of your kids as they learn to be your helpers, they may not want to assist you. Ease up. They are just learning. You are their guide. If something spills, or if many pieces of food fall to the floor, it is part of the process. Every artist makes a mess. Be willing to slow down, because kids love to touch everything. Be prepared for questions. Be open to their suggestions.

Do not make children feel guilty if they do not want to cook or eat foods they do not like.

Ask kids for their opinions during menu planning or in inventing recipes.

Create win-win relationships. Give children healthy food choices. "Do you want steamed vegetables, a salad, or vegetable sticks? Do you want pinto beans or chickpeas? Brown rice or noodles?"

Use a variety of cooking styles. Include foods with different textures, colors, flavors, sizes, and shapes. A simple meal of plain pinto beans, steamed broccoli, baked butternut squash, and noodles with sauce or noodle soup is a big hit; but this meal served every day will get boring. Vary your menus according to the seasons.

You can please everyone. There are foods that everyone likes, and there are variations of meals that everyone likes. Just be willing to dirty an extra pot or two. For example, you may like spicy bean dishes, while your kids do not. Add the spices after you take out some plain beans for them. Also, you can turn a meal into a mini-salad bar, abundant with choices to please everyone.

Children are special. Respect their likes and dislikes. Each child is unique. They may not all like the same things. My six-year-old daughter loves to snack on raw kale and plain beans. My thirteen-year-old daughter will eat plain beans for dinner, but not for snacks. She likes celery sticks, fresh fruits, and dried fruits. My six-year-old does not like celery and occasionally enjoys dried fruits. However, there are many foods they both love: raw carrots, peas, string beans, cooked cauliflower, broccoli, soups with shiitake mushrooms, tofu, baked butternut squash, olives, pickles, fresh fruits, plain cooked grains, beans, and noodles.

Do not pressure kids to eat when they say they are full. Kids will not overeat unless they are tense. Make dining as relaxed as possible.

Children can be very helpful with food shopping. Teach them how to select fruits. Show and tell them what the best produce looks like. Avoid the produce with blemishes and bruises. Pick what smells ripe and sweet, and what they want to eat. Kids also can reserve you a spot in the shortest checkout line while you go fetch one more item, or you can send them for the item, if they are big enough.

Children grow and change. Do not get attached to what they liked yesterday, last week, or last year. Be cautious about stocking up on their favorite foods, unless you like them also.

Encourage your kids to bring friends home for meals and snacks.

Neighborhood suppers and pot lucks ease the burden of daily cooking. My neighborhood has a "rota," a cooking rotation. Anyone in the neighborhood can belong to it. Five nights a week, there are community dinners. Everyone takes turns cooking. (There are so many people on the "rota" that it was necessary to create a computer program to formulate how many times per month members cook. We eat on the "rota" twice a week and only cook once a month. On the twentieth of each month, each member signs up for the next month's "rota".) Most of the members also have a subscription to the community's organic garden and belong to "bulk stores," the community's cool storage room for beans, grains, flours, pasta, oil, etc. This way cooking for twenty is cheap.

Positive eating habits as a child become positive memories. A child who enjoys delicious low-fat, high-fiber foods will continue eating well as an adult.

Here are some recipes for cooking for and with your children. Check the list at the end of this chapter for other recipes included in the book that are also popular with children.

French Toast

A simple, fast, and popular breakfast

1 loaf sourdough or
yeasted raisin bread, sliced
(15 slices)
1-1¼ cups vanilla soy milk
or Rice Dream drink
1 teaspoon-1 tablespoon
canola oil

Put slices of raisin bread in a large bowl. Pour soy milk over the bread. Turn over each slice of raisin bread to wet both sides with soy milk. (Add more soy milk, if needed.) Heat a large frying pan. Add oil. Fry 3-4 slices at a time. Flip them over after about 2-3 minutes. Fry on the other side for about 2 minutes. Serve them with apple sauce or maple syrup.

SERVES 4-6
TIME: 7 MINUTES

Good Morning Strawberry Muffins

Let the kids measure, sift, pour, and mix up the ingredients.

2 cups whole wheat pastry flour
1 tablespoon baking powder
¼ teaspoon sea salt
¼ cup canola oil
¼ cup maple syrup
1 cup apple or other fruit juice
1 teaspoon vanilla
¾ cups sliced strawberries, rinsed

MAKES 1 DOZEN MUFFINS
SERVES 4-6
TIME: 35 MINUTES

Preheat oven to 350 degrees. Sift flour, salt, and baking powder into a large mixing bowl. Add the oil, maple syrup, apple juice, vanilla, and strawberries. (Explain the importance of measuring the oil before the maple syrup: The oil slides the maple syrup out of the measuring cup easily.) Mix up all the ingredients. Smell and taste the batter. (Do you want to add a few more strawberries?) Lightly oil a muffin pan with a pastry brush. Ladle batter into muffin pan. (Who wants to lick the bowl?) Bake for 20 minutes, or until an inserted toothpick comes out dry. Let the muffins cool about 20-30 minutes before taking them out.

Improvisation

Try making these muffins with blueberries or other fruits in seasons.

Emily's Strawberry Drink

***There are many variations to this drink. Emily was 10
years old when she invented most of them.***

*1-2 cups of strawberries
Rice Dream drink or soy milk*

*OPTION #1:
You can add a dash of vanilla
and maple syrup.*

*OPTION #2:
Substitute other berries
or fruits in season,
such as peaches.*

**SERVES 1-2
TIME: 2 MINUTES**

Make strawberries into juice in a blender.
Add Rice Dream drink or soy milk; the proportion of berries to soy milk is up to you
and your child. Some like it half-and-half (1
cup of each), or you can make it with mostly
strawberries.

Cooking Beans For and With Your Children

Colorful beans are often a favorite with children. (See cooking directions for beans on page 117.) Beans double in size after soaking. Show your kids the dry beans and then how much they expand after soaking. Drain and discard the soaking water. Let your kids rinse beans, or show them how you do it. They like to have their hands in water. Keep the beans in the bowl, or transfer them to a colander. Put it in the sink. (If your child cannot reach the sink, get a stool or crate for them to stand on.) Let them run the cold water, turn the beans over with their hands, and drain the water out of the beans. (They may need help, depending on their ages.)

Pinto Beans and Tortillas

A crowd pleaser

1¼ cup dry pinto beans, soaked and drained
1¼ cup water
1 3-inch strip of kelp, ocean ribbon, or dulse (about 3 inches)

For beans and tortillas:
8-10 whole wheat or corn tortillas
shredded lettuce
grated carrots
sliced avocado
olives
salsa

OPTIONAL:
Add a bay leaf or two.

Rinse beans three times and then put them in a bowl or wide-mouthed quart jar with triple their volume of water. Soak beans overnight. Discard the soaking water. Rinse beans well. Put them in a pot. Add water and a sea vegetable. (Show the kids how sea vegetables expand in water.) Simmer beans 30 minutes, or until beans are tender in a cast-iron pot. Stainless steel pots may need more water and more time. Another cooking option is to pressure cook beans in a ceramic pressure cooker insert (see page 118).

Briefly heat each tortilla in a dry skillet, or heat them all together in a warm oven for a minute or two. Everyone takes tortillas and heads for the salad bar.

To assemble tortillas: Put out bowls of fillings, such as rinsed lettuce, shredded carrots, sliced avocado, olives, and salsa. Let your kids assemble their own tortillas with their favorite fillings. It is easy for even a four-year-old to roll up their own tortilla.

Improvisations

1. Start with 3 cups of cooked beans.

2. To round out the meal, make carrot and celery sticks, a salad with sprouts, or steamed vegetables.

3. Try black, anasazi, or kidney beans, or fried tofu wrapped in tortillas.

Roasted Potatoes

15 small, or 10 medium potatoes (8 cups), in slices or bite-sized cubes
10 cloves garlic, sliced
2 teaspoons sea salt
2 tablespoons extra virgin olive oil, or enough to lightly coat the potatoes

SERVES 4-6
TIME: 1 HOUR, 10 MINUTES

Preheat oven to 400 degrees. Wash potatoes with a scrub brush in cold water. Slice them into ¼-½-inch slices or desired shapes. Put potatoes into a baking dish that has a cover or a crock (a good task for a child). Add oil, garlic, and sea salt. Mix all together with your hands, or let your child do it. Cover and bake for one hour. Taste a potato to see if it is tender. If not, bake for a little longer. Serve immediately when ready.

Improvisation

Roast other vegetables, such as yams, onions, string beans, and peppers, with potatoes.

Steamed Vegetables

Children love steamed vegetables, especially broccoli, carrots, cauliflower, and string beans. They are quick and easy to prepare, too. Select one vegetable or a combination of their favorite vegetables.

Steamed Cauliflower

1 large head of cauliflower, cut into florets
½ cup water, or enough to come almost to the bottom of the steamer

SERVES 4
TIME: 10 MINUTES

Put the sliced cauliflower into the steamer basket and put the steamer basket into a large stock pot or pressure cooker. Pressure cooking is faster. Lock on the lid. Bring the pressure cooker to high pressure over high heat. Pressure cook 2-3 minutes. Steam in a regular stock pot 5-10 minutes, or until the cauliflower is as tender or as firm as you and your kids like it.

Improvisations

1. To pressure cook broccoli, string beans, and carrots, bring the pressure cooker up to pressure and then turn it off. These vegetables are ready as soon as the pressure comes down.

2. Steam a variety of vegetables: put the longer cooking vegetables, such as cauliflower, on the bottom of the steamer. Place the quicker cooking leafy vegetables and tofu on the top.

Garlic Bread

6 garlic cloves, pressed
½ teaspoon sea salt
½ cup olive oil
1 loaf French, Italian, or
whole wheat sourdough bread

Preheat oven to 375 degrees. Mix olive oil with pressed garlic and sea salt. Slice bread into individual slices. Spread garlic-olive oil mixture onto one side of each slice. Reform loaf. If there is any mixture left, pour it over the loaf. Wrap loaf in aluminum foil. Bake for 20 minutes, or until the crust is crisp.

SERVES 6-8
TIME: 25 MINUTES

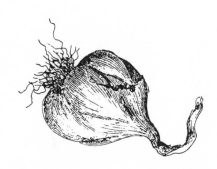

Coffee Cake and Cupcakes

Great for brunch or dessert

2 cups whole wheat
pastry flour
1 tablespoon baking
powder
1¼ teaspoons
cinnamon
¼ teaspoon sea salt
⅓ cup canola oil
⅓ cup maple syrup
1 cup apple juice

Crumb Topping:
½ cup walnuts
1 teaspoon cinnamon
¼ teaspoon vanilla
¼ teaspoon maple
syrup

SERVES 4-6
MAKES 1 DOZEN
CUPCAKES.
TIME: 30 MINUTES

Preheat the oven to 350 degrees. Sift the flour, sea salt, baking powder, and 1¼ teaspoon of cinnamon into a large mixing bowl. Add the apple juice, oil, and maple syrup. (Explain the importance of measuring the oil before the maple syrup: The oil slides the maple syrup out of the measuring cup easily. Mix up all the ingredients. Smell and taste the batter. (Does it have enough cinnamon?) Adjust the flavor, if you like.

Grind up the walnuts in a food processor or nut and seed grinder. Put the ground walnuts in a small bowl. Add 1 teaspoon of cinnamon, ¼ teaspoon maple syrup, and ¼ teaspoon vanilla. Stir together. Smell and taste the mixture. (Is it sweet enough? Does it have enough cinnamon?) Adjust the flavor, if you like.

Like painting, lightly oil a muffin pan with a pastry brush. Ladle the cupcake batter into the muffin pan. Top each cupcake with crumb topping. Bake for twenty minutes, or until an inserted toothpick comes out dry.

For a delicious **Coffee Cake**, pour the batter into an oiled loaf or cake pan. Top with crumb topping. Bake for 30-40 minutes.

Pickles

It is hard to imagine a kid that does not like pickles, especially when they help you make them (see page 105).

Other Recipes Your Children Will Love

Fancy French Onion Soup with Herb Croutons 110

Children's Special Soup 154

Shiitake Barley Mushroom Soup 112

Miso Vegetable Soup 114

Thanks, Grandma 121

Sweet Split Pea Soup 125

Japanese Noodles in Tamari Broth 39

New England Fish Chowder 188

Easy Potato Salad (without the .... onions) 79

Fritters 224

Sauerkraut 104

Japanese Poached Salmon 191

Smoked Fish Hors d'Oeuvres 189

Grains and breads cooked in ceramic pressure cooker insert 199

Greens With Tahini Sauce 165

Sweet Vegetables Lo Mein 157

Shiitake in the Wok 167

Peanut Butter Cookies 237

Vanilla Hazelnut Granola 239

Chocolatey Pancakes 240

Luscious Strawberry Pie 245

Super Chocolate Chip Cookies ... 232

Carob Cookies 249

Chocolate Cake Supreme 258

Teff Applesauce Cake 229

Millet Apple Raisin Cake 212

Apricot Compote 261

Kanten 261

Ginger Bread Cake 252

Corn Bread Cake 253

10

Fish Cookery
Cooking with the Freshest
and Healthiest Fish

Farm-raised seafood and fish from deep in the sea are excellent low-fat, low-calorie sources of protein, vitamins, minerals, and heart-healthy Omega-3 fatty acids. Initiated in Asia about 4,000 years ago, aquaculture is reemerging in response to the growing demand for an abundant and healthy fish supply. Currently, fish farmers grow more than twenty species  of seafood, including: salmon, trout, bass, catfish, shrimp, tilapia, oysters, sturgeon, redfish, carp, lobster, clams, crayfish, bay scallops, mussels, and others. Some fish farmers grow hydroponic herbs, lettuce, wheat grass, watercress, and other vegetables above fish tanks in greenhouses, where they carefully control and monitor the aquatic environment. Breeding fish in greenhouses is a warmer, safer, and more energy-efficient way to catch fish than hunting for them in the open seas. Other fish farmers grow fish in ocean pens and inland tanks. Over-fishing and pollution make aquaculture the natural choice.

Unfortunately, not all farmed seafood is unadulterated. The unethical use of pesticides in aquaculture exists. Some farmers raise fish in crowded conditions where the water exchange is insufficient to disperse the high volume of fish waste. They use antibiotic feed additives to stimulate growth and to prevent and treat disease.

Environmentally friendly aquaculture experts are like organic farmers. They grow their fish in clean water because the fish will taste like the water in which they have lived. They practice water conservation and waste reduction with advanced systems of water circulation that constantly filter the water. Fish manure and other waste products become organic fertilizer used to grow vegetables or sold to organic farmers.

Ecological farmers feed their fish a carefully monitored diet rich in vitamins, grains, and fish meal that exceeds federal standards for purity. They never use antibiotics, hormones, or other additives to grow their fish. Certification for organic farm-raised fish is now being developed.

What about the other varieties of fish that swim in the sea? Fifty percent of Americans live within fifty miles of a shoreline, and their sewage and waste water from factories, commercial farms, and residential and industrial parks go into the sea. Exhaust from cars and smokestacks, toxic chemicals, heavy metals, oils from streets and parking lots, pesticides and fertilizers, manure and garbage, and bacteria and viruses from septic systems move into waterways, upsetting the delicate balance of the ocean's salty waters.

CHOOSING THE SAFEST FISH

You may be able to reduce your exposure to chemical contaminants in fish if you keep in mind two general guidelines: 1) offshore fish are less likely to be contaminated than near-shore or freshwater fish, and 2) within each of these three groups, the fattier the fish, the more likely it is to be contaminated. A few exceptions to these rules include bluefish and striped bass, which tend to be much more contaminated than coastal salmon. (Salmon from the Great Lakes is riskier.)

The following chart lists some of the most popular fish, according to whether they are freshwater, near-shore, or offshore varieties, and in order according to fat content. The safest bets are the fish in the upper left corner—note the exceptions, though.

OFFSHORE	NEAR SHORE	FRESHWATER
cod	✗ stripe bass	yellow perch
haddock	✔ pink salmon	freshwater bass
pollock	✗ bluefish	white perch
yellowfin tuna	✔ chum salmon	brook trout
flounder, sole	✔ sockeye salmon	rainbow trout
ocean perch	sardines	catfish
✗ swordfish	herring	✗ carp
Pacific halibut		lake whitefish
albacore tuna		lake trout

✗ These species probably have high levels of contaminants. **Swordfish** frequently exceed allowable levels of methyl mercury. Migratory fish such as **striped bass** and **bluefish** are frequently tainted with PCBs, even if they're caught offshore. **Catfish** and **carp** are bottom feeders, and are particularly vulnerable to contamination from tainted sediments. Most commercially harvested catfish is farm-raised and relatively uncontaminated with pesticides, but drug residues from aquaculture might be a problem.

As for shellfish, eating them raw may be hazardous to your health; even cooked, they are risky to eat. These stationary bottom feeders absorb and store toxic chemical pollutants, bacteria, and viruses. Farmed shellfish or those harvested from pristine state-certified waters are your best bet.

Buying Tips for Fish

Find an honest fishmonger, one who will guarantee you fresh, healthful seafood, proper fish handling, and accurate information.

When you shop for fish, ask your fishmonger many questions: Is the fish from the sea, or a fish farm? Where is the fish farm? Is the fish in the case from today's delivery? Are there fresher fish in the back? Do your fish come from day boats that catch, land, and deliver the fish the same day, or trawlers that are out on the ocean for a week, or even weeks, before bringing the fish to shore?

Clean hands and proper icing in the hold and at the point of purchase are essential, or the fish will spoil before they reach the dock and the dinner table. Your fishmonger must know where and how long the fish were on the boats, and be willing to tell you how old the "catch of the day" really is.

Expert fishmongers buy farm-raised fish from fish farms that meet high environmental standards. The farmed seafood they stock contains no pesticides or antibiotics. They know their supplier and are not afraid to return any fish that fall below their standards. As for the ocean fish, they consciously choose varieties caught in deep, clean, rapidly moving waters.

The above-average fish store and fish department never sell fish past its prime, nor do they dip fish in chemicals to fool the clientele. They offer money-back guarantees. The average supermarket may discount fish past its prime. They may try to disguise excess age by dipping fish and shrimp in a solution of phosphates, sulfites, or other preservatives. They may dip fish in a toxic solution of chlorine and water to retard spoilage and rinse off surface bacteria. This leaves a residue on the fish skin, undetectable by the consumer. How can you know? If you cook this fish in a sauce, and the sauce turns green, the fish is chlorine-dipped. Don't eat it, and shop elsewhere.

✔ Despite their high fat content, **salmon** (except those caught from the Great Lakes) tend to be relatively free of chemical contaminants.

Reprinted by permission of The Center for Science in the Public Interest

How Can You Tell If The Fish Is Fresh?

Fresh cut fish has a translucent color. It is shiny and moist, with no fishy odor. Ask to smell and see the fish. If it smells fishy, has bruises, spots, odd-colored edges, or is gray, it is probably old and bad.

Whole fresh fish will not smell fishy, except shark or skate, which have a slight ammonia odor when fresh. The skin is shiny and moist, but not slimy. The eyes are clear, not cloudy. The scales are whole and attached, not dry or flaky.

Fresh shrimp is rare. Frozen, thawed, and cooked shrimp is common. Small, medium, large, and jumbo can be meaningless labels; what counts is how many shrimps to a pound. A label such as 16/20 means 16-20 to a pound. Shrimp of 15-30 to a pound usually give the best flavor, value, and are easiest to peel.

Government regulations demand that fresh shrimp (never frozen) have the heads on them. Frozen shrimp must have the heads off.

Black spots on shrimp usually indicate freezer burn, meaning the shrimp were frozen too long or improperly, and the breakdown of the meat has begun. (Black tiger shrimps have black stripes.) Shrimp should not have yellowing shells, or shells that feel gritty. Both indicate the use of a bleaching agent (sodium bisulfite) to remove black spots. Shrimp should smell fresh, like salt water and nothing else. Select shrimp that are firm and fill the shell fully. Shrimp in their shells are fresher than peeled shrimp.

It is best to buy live mussels, clams, and oysters. Choose farmed or harvested shellfish from pristine state-certified waters, such as the waters off central coastal Maine, that have been rinsed, cleaned in a fresh seawater tank, and tested by FDA-approved labs. You are taking a risk when you buy fish from roadside trucks. If buying frozen fish and shellfish, choose odorless fish with no discoloration. Look for recent date codes, packages without holes or rips, and a solid frozen piece of fish. When in doubt, ask.

If you are traveling more than thirty minutes, bring a cooler with you to store the fish. Ask for ice, or bring your own.

Cooking and Storing Tips

It is best to cook fish within twenty-four hours of purchase or freeze it.

Refrigerate live shellfish—such as clams, oysters, bay scallops, and mussels—in a well-ventilated container, not a closed plastic bag or box. Don't use any shellfish that have died in storage.

THE QUICK & EASY ORGANIC GOURMET

Wash your hands, knives, utensils, and your workspace before and after handling fish. Cut the fish on a plate or other non-porous cutting board that is easier to clean.

Always rinse the fish in cold water before marinating or cooking.

Marinate fish in the refrigerator. Thirty to sixty minutes is enough time to marinate fish. Fish will not become more tender with longer marinating.

Cook fish 10 minutes for every inch of thickness measured at the thickest part. Stuffed fish may take longer. A fish in a sauce or wrapped in foil may need an extra five minutes per inch. Check for doneness. See that its color changes to opaque and "flakes" in the center when probed with a fork or knife. Steam mussels, clams, and oysters six minutes. Grill shrimp for four minutes. Steaming shrimp may take less than four minutes. Look to see that their color changes to orange.

Fish are just as versatile as grains and beans. Quick-cooking, fish is ideal for a fast dinner. On the grill, in a soup, poached, fried, sautéed, baked, or broiled, it is up to you. Vary the combinations of vegetables, herbs, spices, and oils. Change a seasoning or cooking method to affect the flavor, texture, and possibly the ethnicity of the dish. Look back over the recipes in the other chapters. Add some fish to the chili, sweet-and-sour dishes, stir fries, vegetable and noodle soups, etc.

Per-person portions range from $1/3$ to ½ pound for filets, steaks, and shrimps in the shell. For some adults and children, ¼ pound is enough. Whole fish portions are slightly larger, ½ to ¾ pound, since you are paying for the head, skin, and the bones. Ten to eighteen mussels a person cover most appetites. Ten bay scallops per person, or a pound for two, are enough.

New England Fish Chowder

Simply delicious!

*4 cups water
2 onions (at least 1½ cups) or leeks, chopped
4 potatoes, or 1 medium cauliflower (3-4 cups), sliced
3 stalks celery, or a carrot and a yellow squash*, sliced
1 pound scrod, or an assortment of cusk, cod, and monkfish
¼ teaspoon sea salt
pinch-¼ teaspoon pepper
pinch of nutmeg
chopped parsley, chives, or scallions for garnish*

**SERVES 4
TIME: 40 MINUTES**

Boil water. Chop and add the onions. Simmer 10-60 minutes. (The longer the onions simmer, the sweeter the soup.) Rinse, slice, and add cauliflower or potatoes and/or carrots and squash. Simmer 10 minutes for cauliflower and 15-20 minutes for potatoes. Add celery. Rinse and slice the fish into 1–2-inch pieces. Add it to the broth. Simmer 2-3 minutes, until the fish is tender. Add salt, pepper, and nutmeg. Taste and adjust the seasonings, if desired. Garnish with chopped parsley, scallions, or chives.

Improvisations

1. Add corn.

2. Sauté onions or leeks before simmering them in the soup.

3. Season the soup with thyme, basil, bay leaf, or sage.

4. Increase the portion of fish.

---

* Use carrots and winter or summer squash for a sweet chowder.

Smoked Fish Hors d'Oeuvres

With little fuss and plenty of gourmet savvy, smoked fish platters are a pure indulgence.

Choose one variety or an assortment of smoked, farm-raised fish: trout, salmon, scallops, shrimp, mussels, or sturgeon. Naturally smoked, peppered mackerel, herbed mackerel, tuna, haddock, cod, or pollack add pizzazz.

OPTIONAL:
If you choose smoked salmon and herbed mackerel, you could serve them with **Frey Vineyard's Organic Cabernet Sauvignon** *or* **Four Chimney's Organic Celestial Peach Wine.** *An organic white wine is also nice.*

**BUY ¼ POUND OF SMOKED FISH PER PERSON
TIME: 10 MINUTES**

Smoked fish is best served at room temperature. Set up a platter with (rinsed) lettuce or purple kale leaves. Lay the fish on top of the greens. Surround the smoked fish with slices of zucchini, turnip, cucumber, fennel, apples, melon, and crackers. A bowl of cherry tomatoes and olives also adds to the fun.

Smoked Fish Salads

Add pieces of smoked fish to a tossed salad for an easy and elegant meal.

There are several varieties of smoked farm-raised fish to choose from: trout, salmon, scallops, shrimp, mussels, and sturgeon. Naturally smoked, peppered mackerel, herbed mackerel, tuna, haddock, cod, and pollack also add pizzazz.

**BUY ⅓-½ POUND OF SMOKED FISH PER PERSON
TIME: 10 MINUTES**

To prepare your fish salad, rinse your greens—lettuce and parsley, for example. Tear lettuce into bite-sized pieces and chop up the parsley. Put greens in a bowl. Add slices of cucumber and diced red onion. Top with flakes of (room temperature) smoked trout or salmon and capers.

Japanese Poached Salmon

1⅓ pounds salmon fillet
2 tablespoons sesame oil
2 tablespoons tamari
or shoyu
2 tablespoons mirin or
white wine
¼ cup water or
enough water to reach
halfway up the fish

OPTIONAL:
Use 1 teaspoon grated ginger.

SERVES 4
TIME: 25 MINUTES

Preheat oven to 400 degrees. Rinse fish in cold water. Place it skin side down in an uncovered baking dish. Pour the oil, tamari, and mirin on top of fish. Add water to the pan. Bake for about 20 minutes, or until fish is tender. Cook fish 10 minutes for every inch of thickness measured at the thickest part.

Improvisations

1. Poach a different fish, such as flounder, catfish, rainbow trout, or cod.

2. Poach a combination of fishes together, such as salmon and cod.

3. **Savory Fish Stew:** Add vegetables, such as potatoes, yams, and carrots. Add a little bit more water, too.

4. Omit the oil.

---

* Instead of tamari and mirin, you could use one of *Four Chimneys'* organic cooking wines, such as the one that includes soy sauce.

Chinese Stir-fry

2 tablespoons sesame oil
4 tablespoons mirin
4 tablespoons tamari
or shoyu
3-inch piece of ginger,
peeled and grated
6 cloves of garlic, sliced
2 onions, sliced
2 large carrots, sliced
into match sticks
4 stalks celery, sliced
1 pound cod, rinsed and
cut into bite-sized
pieces or larger*
½ pound mushrooms,
rinsed and sliced
2 bunches mizuna or
watercress, rinsed and sliced
into bite-sized pieces

SERVES 4
TIME: 15 MINUTES

Heat wok. Add ginger, oil, mirin, and tamari. Stir and then add onions, garlic, and carrots. Cover and fry for 5 minutes. Add celery, mushrooms, and cod. Stir fry for 3 minutes. Then add the mizuna. Stir fry for 2 minutes. The cod will flake and almost dissolve into the vegetables' juices. (If the cod is thin, it will take 5 minutes; if it is at least an inch thick, add the cod with the onions and carrots to allow it 10 minutes to cook).

Improvisations

1. **Italian-style:** Sauté onions, tomatoes, and peppers in olive oil and garlic. Add a bunch of chopped basil, too. Season to taste with salt and pepper. Garnish with fresh sprigs of oregano, thyme, or basil leaves.

2. **Hot and Spicy:** Add 1 teaspoon crushed red pepper flakes or a fresh, sliced hot pepper to the oil, or use hot pepper sesame oil to sauté.

3. Substitute farm-raised shrimp, salmon, or bay scallops for cod.

4. Use a larger portion of fish.

---

* Cut the cod in larger pieces so it will end up being in bite-sized pieces.

Honey Shrimp Kabobs

4 tablespoons sesame oil
4 tablespoons honey
4 tablespoons wet mustard
2 pounds shrimp, shelled,
deveined, and rinsed

SERVES 4-6
TIME: 25 MINUTES

Mix up the oil, honey, and mustard in a large bowl. Taste and adjust the seasoning, if desired. Peel, devein, and rinse shrimp. Put shrimp in the bowl. Put the bowl in the refrigerator for 15-60 minutes. Take shrimp out of the refrigerator. Put shrimp on skewers, leaving spaces between each one. Put the skewers in a large glass baking dish and pour remaining marinade over the shrimp. Broil for 4 minutes, or until shrimp turn orange. Serve on top of rice or pasta with a green salad or steamed vegetables on the side.

Improvisations

1. Grill instead of broil.

2. Add fresh or marinated vegetables, such as onions, mushrooms, zucchini, peppers, or yellow squash to the skewers . Make extra marinade for the vegetables. Marinate the vegetables in their own separate bowl. Be sure to leave spaces between the vegetables and shrimp so that the shrimp cook evenly.

Dorothy's Steamed Bay Scallops

1 onion, sliced
3 cloves garlic, sliced
water, white wine, or
vegetable stock for steaming
1 pound farm-raised bay
scallops in their shells, rinsed

SERVES 2
TIME: 10 MINUTES

Put the sliced onions and garlic in the bottom of the steamer pot. Rinse the scallops and put them in the steamer basket. Pour water, white wine, or vegetable stock on top of the scallops to reach the bottom of the steamer basket. Steam for 5-10 minutes until the shells open. Serve scallops in their shells with side dishes such as baked yams, kasha and mushrooms, and green salad.

Broiled Farm-raised Trout

1 whole trout per person
1 teaspoon extra virgin
olive oil

OPTION #1:
Add 1-2 cloves garlic.

OPTION #2:
Add 1 teaspoon of chopped dill, cilantro, marjoram, or oregano, and/or chopped nuts.

OPTION #3:
Add 1 tablespoon of bread crumbs. Garnish with a wedge of lemon or lime, parsley sprigs, or chopped chives.

SERVES 1
TIME: 15 MINUTES

Rinse fish in cold water. Place trout cut in half the long way in a baking dish. Top with 1-2 cloves of crushed garlic, and/or herbs and/or chopped nuts, and 1 teaspoon of olive oil. Broil 10-15 minutes, until the flesh changes color.

Improvisation

Bake the trout uncovered for 10-15 minutes in a 400-degree oven.

The Quick & Easy Organic Gourmet

Striped Bass, Trout, or Tilapia*
Stuffed With Herbed Croutons

Tilapia has a mild taste, like Dover sole.

*6 slices of bread (1 quart), cut
into ½-inch cubes
2 teaspoons dried oregano
2 teaspoons dried basil
2 teaspoons dried thyme
2 cloves garlic,
pressed or minced
5 tablespoons extra
virgin olive oil
¼ teaspoon sea salt
4-6 whole trout, or
2-4 whole tilapia or
striped bass*

OPTIONAL:
*Pour just enough white wine,
vegetable stock, or water to
cover the bottom of the pan;
then bake.*

**SERVES 4-6
TIME: 25 MINUTES**

Preheat the oven to 400 degrees. Mix up the crouton ingredients (slices of bread, herbs, garlic, sea salt, and olive oil) in a bowl. Rinse the fish in cold water. Place the fish in a baking pan. Stuff each fish with croutons. (If there are extra croutons, put them on the bottom of the baking dish and put the fish on top of the extra croutons.) Bake for 15-20 minutes, or until a toothpick or fork easily pierces the skin of the fish.

Improvisations

1. Stuff fish with your favorite vegetables.

2. Lay fish on a bed of thinly sliced onions or your favorite vegetables.

3. Score three diagonal lines across the fish and insert lemon slices.

---

* Whole tilapia and hybrid bass are bigger than trout. One trout serves one person.

Quick-fried Bass With Tartar Sauce

½ cup cornmeal
2 tablespoons sesame, corn,
peanut, or extra virgin
olive oil
2 pounds or 4-6 fresh, hybrid,
farm-raised bass fillets
tarter sauce

SERVES 4-6
TIME: 10 MINUTES

Put cornmeal on a plate. Heat a large, heavy skillet on medium. Add oil. Rinse the fillets in cold water. Dip fillets in the cornmeal to coat both sides. Place them in the hot pan. Listen for the sizzle as the quick crust forms on the outside. Fry for about 4 minutes on each side. Check for doneness. Remove to a paper towel or brown paper bag to drain off excess oil.

Tartar Sauce: Mix up soy mayonnaise or soft tofu with pickle relish or chopped pickles to taste.

Improvisations

1. Substitute tilapia fillets, tuna, or a white meat fish (scrod, flounder, cusk, sole).

2. Sauté garlic and onions in the pan first; remove them before adding the fish. Serve fish topped with garlic and onions.

Pan-fried Fish

Cajun: Season the fish with a mixture of onion, garlic, paprika, red pepper, and oregano. Another excellent Cajun seasoning* combination is cayenne, chili powder, ground cumin, salt and black pepper. Pan fry in corn oil, extra virgin olive oil, sesame, or peanut oil. Optional: Mix herbs and spices with flour or arrowroot before frying the fish.

French: Pan fry fillets or shrimp in extra virgin olive oil, garlic, onions, white wine, thyme, savory, bay leaves, and/or a touch of black pepper for a grand entrée.

Improvisation: Grill fish with fennel, lemon, extra virgin olive oil, oregano, or savory.

Japanese: Pan fry fillets or shrimp in sesame oil, mirin, tamari, garlic, and ginger. You can also first marinate the fillets in the mixture for up to an hour in the refrigerator before sautéing.

Italian: Pan fry fillets or shrimp in extra virgin olive oil, garlic, bay leaves, and rosemary. Tomatoes, mushrooms, and olives fried in olive oil with fish is also a fine variation.

American: Pan fry fillets or shrimp in extra virgin olive oil and garlic or dill. Serve with a wedge of lemon.

---

* See chapter 5, "The Art of the Stir Fry and Sauté," for more information about using herbs and spices for ethnic accents.

11

Grain Cookery

A fabulous variety of grains provides culinary excitement without hours of labor. I will teach you how to simmer and pressure cook grains alone and together with other grains, in infinite combinations with spices, vegetables, nuts, and seeds. Once you know the proportion of liquid to grain you can make up your own combinations. Sometimes it may require a little math, because some grains require more cooking liquid than others. Don't let the math stop you. Go a little wild and improvise. Add cooked grains to a salad, stir-fry, or soup, or garnish them with fresh herbs or toasted seeds.

Rinse your grains. Place a measured amount of grain in a pot, pressure cooker insert, or large bowl. Cover grain with three to four inches of water. Swirl grain with a chopstick or wooden spoon. Pour off any floating debris, grain hulls, twigs, etc. Repeat rinse until the water is clear. Some grains, such as barley, oats, and millet, are dustier than others and require more rinsing. Spelt, wild rice, and kamut are fairly clean and rinse quickly. Don't bother rinsing teff. It is too tiny, and has already been cleaned before packaging. I also never rinse kasha (buckwheat groats) or flaked or cracked grains like rolled oats, spelt flakes, kamut flakes, corn grits, bulgar wheat, spelt cous, or cous cous.

Cooking. Boil and simmer 1 cup of these grains with two cups of water and a pinch of sea salt:

brown rice	quinoa	kasha (buckwheat groats)
sweet brown rice	basmati rice	wehani rice
spelt	cous cous	bulgar wheat

Cut the water or cooking liquid in half when you pressure cook these grains in a ceramic pressure cooker insert, also known as a rice crock, insert, or Ohsawa pot, so that you cook 1 cup grain to 1 cup water. For moister and softer grains, try 1 cup grain to 1¼ cups liquid. If you pressure cook any of these grains without an insert, use 1¼-1½ cups of water per cup of these grains.

Boil and simmer 1 cup of these grains with 3 cups of water and a pinch of sea salt:

millet	teff	rye berries
amaranth	kamut	whole oats
barley	corn grits	job's tears
wheat berries	wild rice	triticale berries

Cut the water in half and cook 1 cup grain to 1½ cups of liquid when pressure cooking them in a ceramic insert.

Another cooking option is to bake grains. Use the same amount of water as for simmering. Preheat the oven to 350 degrees and bake them for 10 minutes longer than the recipes suggest you simmer them. Baked grains are soft, golden, slightly sticky, and open. You can dry roast, sauté, or soak grains before you bake them.

Cooking Liquids: Remember, you can also cook grains in nut milk, juice, wine, beer, mirin, or vegetable or noodle stock. Wine, beer, and mirin are strong in flavor. It's best to combine them with water, nut milk, or vegetable stock.

Pressure Cooking With Confidence

I got my first 6-quart pressure cooker in 1985. I spent more time scouring its thin, burnt, stainless steel bottom than cooking in it. Then, I got my first Ohsawa pot, also known as a rice crock, and discovered many advantages to using it:

1. **It is impossible to burn the foods cooked inside.**

   Put 1 quart of water in the pressure cooker before you place the insert inside. Foods never contact the bottom of the pressure cooker. Even if you fail to turn off the pressure cooker on time, foods won't burn. After several hours, however, the water (around the crock) will boil away and the insert could crack.

2. **Foods taste sweeter cooked inside the ceramic insert.**

3. **Foods have no metallic flavor.**

4. **You can make fancy layered dishes.**

   The surrounding water gently rocks the foods. Normal pressure cooking agitates foods, like a washing machine, mixing them up.

5. **Foods cooked inside the insert stay warm for hours** without being over-cooked. The insert is ideal for transporting a hot dish to a dinner party and for keeping foods hot when you want to serve them later that day.

6. **Use half the cooking liquid used for simmering.** Convert any soup, stew, grain or bean recipe for pressure cooking by cutting the cooking liquid in half. For example, cook 2 cups of brown rice with 2 cups of water. Normal simmering uses 4 cups of water.

7. **You can cook beans and cereals** that normally would clog up the vents of the pressure cookers.

8. **Consider making large amounts.** A medium insert has a 7-cup capacity. You can cook, serve, store, and reheat grains in the insert. Make extra grains to have on hand for stir-fries, breakfast, etc. during the week.

9. **Reheat cooked grains or other entrees without drying them out**. Simply put the insert back into the pressure cooker. (Be sure to surround it half-way up with water.) Bring it up to pressure and cook 5 minutes.

10. **Cleanup is quick and easy**. Empty the hot water out of the pressure cooker. Air dry it and put it away. Wash the insert by hand or in the dish washer.

11. **If you need to turn off the pressure cooker prematurely,** grains can finish cooking with the residual heat available.

How to Use a Rice Crock in a Pressure Cooker

1. **Measure** grains.

2. **Rinse grains in your insert** (see page 199).

3. **Add a salty seasoning:** a pinch of sea salt, small piece of a sea vegetable, an umeboshi plum, a shiso leaf, or tablespoon of sauerkraut.

4. **Add water, vegetable stock, or fruit juice.**

5. **Add other ingredients,** such as nuts, seeds, vegetables, and spices. These change the texture and flavor. As far as herbs go, their flavors are very delicate and easily destroyed by high heat. Add herbs after cooking grains.

6. **Put the lid on the insert.**

7. **Add 1 quart of water to the pressure cooker.** To save a little cooking time and energy, use warm but not boiling water, so not to shock the stone-ware and crack it.

8. **Place the insert inside the pressure cooker.** (Some models have a rope for easy lowering and lifting of the insert into and out of the pressure cooker.) The hot tap water reaches halfway up the side of the crock.

9. **Attach the lid to the pressure cooker.**

10. **Place over high heat and bring to full pressure.**

11. **After about a minute, reduce the heat to low.**

12. **Cook at low pressure** according to recipe (20-40 minutes, depending on the grain). When pressure cooking two grains that have different cooking times, such as millet and brown rice, always cook the grains for the longer cooking time. The times for these recipes are based on cooking on a gas stove. Owners of electric stoves may need to make small adjustments in timing, such as turning the burner off a few minutes early. Electric burners take a while to cool down.

13. **Turn off the heat.** Wait for the pressure to come down naturally. In a hurry? Put pressure cooker in the sink and run cold water over it, which will cause the pressure to come down quickly.

14. **Open the pressure cooker** and remove the lid.

15. **Is it done?** If the answer is yes, then serve it. Sometimes, particularly with millet, some batches need extra water. When I open the insert and stick a rice paddle in it, if I see uncooked millet kernels, I then add more liquid and pressure cook a little longer.

Special Ways of Cooking Grains

1. *Before cooking, dry roast* rinsed grains alone or with

    spices   nuts and/or seeds

    to make them fluffy, light, individual, dry, and nutty-flavored.

2. *Sauté* rinsed, uncooked grains alone or with

    vegetables   spices   herbs

    to make them moist, tender, individual, rich and flavorful. Then, cook as usual.

    Use sesame, toasted sesame, extra virgin olive, canola, corn, almond, peanut, hazelnut, high oleic sunflower, or high oleic safflower oil.

3. *Soak* rinsed grains in their cooking liquid overnight or 6-8 hours before cooking them. This makes them softer and easier to digest.

Something sublime happens when you garnish grains with herbs and season them with spices. With a little imagination and minor experiments, you can push the creative limits of grain cookery. Try my recipes, or you can further tease the senses by adding any one of these suggested seasonings or garnishes:

Suggested Garnishes: chopped scallions, parsley, chives, cilantro, toasted sunflower seeds, or strips of nori.

Suggested Seasonings: ½-1 teaspoon of pan-toasted mustard, cumin, and coriander seeds for an Indian accent; 1 tablespoon raw or pan-toasted sesame seeds; 1 teaspoon of caraway, celery and/or dill seeds; ½ cup sunflower seeds; 1-2 bay leaves.

Sautéed Aromatic Vegetables: leeks, onions, shallots, celery, peppers, mushrooms.

Colorful Vegetables: carrots, yams, winter squash, turnips, cauliflower, parsnips, daikon, red, green, purple or yellow peppers.

Raw or Sautéed Spices: 1-5 garlic cloves, 1 slice or more of ginger, a cinnamon stick, curry powder, a pinch of dried or a whole fresh chili pepper. ⅓ cup shredded coconut, with or without a jalapeno chili; 1 strip of lemon, lime, or orange zest, with a pinch of dried crushed chili peppers or a slice of ginger.

Nuts: ½ cup almonds, walnuts, filberts, peanuts, pecans, pistachios, cashews, chestnuts, or pine nuts.

Seasonal Fresh Fruits: apple, pear, peach, blueberry, cranberry, strawberry, papaya, nectarine, and date.

Dried Fruits: apple, apricot, currant, date, fig, nectarine, papaya, peach, pear, persimmon, pineapple, raisins, and prunes.

Cooking Liquids: water; juice for sweetness; vegetable stock for adding minerals and flavor. Use more liquid for softer grains. You can also mix wine, beer, or mirin with water, nut milk, or stock.

Basic Brown Rice

2½ cups brown rice
(any length), or brown
basmati rice
5 cups water for simmering,
or 3 cups for pressure cooking
in a rice crock
pinch or ⅛ teaspoon
of sea salt

OPTIONAL:
Garnish with fresh chopped
parsley or scallions.

SERVES 4 (FOR TWO MEALS)
TIME: 50 MINUTES

Rinse rice. Boil water and salt. Add rice and simmer covered for 45-60 minutes. To pressure cook in an insert: Combine rinsed rice, cold water, and sea salt in an insert. Pressure cook for 40 minutes.

A Taste of India

½ teaspoon brown
mustard seeds
½ teaspoon cumin seeds
½ teaspoon sesame
or almond oil
2 cloves garlic, sliced
1-inch piece of ginger,
peeled and grated
1 onion, sliced
1-3 carrots (1¼- 1½ cups),
sliced
2 cups brown basmati
rice, rinsed
¼ teaspoon sea salt
5 cups water if simmering, or
3 cups if pressure cooking in
an insert

SERVES 6-12
TIME: 50 MINUTES

Dry roast cumin and mustard seeds in a covered fry pan until they pop, about a minute. Add oil, garlic, and ginger, and sauté for about a minute. Add onions and carrots, and sauté for 5 minutes. Add rice, salt, and water. Bring to a boil and then simmer for 40-50 minutes.

To pressure cook in an insert: rinse the basmati rice in the insert. Add sautéed vegetables, spices, water, and sea salt, pressure cook for 30-40 minutes.

Improvisations

1. Substitute cloves, peppercorns, coriander seeds, or cardamom pods.

2. Substitute other grains for rice.

Barley Rice

1 cup brown rice
1 cup barley
5 cups water if simmering,
or 2½ cups if pressure
cooking in an insert
pinch of sea salt

OPTIONAL:
Add ½ cup sunflower seeds.

SERVES 6-12
TIME: 50 MINUTES

Rinse grains. Combine all the ingredients in a 2-3-quart saucepan. Boil and simmer covered for 50-60 minutes.

Or:

Combine all the ingredients and pressure cook in an insert for 40 minutes.

Short and Sweet

2 cups short-, medium-,
or long-grain brown rice
½ cup sweet brown rice
5 cups for steeping
or 3¼ cups water
in an insert
pinch of sea salt

OPTIONAL:
Add slices of ginger.

SERVES 6-10
TIME: 50 MINUTES

Rinse grains. Boil and then simmer covered for 50-60 minutes. Serve immediately, or wait for rice to cool and roll rice into nori rice rolls (see directions on page 161).

Or:

Combine all the ingredients in an insert and pressure cook for 40 minutes.

Improvisations

1. **Nutty Grain Balls:** Toast and grind nuts or seeds, such as sesame seeds, sunflower seeds, or walnuts. Put ground nuts or seeds on a large plate or cutting board. When it is cool enough to handle with your hands, shape cooked grain into 2-inch round balls. Roll grain balls onto toasted nuts. Serve on a bed of kale or surrounded by parsley.

2. Try half-and-half-sweet brown rice to brown rice.

Spelt Good

2 cups brown rice, or
1¼ cups millet
½ cup spelt grain
5 cups water for simmering
or 2½-3 cups for pressure
cooking in an insert
pinch of sea salt
chopped chives, scallions, or
parsley for garnish

OPTION #1:
Dry roast grains.

OPTION #2:
*Add sautéed onions, garlic,
celery, and carrots.*

SERVES 5-10
TIME: 45 MINUTES

Rinse grains. Combine all the ingredients in a 2-3-quart saucepan. Boil and simmer covered for 45-60 minutes.

Or:

Pressure cook in an insert for 40 minutes.

Wild and Wonderful

1½ cups long-grain brown rice, or brown basmati rice
¼ cup wild rice
3¾-4 cups water if simmering, or 2-2½ cups if pressure cooking in an insert
pinch of sea salt

OPTION #1:
Add sautéed vegetables, such as leeks, celery, and mushrooms (you could use onions or shallots for leeks).

OPTION #2:
Add 2 bay leaves and/or 3 cloves of garlic

OPTION #3:
Add grated orange zest (peel), currants, and pine nuts

SERVES 4-8
TIME: 50 MINUTES

Rinse grains. Combine all the ingredients in a 2-3-quart saucepan. Boil and then simmer covered for 50-60 minutes.

Or:

Pressure cook in an insert for 40 minutes.

Three Sisters Grains

1 cup long-grain brown rice
½ cup millet
½ cup kamut
¼ teaspoon sea salt
5 cups water for simmering or
3 cups water for pressure
cooking in an insert

OPTIONAL:
Top with **Sweet
and Sour Sauce** or
Vegetable Gravy (see pages
140 and 147 for directions).

SERVES 6-12
TIME: 1 HOUR

Rinse grains. Boil water and salt. Add grains. Simmer covered for at least one hour.

Or:

Combine all the ingredients in an insert and pressure cook for 1 hour.

Freckles

1 cup millet, rinsed
½ cup whole oats or
teff grain, rinsed
4½-5 cups water
for simmering, or 3 cups for
pressure cooking
in an insert
pinch of sea salt

SERVES 5-8
TIME: 15 MINUTES FOR MILLET
AND TEFF IN AN INSERT,
20 MINUTES SIMMERED; AND
40 MINUTES FOR MILLET AND
OATS IN A PRESSURE COOKER
INSERT, OR 1 HOUR SIMMERED

Combine all the ingredients in a 2-3-quart saucepan. Boil and then simmer covered for 1 hour.

Or:

Pressure cook in an insert for 40 minutes for millet and oats, and 15 minutes for millet and teff.

THE QUICK & EASY ORGANIC GOURMET

Aztec Two-step

1½ cups millet, rinsed
½ cup amaranth, rinsed
6 cups water if simmering,
or 3 cups water or vegetable
stock for pressure cooking in
an insert
pinch of sea salt

OPTION #1:
Add currants, dates,
or raisins.

OPTION #2:
Sauté grains with garlic
and onions.

TIME: 25 MINUTES
SERVES 6-10

Rinse grains. Combine all the ingredients in a 3-quart saucepan. Boil and then simmer covered for 20-25 minutes.

Or:

Pressure cook in an insert for 15-20 minutes.

King Tut Special

1¼ cup millet, rinsed
⅓ cup kamut, rinsed
4½ cups water for
simmering, or 2½ cups for
pressure cooking
in an insert
pinch of sea salt

OPTION #1:
Dry roast grains first.

OPTION #2:
Add sautéed leeks,
mushrooms, and peppers.

SERVES 4-8
TIME: 1 HOUR

Combine all the ingredients in a 2-3-quart saucepan. Boil and then simmer covered for at least 1 hour.

Or:

Pressure cook in an insert for 40 minutes. Top with a *Sweet and Sour Sauce, Onion Sauce* or *Ginger Burdock Sauce* (see page 145).

Sunny Mountain Rice

2 cups brown rice, rinsed
1 cup quinoa, rinsed
½ cup sunflower seeds
6 cups water if simmering,
or 3½ cups if pressure
cooking in an insert
pinch of sea salt
fresh chopped parsley or
scallions for garnish

OPTION:
Another great trio is:
1½ cups short brown rice
½ cup quinoa
½ cup wild rice
1 bay leaf
a pinch of sea salt
5 cups water if simmering, or
3 cups if pressure cooking in
an insert

SERVES 6-12
TIME: 45 MINUTES

Boil water; add grains, salt, and seeds. Simmer covered for 45-60 minutes.

Or:

Combine all the ingredients in the insert. Pressure cook for 40 minutes. Garnish with fresh chopped parsley or scallions.

Sweet Millet

1½ cups millet, well rinsed
3 large carrots, sliced, or 1
medium butternut squash,
peeled and sliced
1 onion, sliced
4½ cups water if simmering,
or 2½ cups if pressure
cooking in an insert
pinch of sea salt

OPTIONAL:
Use fewer carrots and add
leeks, cauliflower, or other
vegetables.

SERVES 4-8
TIME: 20 MINUTES

Combine all the ingredients in a 2-3-quart saucepan. Boil and then simmer covered for 20-25 minutes.

Or:

Pressure cook in an insert for 15-20 minutes.

Improvisations

1. **Millet Croquettes:** When the millet and carrots are cool enough to handle, shape them into balls or patties and fry or deep fry them.

2. **Millet Veggie Loaf:** Transfer hot millet and carrots to a loaf pan. When cool, slice and serve with a hot mushroom or onion sauce.

Millet Apple Raisin Cake

*1 cup millet, rinsed
and drained
3 cups apple juice
or your favorite fruit juice
pinch of sea salt
1 cup of raisins*

SERVES 6
TIME: 20 MINUTES

Rinse the millet completely so the water runs clear. Put all the ingredients in a stock pot and boil and simmer about 20 minutes.

Or:

Put all the ingredients in a pressure cooker. Lock the lid in place and bring it up to pressure over high heat. Reduce heat to low, so it's just enough to maintain pressure, and cook 15 minutes. Use a heat deflector if the bottom of your pressure cooker is thin.

Open the pot and stir up the millet and raisins. Pour mixture into a cake pan. Let it cool. Slice and serve it like brownies.

Improvisations

1. Use a combination of other fresh or dried fruits, such as pears, apples, apricots, peaches, and/or currants.

2. You can stir in cinnamon or vanilla before pouring grain into the pan.

3. You can serve it hot for a breakfast cereal.

4. Use corn grits instead of millet, or a combination of the two.

Chestnutty Rice

⅛ *cup dried chestnuts,*
soaked overnight (expands
to ¼ cup)
2 cups short-grain
brown rice, rinsed
⅛ *cup aduki beans,*
presoaked overnight
(expands to ¼ cup)
5 cups water to simmer
or 3 cups to pressure cook in
an insert
pinch of sea salt, or a
1-2-inch piece of kelp or
kombu
Garnish with fresh, sliced
scallions or top with **Quick**
Ginger Scallion Sauce *(see*
page 144)

OPTION #1:
You can change the
combination to:
1½ cups brown rice
1½ cups sliced carrots*
⅛ *teaspoon sea salt*
⅜ *cups dried chestnuts*
soaked overnight (expands
to ¾ cups)
4 cups water if simmering or
2½ cups water if pressure
cooking in an insert

SERVES 6-12
TIME: 50 MINUTES

Rinse rice and adukis. Drain the chestnuts, and save the chestnut soaking water in a measuring cup. Add enough fresh water to make 5 cups liquid or 3 cups if pressure cooking. Put adukis, rice, salt, water, and chestnuts in the insert or stock pot, and mix. Place kelp on top. Pressure cook 45 minutes or simmer 45-60 minutes. Try this grain combination in a sourdough bread (see pages 216-218).

Improvisation

If you use the insert, you can make this a fancy layered dish by not mixing up the ingredients. Put rice on the bottom, carrots next, and chestnuts on top; or create your own arrangement. Use a pie server to take out a layered wedge, or, if time permits, take the crock out of the pressure cooker and let it cool. Use a rubber spatula to loosen the sides, and slide it out like a cake upside down onto a dish.

---

* You can sauté carrots with onions, celery, or celery seed.

Kasha

3 cups boiled water or
vegetable stock
1½ cups of kasha
pinch of sea salt

SERVES 4-6
TIME: 10 MINUTES

Boil water. Dry roast kasha and sea salt in a skillet. Remove from heat. Add boiling water. Simmer 10 minutes, or until water is absorbed.

Serve plain, mixed with macaroni or spirals, or topped with onion or mushroom herb sauces (see page 146). Add cooked kasha to soups. Marinate it with fresh, diced vegetables. Serve kasha topped with a stir-fry, baked in knishes or other pastries, deep-fried with other grains and seeds in croquettes, refried with vegetables, or braised with vegetables, herbs, and spices.

Improvisation

Sauté kasha in olive oil with onions, mushrooms, and dill before adding boiling water.

Kasha Cous

3 cups water
¾ cup couscous
¾ cup kasha
pinch sea salt

Boil water. Dry roast the grains and sea salt together. Remove from heat. Add boiling water. Simmer 10 minutes, or until the water is absorbed.

SERVES 4
TIME: 15 MINUTES

THE QUICK & EASY ORGANIC GOURMET

Couscous and Teff

4 cups water
1 cup couscous
²/₃ cup teff (Use brown teff if
you want to contrast with the
tan color of the couscous. Use
ivory teff to keep
the colors alike.)
pinch of sea salt

SERVES 4-6
TIME: 15 MINUTES

Boil the water. Briefly roast the grains and salt. Remove from heat. Add boiling water to grain. Simmer 15 minutes, or until water is absorbed.

Improvisations

1. Cool before serving in a cake pan, and cut like a brownie.

2. After it cools, cut and deep-fry it.

Bronze Delight

3½ cups water
1 cup kasha
½ cup brown or ivory teff
(Contrast the brown kasha
with ivory teff, or match it
with brown teff.)
pinch of sea salt

SERVES 4
TIME: 15 MINUTES

Boil the water. Briefly roast the grains and salt. Remove from heat. Add boiling water to grain. Simmer 15 minutes, or until water is absorbed. Serve with *Mushroom Leek Sauce* (see page 146) garnished with chopped parsley or scallions.

Bread Making

These sourdough breads are delicious, moist, and chewy. Mix it up in the morning, knead it after dinner, and bake or pressure cook it the next morning.

Rice Bread #1

Simple to make

3 cups leftover rice, even better if sour
3 cups whole wheat bread flour
½ teaspoon sea salt
water to knead, about ⅛-¼ cup
1 teaspoon sesame, corn, or canola oil

TIME: 2 HOURS WITH 2 OVERNIGHT RISINGS

Put rice and flour in a mixing bowl. Rub them together to break up the rice. Add salt and water. Use your hands to knead into a dough. Knead for 10 minutes. Cover with a damp, warm, thin towel. Let rise for 8 hours.

Knead the dough again for 10 minutes in a big mixing bowl or on a lightly floured pastry board. Add more wheat or other kind of flour, if dough is very sticky. Oil the insert or a bread pan. Put the bread dough inside. Cover with a warm damp towel. Let rise again at least 8 hours or overnight.

Take off the towel! Pressure cook in the insert for 1½ hours.

Open the insert when the pressure comes down. When you look at bread, the top may seem wet, but it will dry out as it cools. Take out the insert. When it is cool enough to handle, turn it upside down onto a cooling rack. Bread slides out easily.

Or:

You can bake the bread at 300 degrees for 15 minutes, then at 350 degrees for 1½-2 hours.

1. Substitute spelt or whole wheat pastry flour for some or all the whole wheat bread flour.

2. You can use kamut instead of wheat flour. Use a little bit more (¼-½ cup) water.

3. You can substitute sesame, canola, or corn oil for water. Oil makes a richer tasting bread.

4. You can substitute any leftover grain for rice. If you use a softer, creamier grain, such as breakfast oatmeal, you can use less or no water.

5. You can reduce the amount of wheat flour by 10 to 20%. Replace it with 10-20% of another whole grain flour. (See "Bread Making Improvisations" on page 218 for ideas).

Rice Bread #2

1 cup leftover brown rice
4 cups whole wheat bread flour
1 tablespoon barley malt
½ teaspoon sea salt
about 1½ cups of water, enough to make a kneadable dough

TIME: 2 HOURS WITH
2 OVERNIGHT RISINGS

Follow the same procedure as for *Rice Bread # 1* above.

Brown Rice and Barley Bread

1 cup leftover brown rice
3½ cups whole
wheat bread flour
½ cup barley flour
½ teaspoon sea salt
1½ cups water
2 teaspoons poppy
seeds

Follow the same procedure as for *Rice Breads #1 and #2*, on previous pages. Sprinkle poppy seeds on top of bread dough before you pressure cook it.

TIME: 2 HOURS WITH
2 OVERNIGHT RISINGS

Bread Making Improvisations

Use a variety of whole grain flours with and without cooked grains.

Use mostly whole wheat or spelt flours, with smaller percentages (10–20%) of other whole grain flours for different tastes and textures.

Spelt and kamut whole grain flours are ancient relatives of wheat. They are non-hybridized wheat ideal for most people allergic to wheat. Spelt and kamut are considered high energy grains, preferable for athletic training and building stamina because they have more protein, fiber, fat, iron, zinc, copper, and vitamins B1 and B2 than wheat.

Spelt is quicker and easier to digest than most grains because of its bio-availability or water-solubility. Its nutrients dissolve rapidly in liquid and are available with only a minimum of digestive work. When baking, use about ¼ less liquid than when using wheat flour. I love spelt's rich, nutty flavor, and I am not allergic to wheat.

Kamut, an ancient relative of durum (pasta) wheat, has a low gluten content, lighter texture, and requires a little more liquid than spelt or whole wheat flour. Spelt and kamut flours are more nutritious and expensive than whole wheat flour and better tolerated by those with gluten and wheat sensitivities.

Barley flour adds a sweet, moist, cake like quality. Dry-roasted barley flour has a nutty flavor.

Use 10-50% rye flour with a teaspoon of caraway seed for a strong, hearty bread. If your bread has a granular quality, add rye flour for moisture and smoothness.

Yellow-orange corn meal is sweet and coarse. It gives breads a crumbly texture. If your bread batter is too moist, add some corn meal.

Rolled oats add sweetness. They make breads chewy and moist. Buzz them in a blender to make your own oat flour.

Brown rice flour makes breads sweet, moist, dense, and smooth.

Buckwheat flour has a strong, distinct flavor. It adds warmth and heaviness.

Millet flour gives bread a beautiful color and a fine cake-like quality.

Doughs made with cooked grains need less water than doughs made with mostly flour.

For a lighter bread, use some white flour.

For Variety

❖ **Add a teaspoon of cinnamon.**

❖ **Add about ⅓ cup of nuts** to the batter: peanuts, almonds, cashews, etc.

❖ **Add about ⅓ cup seeds** to the batter, or sprinkle some on top of the bread before pressure cooking or baking: sunflower, sesame, poppy, caraway, dill seeds, etc.

❖ **Add about ⅓ cup dried fruits or fresh berries:** currants, raisins, dates, blueberries, etc.

❖ **You can use leftovers** besides cooked grains, such as sautéed vegetables, beans, soups, salads, pureed vegetables or fruits, etc.

12

Teff: Gem of Grains

Oat bran is not the only whole grain that helps reduce cholesterol. A tiny grain from the hills of Northeast Africa is making
its way, via the plateaus of Idaho, to the tables of health-con-
scious Americans. Gruffly named "teff," it's smaller than a
poppy seed. Early botanists called it *Eragrotis tef. (Eros* means
love and *grotis* means grass.) Yet, when it comes to high fiber and a wallop of nutrients, teff is as much a powerhouse
as brown rice, whole wheat, corn, or oat bran.

How did teff get to America? In 1973, Wayne Carlson,
an American biologist working in the Ethiopian highlands,
developed a taste for *injera*, a two-foot-round sourdough
flatbread made from teff flour. Carlson, a Californian, not only
enjoyed the taste, but also recognized the food's nutritional value: Teff is an
abundant source of calcium, iron, and fiber.

Three years later, Carlson joined the Idaho Health Department. Observing
the similarity of the state's landscape to that of Ethiopia, he began experiment-
ing with growing teff, both ivory and brown varieties, intending to supply the
grain to Ethiopians living in America. He succeeded in growing an abundance.

Teff has a moist, poppy-seed like texture, and a mildly sweet flavor reminiscent of chocolate and molasses. It cooks in 20 minutes, about half the time it
takes to cook brown rice, oats, or barley. There is no need to rinse teff—another
time-saver. It is just too tiny, and it is clean, having passed through a series of
screens after its harvest.

A cup of cooked teff contains 387 milligrams of calcium (40% of the USRDA
for calcium), 840 milligrams of potassium, and 15 milligrams of iron (100% of
the USRDA for iron). By comparison, a cup of milk contains 300 milligrams of
calcium. Teff is an ideal non-dairy source of this mineral. Both an extra large
egg and two ounces of teff have seven grams of protein, but teff has no cholesterol. It is also low in fat (1 gram per 2-ounce serving) and high in fiber (8
grams per 2-ounce serving). It's about 14% fiber. The brown variety is slightly

richer in iron; the ivory is slightly higher in protein. Also, teff is a good source of vitamins—niacin, thiamin, riboflavin—and minerals—zinc, magnesium, copper, manganese, boron, and phosphorous.

Unlike other grains, teff will never lose any of its nutritional value through polishing, parboiling, flaking, or other modern refinements, because teff is too tiny for any such processing. It is smaller than the period at the end of this sentence. One hundred and fifty grains of teff weigh as much as one wheat kernel.

Bought whole or already stone ground as a flour, either brown or ivory teff can be used rather than wheat. This is an advantage for people who are allergic to gluten, which helps dough rise and gives it cohesiveness. With only traces of gluten, teff flour is more suitable to pastries and flat breads than to high-rising sandwich breads.

More versatile than wheat, teff grain or flour can be used for crusts for a main course quiche or for dessert pies. See *Elegant Vegetable Quiche* on page 227, *Coffee Tofu Apricot Pie* on page 228 , and *Apple Crumb Pie* on page 233. Teff flour replaces and even improves upon wheat in pancakes, cookies, pie crusts, granola, and muffins. Its flavor is the reason why.

Imagination elevates teff into high cuisine. You can simmer, pressure cook (in a ceramic pressure cooker insert), dry roast, fry, and bake teff. The grain blends well with vegetables, other grains, tofu, beans, and herbs, spices, fresh and dried fruit. There are infinite variations of combinations of vegetables and fruits cooked and served with teff grain and teff flour. Consider those which are fresh, organically grown, and in season.

Teff is another ancient grain like quinoa, kamut, and spelt. The key to success in eating a grain-based diet is variety, versatility, and flavor. I am proud to provide you with delicious recipes and improvisational techniques for the renaissance of teff.

Basic Teff

3 cups water
1 cup brown or ivory teff
grain
pinch of sea salt

SERVES 4-6
TIME: 20 MINUTES

Boil water. Add teff and sea salt. Cover and simmer 15-20 minutes, or until all the water is absorbed. (Often, after 15 minutes of cooking, there is a creamy liquid on top. Turn off the heat. Stir grain, and you will see the liquid quickly absorbed.)

Teff Plus Other Grains

Cooking teff in combination with millet, couscous, oatmeal, buckwheat groats (kasha), and corn meal is delicious. The total ratio of grain to boiling water is still 1:3. The ratio of teff to other grains is up to you. With couscous, half and half is nice. With millet, I prefer twice as much millet to teff. To add extra flavor, dry roast grains before adding boiling water to them.

Fritters

***Friday is 'fritter night' at our house. The brown
teff makes a nice contrast to orange corn meal.***

4 cups water
1 cup corn meal
⅓ cup teff grain
pinch of sea salt
*3 tablespoons extra
virgin olive oil*
3 tablespoons tamari

SERVES 4
TIME: 30 MINUTES
PLUS AT LEAST 2 HOURS FOR
TEFF AND CORNMEAL TO COOL

Boil water. Lightly roast the teff and corn-meal in a large, unoiled skillet until the grains are hot or you smell a nutty aroma (about 5 minutes). Turn off the heat. Add boiling water and a pinch of sea salt to the roasted grains. Simmer and stir occasionally to prevent lumps until all the water is absorbed (10-20 minutes).

Let the teff and cornmeal cool for at least 2 hours. Then it will be easy to cut. (I prefer to make the teff and cornmeal in the morning, let it set all day, and then fry the fritters for dinner). Heat a large skillet. Add olive oil and tamari. After about a moment, use a spatula to slice the cooked cornmeal and teff into triangles or other shapes. Place them in the hot pan. Deep fry fritters a few at a time until golden brown on both sides. Serve fritters immediately or keep them hot in a covered dish in a warm oven (250 degrees). They are a great complement to bean dishes and steamed vegetables.

Improvisations

1. Fry other grains cooked in combination with teff, such as millet.

2. Cooked millet and corn grits also stick together once they have cooled. Make fritters with them, too.

Millet and Teff with Squash and Onions

A colorful, sweet, autumn dish

1 butternut squash, sliced
1 large onion or leek, sliced
1 cup millet, rinsed
½ cup teff grain
4½ cups water
pinch of sea salt

SERVES 4-6
TIME: 25 MINUTES

Wash the squash by scrubbing the skin with a vegetable brush. Cut the squash into 1-inch rounds. Scoop out the seeds with a spoon. Trim away the skin, and cut the squash into bite-sized pieces.

Slice the onion into bite-sized pieces, or smaller if you want it to disappear and melt into the other ingredients. Combine rinsed millet, squash, onions, teff, water, and sea salt. Gently mix together. Cover and simmer 20 minutes, or until all the water is absorbed.

Improvisations

1. For a richer flavor, you can sauté the vegetables before simmering and/or dry roast the grains.

2. You can bake these ingredients in a covered casserole dish in a 350 degree oven for twenty minutes instead of simmering.

3. You can substitute other varieties of winter squash, such as delicata or buttercup. In summer, you can use carrots and yellow squash.

Deluxe Morning Breakfast

½ cup teff grain
1 cup rolled oats,
or spelt or kamut flakes, or
both combined
4½ cups water
½-1 cup of dried fruits:
apples, pears, peaches,
apricots, and/or dates, or a
combination of fresh fruits
pinch of sea salt
1 tablespoon vanilla
1 teaspoon cinnamon

OPTION #1:
Garnish with fresh roasted
walnuts or pecans.

OPTIONAL #2:
Serve topped with Rice Dream
drink or soy milk.

OPTION #3:
Add a little maple syrup for
a sweeter version.

SERVES 4
TIME: 25 MINUTES

Put the teff, oatmeal, dried fruit, water, and sea salt in a pot and simmer for 20 minutes. Add cinnamon and vanilla. Taste and add maple syrup, if desired.

Improvisations

1. You can vary the amounts of teff to oatmeal.

2. If leftover grains, such as brown rice are available, add to the cooking porridge with more water. For example, if you add ⅓ cup of cooked brown rice, add at least ½ cup of water with it.

3. Try this dish baked in a cast-iron pot or covered dish.

THE QUICK & EASY ORGANIC GOURMET

Elegant Vegetable Quiche

It is unusual to think of cooking a grain and then using it for a pie crust, but teff is incredibly versatile.

The Crust: Basic Teff
3 cups water
1 cup uncooked whole teff grain
pinch of sea salt

The Filling:
1 pound extra firm tofu*
2 tablespoons umeboshi vinegar
1 bunch fresh dill or basil (or 1 teaspoon of either herb dried)
1 teaspoon cold-pressed extra virgin olive oil
2 cloves garlic, sliced
1 large onion or leek, sliced
½ pound mushrooms, sliced
1 stalk (with florets) broccoli, sliced

OPTIONAL:
Add ⅛-¼ cup water*.

SERVERS 6
TIME: 40 MINUTES

This recipe balances teff's moist, poppy seed texture with soft, whipped tofu for a complete protein; its chocolate flavor with spicy onions, leeks, and garlic; and its brown color with the green of leafy vegetables.

Using three cooking styles—simmering, sautéing, and baking—this quiche is a delightful blend of salty, sour, pungent, and bitter flavors. Serve it with a soup, salad, or steamed vegetables, and it becomes the centerpiece of a meal. Heat any leftovers in a steamer to preserve the luscious texture.

Preheat the oven to 350 degrees. Boil 3 cups of water in a saucepan. Add 1 cup of teff grain plus a pinch of sea salt. Simmer for 15 minutes, or until all the water is absorbed. Pour cooked teff into a casserole dish or large pie pan, spreading it around to form a crust. Blend tofu, water, umeboshi vinegar, and herbs. Sauté the vegetables and garlic in olive oil. Combine tofu mixture and sautéed vegetables in a large bowl and pour onto the teff crust. Bake for 10 minutes, or until tofu turns light brown.

1. Substitute vegetables in season, such as several leaves of kale or a small bunch of asparagus, for broccoli and mushrooms.

2. Omit the herbs and blend the tofu with 1 teaspoon of shiso leaves. Sauté the vegetables with an extra 2 tablespoons of umeboshi vinegar. (This makes a total of 4 tablespoons of umeboshi vinegar, 2 blended with the tofu and 2 sautéed with the vegetables.)

---

* Adding water to an extra firm tofu gives you more for your money than if you used a soft or silky tofu.

Coffee Apricot Tofu Pie

Teff Whole-grain Crust:
2 cups boiling water
²/₃ cup brown or ivory teff grain
1 cup dried apricots or other dried fruits
pinch of sea salt

Filling:
1 pound tofu
½-²/₃ cup rice syrup, or ¹/₃ cup maple syrup
¼ cup tahini
¹/₃ cup grain coffee

OPTIONAL:
Add 1 teaspoon vanilla.

SERVES 6
TIME: 30 MINUTES

Preheat the oven to 375 degrees. Boil the water. Add teff, dried apricots, and sea salt. Simmer 15-20 minutes until the water is absorbed. Pour and spread cooked teff and apricots evenly into a casserole dish or large pie pan. Blend the tofu, tahini, grain coffee, vanilla, and sweetener in a food processor. Pour and spread coffee-tofu filling on top of the teff crust. Bake 10 minutes, or until the top of the coffee tofu is a slightly darker brown.

Improvisations

1. Use a teff flour crust (see page 231), or any other pie crust from the dessert chapter.

2. Leave out the apricots from the crust. Create a design with fresh fruit slices or berries on top, or you can use the *Apricot Compote* on page 261 for the topping.

Teff Applesauce Cake

Here is an easy autumn dessert that both kids and grownups love.

4¼ cups water
1⅓ cups teff grain
1 cup raisins or other dried fruits: pears, figs, or apricots
⅛ cup rice syrup
2 pinches of sea salt
7 cups apples or a combination of fresh fruits in season

SERVES 6
TIME: 25 MINUTES

Boil 4 cups of water in a large stock pot. Add teff, rice syrup, raisins, and a pinch of sea salt. Simmer for 15-20 minutes, until the water is absorbed.

While waiting for the water to boil, wash and thinly slice the apples. (Leaving the peels on the apples turns the sauce a pretty pink color.) Simmer apples, ¼ cup of water, and a pinch of sea salt for about 20 minutes, or until the apples turn to sauce. Stir occasionally.

Pour the cooked teff and raisins into a pie pan, cake pan, or casserole dish. Top with the fresh, hot applesauce. When cool, you can cut the teff into squares, like brownies.

Improvisations

1. You can cook fruit with teff for a fruit cake.

2. You can serve the cooled, cooked teff cut as a brownie and smothered with hot applesauce.

Lemon Poppy Seed Cake

A classic!

½ cup brown teff grain
¼ cup water, boiled
1 cup teff flour
3 cups whole wheat
pastry flour
½ teaspoon sea salt
2 tablespoons
baking powder
½ cup poppy seeds
1½ cups apple juice
1 cup maple syrup
½ cup corn or canola oil
½ cup freshly
squeezed lemon juice
(1-2 lemons)
½ cup vanilla soy milk
1 tablespoon vanilla

TIME: 1 HOUR

Preheat the oven to 350 degrees. In a small mixing bowl, pour ¼ cup boiling water over ½ cup of teff grain. Let it stand for 10 minutes. Combine dry ingredients without sifting in a large mixing bowl. Blend the wet ingredients except the teff in a food processor or blender. Pour the wet ingredients onto the dry. Add the wet teff grain. Mix all the ingredients together. Brush a large (9x13x2-inch) cake pan with oil (or use a pair of 9-inch pans). Pour in batter. Bake for 45 minutes, or until an inserted knife or toothpick comes out dry.

Improvisation

If you are out of fresh lemons, you can substitute an equal amount of a natural lemonade or lemon recharge drink.

Wheat-free Baking With Teff Flour

Dessert Pie Crust

Without rolling or refrigerating, this pie crust is quick and simply delicious.

2 cups teff flour
½ cup maple syrup
½ cup unrefined corn
or canola oil
½ teaspoon sea salt

TIME: 15 MINUTES

Preheat oven to 375 degrees. Combine ingredients and form into a dough. Press dough with your fingers into a lightly oiled pie plate. Poke holes in the dough with a fork. Bake for 10 minutes; add filling.

Improvisation

You can substitute water for maple syrup and use this crust for a vegetable quiche or pie.

Super Chocolate Chip Cookies

Add some chocolate chips, nuts, and voilà!
Here is a simple variation of the pie crust recipe.

2 cups teff flour
½ cup maple syrup
½ cup corn or canola oil
½ teaspoon sea salt
1 tablespoon vanilla
¼-½ cup chocolate chips

OPTIONAL:
Add ¼ cup walnuts.

MAKES 18 COOKIES
TIME: 25 MINUTES

Preheat the oven to 350 degrees. Mix all the ingredients together. Shape the dough into 2-inch round cookies with your hands. Place them on a lightly oiled cookie sheet. Bake for 15 minutes. Let them cool for about 10 minutes before transferring to a cooling rack or platter.

Improvisations

1. Substitute carob chips for chocolate chips.

2. Shape the cookies into smaller or larger sizes.

3. You can bake the cookies for only 10 minutes at 375 degrees.

Apple Crumb Pie

This pie is pure, sweet indulgence.

Pie Crust:
1 recipe for Dessert Pie Crust
(see page 231)

Filling:
5 large apples (such as Rome,
Macintosh, or Cortland)
pinch of sea salt
½ cup water
1 tablespoon kudzu
or arrowroot
1½ teaspoons cinnamon

OPTIONAL:
Simmer apples in a little
water to make applesauce,
and omit the kudzu.

TIME: 45 MINUTES

Preheat the oven to 375 degrees. Mix up the pie crust and reserve (do not bake) ½ cup of pie dough for crumb topping. Press the remainder of the dough into lightly oiled pie pan. Poke holes in the dough with a fork. Bake for 10 minutes. While crust is baking, thinly slice apples. Place them in a 2-quart sauce pan with ¼ cup water and a pinch of sea salt. Simmer for about 20 minutes, or until the apples are tender and juicy. Dissolve kudzu in ¼ cup cold water. Stir it into the cooked apples. Stir in the cinnamon. Taste, and adjust the seasonings, if desired. You can add more cinnamon or sweetening. Then pour filling into the baked pie crust. Crumble remaining teff dough on top. Bake for 10 minutes, or until crumbs turn a slightly darker brown.

Improvisations

1. You can change the filling: simmer ½ cup of raisins, 3 sliced apples, and 2 thinly sliced pears with a pinch of sea salt. As above, add cinnamon and diluted kudzu or arrowroot.

2. You can use a combination of apples and peaches.

3. **Peach Crumb Pie:** Substitute 5 fresh, sliced, peaches for apples. You can simmer the peaches as the apples, or add them fresh to the baked pie crust. Crumble remaining dough on top of peaches. Bake for 10 minutes, or until the peaches are tender.

4. **Blueberry Crumb Pie:** Rinse 2 cups of blueberries. Add them to baked crust. Crumble remaining dough on top of blueberries. Bake for 10 minutes.

Topless Blueberry Pie

Pie Crust:
1½ cups teff flour
½ cup date sugar
½ canola oil
⅓ cup water
½ teaspoon sea salt

The Filling:
2 cups blueberries
¼ cup cold water
pinch of sea salt
¼ cup rice syrup
1 tablespoon kudzu

Preheat oven to 375 degrees. Mix up pie crust ingredients. Lightly oil a pie plate. Press crust into pie pan. Make several holes in the pie crust with a fork. Bake for 10 minutes. Add filling.

Simmer blueberries with a pinch of sea salt for a few minutes. Add rice syrup, stir, and simmer briefly. (A short cooking time keeps the blueberries whole.) Add kudzu dissolved in cold water. Stir. Taste and add more rice syrup for a sweeter flavor. Pour into baked pie crust. Let it cool before serving.

TIME: 25 MINUTES

Berry Good Tofu Pie

Pie Crust:
*1 recipe for Dessert Pie Crust
(see page 231)*

Filling:
*1 pound tofu (Silky or soft
varieties make a creamy
filling, and extra firm and
firm tofu make a more solid
filling, unless you add more
water when blending.)*
*½-²/₃ cup rice syrup or
⅓ cup maple syrup*
¼ cup tahini
1 tablespoon vanilla
*1 cup blueberries, straw-
berries, or raspberries*

OPTIONAL:
*Add ⅛ cup water to firmer
tofu.*

TIME: 30 MINUTES

Preheat the oven to 375 degrees. Prepare and bake the whole crust. Whip up the tofu, sweetener, vanilla, and tahini in a food processor. (If using an extra firm or firm tofu, add ⅛ cup of water for a creamier filling.) Taste and adjust the flavor by adding more sweetener or vanilla, if desired. Then pour sweetened tofu into baked pie crust. Make a design with the fresh berries on top and bake for 10 minutes, until the sweetened tofu filling has a golden brown color.

Improvisations

1. You can make a design on top with more than one kind of berry.

2. You can cook the cup of berries with a little rice syrup or maple syrup to taste (1-2 tablespoons). Add 1 teaspoon of kudzu diluted in ⅓ cup of cold water to the cooked berries. Taste and add more sweetener, if desired. If you want it to be thicker, add more diluted kudzu. Next, pour the cooked berries on top of the tofu filling. Bake for 10 minutes.

3. You can bake the tofu filling for 10 minutes and then top with the fresh or cooked berries, or other favorite (raw or cooked) fruits in season.

Bananarama Tofu Pie

Use the same dessert pie crust and change the filling.

Pie Crust:
1 recipe for Dessert Pie Crust,
(see pages 231 and 234)
Filling:
1 ripe banana
⅛ cup maple syrup
⅛ cup tahini
1 pound extra firm
or firm tofu
⅛ cup water

Preheat oven to 375 degrees. Make the pie crust recipe on either page 231 or 234. Blend all of the ingredients for the filling in a food processor. Pour filling into baked pie crust and bake for 10 minutes.

Improvisation

You can use a soft or silky tofu, and leave out the ⅛ cup of water.

TIME: 30 MINUTES

Espresso Scones

These are wonderful for tea time or dessert.

2½ cups teff flour
½ cup grain coffee
1 tablespoon arrowroot
1 tablespoon baking
powder
½ teaspoon sea salt
1 teaspoon vanilla
⅔ cup canola oil
⅔ cup maple syrup
¾ cup dried fruit, such
as, figs or apricots,
cut up small pieces

Preheat oven to 350 degrees. Combine and mix together all the ingredients. Using your hands, shape the dough into round patties about ½-inch thick and 2 inches round. Bake for 20 minutes.

Improvisations

1. You can use jam instead of dried fruit. Gently press your thumb into the center of the scone; fill each cookie with ½ teaspoon of jam.

2. Change the amount of oil and maple syrup to ⅓ cup each, and use 1 tablespoon instead of 1 teaspoon of vanilla for crispier scone.

MAKES 2 DOZEN
TIME: 25 MINUTES

THE QUICK & EASY ORGANIC GOURMET

Peanut Butter Cookies

Kids love to make these.

1½ cups teff flour
½ teaspoon sea salt
½ cup maple syrup
½ cup corn or
canola oil
1 teaspoon vanilla
1 cup peanut butter

MAKES 2 DOZEN
TIME: 25 MINUTES

Preheat the oven to 350 degrees. In a large mixing bowl, combine the teff flour and sea salt. Blend the peanut butter, maple syrup, oil, and vanilla in a food processor until creamy. Then pour the wet ingredients into the bowl with the flour and salt, and stir all together. Shape the dough into walnut-sized balls. Flatten these gently with a fork on an unoiled cookie sheet. Bake for 15 minutes. Take them out of the oven and allow them to cool before handling them, or they may crumble. Teff flour cookies are usually soft when hot, but when they are cool, they are just the right texture.

Improvisations

1. You can substitute cashew or almond butter.

2. For a crisper cookie, you can try ⅔ cup nut butter and ⅓ cup canola oil.

3. **Peanut Butter Chocolate Chip Cookies:** Add some chocolate chips.

4. You can substitute kamut flour for teff flour.

Hazlenut Butter Cookies

**Rich like Viennese butter cookies,
and they are so easy to make.**

OPTIONAL:
*Add a drop of raspberry jam
to each cookie before baking.*

Follow the same recipe and procedure as *Peanut Butter Cookies* (on the previous page), with a few exceptions:

Use 2 cups teff flour and omit the vanilla. Use hazelnut butter instead of peanut butter.

MAKES 34 COOKIES
TIME: 25 MINUTES

Fruit Paradise

Once again, teff flour replaces and surpasses wheat flour.

*4 large apples or pears
(1½-2 pounds), sliced
½ teaspoon cinnamon
pinch of sea salt
1 cup fruit juice,
such as apple or pear juice*

*Crisp ingredients:
1½ cups rolled oats
½ cup teff flour
¼ cup rice syrup, or
¼ cup maple syrup
for a sweeter taste
¼ cup unrefined corn
or canola oil
½ teaspoon cinnamon
pinch of sea salt*

Preheat the oven to 350 degrees. Thinly slice fruit. Place in a 9x13x2-inch baking dish. Sprinkle with ½ teaspoon of cinnamon and a pinch of sea salt. Cover with 1 cup apple or pear juice. Next, mix together the crisp ingredients and crumble them on top of the sliced fruit. Bake for 30 minutes for apples and 45 minutes for pears, or until the crisp is crunchy and the fruit is soft.

Improvisation

Use a combination of seasonal fruits, such as cherries, plums, nectarines, or peaches.

SERVES 6 OR MORE
TIME: 45 MINUTES

Vanilla Hazelnut Granola

World's best granola!

3 cups rolled oats
1 cup hazelnuts
½ cup teff flour
½ cup maple syrup
⅓ cup canola oil
2 tablespoons vanilla
½ teaspoon cinnamon
pinch of sea salt

MAKES ABOUT 5 CUPS
SERVES 6 OR MORE
TIME: 1 HOUR

Preheat the oven to 325 degrees. Mix all the ingredients together in a large mixing bowl. Lightly oil a cookie sheet or large casserole dish. Pour the ingredients onto it. Bake for 50 minutes.

Improvisation

You can use different kinds of nuts: almonds, pecans, or a combination.

Scrumptious Muffins

2 cups rolled oats
1 cup teff flour
¼ teaspoon sea salt
1 tablespoon arrowroot
1 tablespoon baking powder
½ teaspoon cinnamon
1 teaspoon vanilla
½ cup maple syrup
½ cup corn or canola oil
⅔ cup water

MAKES 12 MUFFINS
TIME: 30 MINUTES

Preheat the oven to 375 degrees. Sift the teff flour, sea salt, arrowroot, baking powder, and cinnamon into a large mixing bowl. Add rolled oats, vanilla, maple syrup, oil, and water. Mix all the ingredients together. Oil a muffin tin; fill muffin cups ⅔ full. Bake for 25 minutes.

Improvisations

1. You can add ¼ cup raisins.

2. You can substitute ¼ teaspoon almond extract for vanilla.

Chocolatey Pancakes

Great topped with applesauce!

1½ cups teff flour
1 tablespoon baking powder
1 tablespoon arrowroot
¼ teaspoon sea salt
1 tablespoon plus 1 teaspoon canola or unrefined corn oil
1 tablespoon vanilla
1½ cups fruit juice (apple, pear, raspberry), or 1 cup fruit juice and ½ cup amasake (rice nectar), or 1 cup soy milk or Rice Dream drink and ½ cup fruit juice

SERVES 3-4
(MAKES 18 PANCAKES)
TIME: 20 MINUTES

Without sifting, mix the dry and wet ingredients (use only 1 tablespoon oil) together in a bowl. Brush a large frying pan with 1 teaspoon oil. Heat the frying pan and add batter when pan is hot. Test by adding a little batter, or look for the wavy lines of oil. Fry 4 pancakes at a time. Fry them for a few minutes, until you see little holes in the pancakes; then flip them over and fry for a couple of minutes more.

Improvisation

Should there be any pancake batter left over, pour it into an oiled muffin pan. Bake in a preheated 350-degree oven for 20-30 minutes, or until an inserted knife or toothpick comes out dry. You can frost these muffins, too.

13

Guilt-free Desserts

You can create many great desserts with maple syrup, rice syrup, barley malt, date sugar, fruit juices, and fresh and dried fruit. Without white sugar, white flour, eggs and dairy (cholesterol), you can bake your cake and eat it, too. These marvelous desserts will please even the sweetest tooth in town.

Sweet Alternatives and Unrefined Sweeteners

Excessive sugar intake is the cause of a host of health problems, from diabetes to tooth decay. Yet the average American consumes about 100 pounds of sugar a year.

Regardless of the sugar's source, table sugar, corn syrup, molasses, and honey become glucose in the body. Normally glucose levels in the bloodstream are kept in balance by the insulin that the body generates. Our bodies need glucose to function, but complex carbohydrates provide glucose more nutritiously and economically than sugar.

The problem with table sugar (sucrose) is that it provides empty calories. There is no other nutritional benefit. It is a myth that brown and raw (unrefined) sugar are more healthful than white (refined) sugar. Nor is turbinado, a partially refined sugar, any more nutritious than the others.

How the alternatives to table sugar stack up:

Corn sweeteners, such as dextrose, corn syrup, and high fructose corn sweetener (HFCS) are all refined from corn starch and are as nutritiously bankrupt as cane and beet sugars.

Sucanat is made by evaporating the juice of organic sugar canes and milling it into powdered form. All the vitamins, minerals, and other nutrients are intact—all 3% of them, as it is 97% sugar.

Black strap molasses (made from sugar cane) and **sorghum** (made from the sorghum plant) have varying amounts of iron, calcium, potassium, and B vitamins. The darker the color, the more nutritious it is. One tablespoon of molasses has 3% of the US RDA for certain B vitamins and 15% of the daily requirement for iron and calcium. It has 50-70% sugar.

Fresh fruits have 10-25% fructose and glucose, plus fiber, minerals, and vitamins. **Dried fruits** are much sweeter, but they do contain iron. Substitute date sugar (dried crushed dates) for other sugars in baking. Use ½-⅔ the date sugar as regular sugar. Grind it in food processor or coffee grinder for a smooth consistency, or use it coarse. Date sugar is 65% sugar.

Complex carbohydrates, such as whole grains, whole grain flours, and seeds like sunflower and sesame, are a good source of glucose and other important nutrients. Grain-based syrups, such as barley malt, rice syrup, and amasake (made from fermented sweet brown rice) are somewhat more nutritious than other sweeteners. Rice syrup, depending on the brand, is 35-50% sugar; barley malt is 60%.

Maple sap straight from the tree is only 3% sucrose (and quite delicious), but the syrup made from boiling down the sap is 65% sucrose. Imitation maple syrup is 97% sucrose. Although maple syrup contains some calcium and potassium, it is not a prime source of either.

Bottom line: Use the least refined sweetener possible to avoid the sugar blues.

Replace 1 cup of sugar with:

1 cup sucanat
⅔ cup date sugar
½-¾ cup maple syrup minus ¼ cup of other liquid ingredients
½ cup molasses minus ¼ cup of other liquid ingredients
1-1¼ cup rice syrup or barley malt minus ¼ cup of other liquid ingredients
½ cup honey minus ¼ cup of other liquid ingredients

Will these sweeteners taste just as sweet as sugar?

Sucanat and maple syrup will; and honey is even sweeter.

Date sugar and molasses almost will; they are 70% as sweet as sugar.

Rice syrup won't; it is only 25% as sweet as sugar.

Barley malt won't either; it is 50% as sweet as sugar.

Spelt and Kamut Whole Grain Flours

Spelt and kamut are ancient relatives of wheat. They are non-hybridized wheat ideal for most people allergic to wheat. Spelt and kamut are considered high energy grains, preferable for athletic training and building stamina because they have more protein, fiber, fat, iron, zinc, copper, and vitamins B1 and B2 than wheat.

Spelt is more quickly and easily digested than most grains because of its bio-availability, or water-solubility. Its nutrients dissolve rapidly in liquid and are available with only a minimum of digestive work. When baking, use about ¼ less liquid than when using wheat flour. I love spelt's rich, nutty flavor, and I am not allergic to wheat.

Kamut flour is ideal for pasta making and pastries. Because of its low gluten content, it is not recommended for making bread, unless it is flat bread. Kamut has a lighter and richer taste than wheat. Hybridized common wheat tastes bland to me after eating kamut.

Why were these grains forgotten?

Spelt's thick, hard, inedible, outer husk is a mixed blessing. Harvested wheat is dehulled in the combine; harvested spelt is stored with its hull intact. Thus its nutrients are protected from airborne pollutants. Spelt grain must be mechanically dehulled, which adds an extra step and the cost of specialized equipment. In our speedy, standardized world with our over-reliance on chemical agriculture, kamut and spelt have been forgotten in favor of higher yielding wheat. Kamut and spelt thrive without pesticides and can grow in areas that are too dry for wheat.

Spelt and kamut are tasty alternatives to wheat. When baking with spelt flour, I have found that I can substitute it cup for cup in my whole wheat pastry cookie and pie crust recipes, but its greater water solubility reduces the liquid amounts by 25% for cake recipes. Kamut is drier than wheat. Like teff, it requires a little more liquid. If you are a novice pastry chef, try the cake recipes in this chapter first. Then improvise, once you know how to recognize the right consistency for a cake batter.

Baking Oils

Use an expeller-pressed mechanically extracted oil, as opposed to chemically extracted canola oil. Unrefined corn, sesame, safflower, sunflower, and hazelnut oils are also good for baking.

Pies and Pie Crusts

Feel free to mix and match pie crusts and fillings.

Banana Date Tofu Pie

Pie Crust:
1½ cups spelt flour
½ cup toasted and ground almonds
¼ cup canola, corn, or safflower oil
⅓ cup maple syrup
¼ teaspoon sea salt

Banana Date Filling #1:
1 pound extra firm tofu
6 small, ripe bananas (the riper, the sweeter)
9 bardhi or other soft, gooey dates

Banana Date Filling #2:
1 pound firm or extra firm tofu*
2 ripe bananas
⅓ cup date sugar
1 tablespoon vanilla
¼ cup water

TIME: 25 MINUTES

Preheat the oven to 375 degrees. Roast almonds for 10 minutes. Grind almonds into a meal in a food processor. Combine the almond meal with the other pie crust ingredients in a mixing bowl. Stir them together. Brush a light coat of oil onto a 9-inch pie pan. Use your hands to press the dough into the pie pan. Poke several holes in the dough with a fork. Bake for 10 minutes. Add filling.

Blend tofu, bananas, and dates in a food processor on high until tofu is creamy. Taste. (Add more dates for a sweeter flavor.) Fill the baked pie crust, and bake for 10 minutes. Serve at room temperature.

Date sugar replaces dates for another delicious variation: Blend all the filling ingredients in a food processor. Pour it into the baked pie crust. Bake 10 minutes or until top is golden brown. Serve at room temperature.

Improvisations

1. You can substitute whole wheat pastry flour for the spelt flour. You may need a little more liquid with wheat flour.

2. You can substitute walnuts, filberts, or other ground nuts for almonds.

---

* You can substitute soft or silken tofu and omit the water.

Luscious Strawberry Pie

Pie Crust:
2 cups whole wheat pastry flour
⅓ cup maple syrup
⅓ cup canola oil
¼ teaspoon sea salt

Filling:
1 pound extra firm tofu
½ cup rice syrup, or
⅛ cup maple syrup
1 tablespoon vanilla
1 tablespoon tahini

10 strawberries, rinsed

OPTION #1:
Add 1 teaspoon vanilla or ⅛ teaspoon almond extract.

OPTION #2:
Add a little rice syrup to the filling or drizzle it on top before or after baking the pie.

TIME: 25 MINUTES

Preheat oven to 375 degrees. Mix up pie crust and press it into a lightly oiled pie pan. Poke several holes in the pie dough with a fork. Bake 10 minutes. Blend all the filling ingredients except the strawberries in a food processor until creamy. Taste. Add more sweetener or vanilla, if you like. Pour the whipped tofu filling into the baked pie shell. Bake for 10 minutes, or until the tofu is a golden color.

Improvisations

1. Decorate the pie with fresh strawberries before or after baking.

2. Briefly simmer the strawberries with a pinch of sea salt. When the strawberries are soft, taste them. Dilute a little kudzu or arrowroot in a little cold water. Stir it into the cooked berries to thicken the sauce. Pour cooked strawberries on top of the tofu before or after baking.

3. Blend fresh or cooked berries into the tofu filling.

4. Substitute blueberries or other seasonal fresh fruits for strawberries.

Creamy Chocolate Truffle Pie

Intoxicating! A small piece of dessert has never
satisfied me until I made this one!

Pie Crust:
2 cups teff flour
½ cup maple syrup
2 tablespoons hazelnut
butter
2 tablespoons canola oil
¼ teaspoon sea salt

Chocolate Truffle Filling
or Pudding:
1¼ cups chocolate chips
(Barats or Sunspire)
1 pound silken tofu
2 tablespoons roasted
almond butter
½ teaspoon vanilla

OPTIONAL:
Decorate pie with almonds
before baking or strawber-
ries after baking.

TIME: 30 MINUTES

Preheat oven to 375 degrees. Mix up pie crust ingredients and press into a lightly oiled pie pan. Poke several holes in the pie dough with a fork. Bake for 15 minutes.

In a small sauce pan, melt chocolate chips over low heat, stirring constantly. Put tofu, vanilla, and almond butter in a food processor. Add melted chips, and blend until creamy. Bake 7 minutes, or until edges of the filling darken. Let pie sit in warm oven for 3 minutes.

Improvisation

Chocolate Pudding: Double the filling recipe and skip the crust and the baking. Pour into pudding cups.

Walnut Pie

Pie Crust:

2 cups spelt or whole wheat
pastry flour
⅓ cup canola oil
⅓ cup water
1 tablespoon vanilla
½ teaspoon sea salt
1 tablespoon sucanat

Filling:

1½ cups rice syrup, or
1 cup barley malt with
¼ cup honey
1½ cups water, or fruit
juice, such as cherry
3-4 tablespoons of agar
agar flakes (use 4 for a
firmer filling)
¼ teaspoon of sea salt
½ teaspoon cinnamon
½ teaspoon arrowroot
or kudzu and enough water
to barely cover it (about 2
tablespoons)
2 cups raw or
roasted walnuts
1-2 teaspoons vanilla

OPTIONAL:
Roast walnuts in the oven
while the pie crust bakes.

TIME: 35 MINUTES

Preheat oven to 375 degrees. Mix all the pie crust ingredients together except the sucanat. Press dough into a lightly oiled pie pan. Poke several holes in the pie crust with a fork. Sprinkle sucanat on top of pie crust and bake 12 minutes for spelt flour or 10 minutes for whole wheat pastry flour.

Whisk the sweetener(s), water (or juice), agar agar, cinnamon, and salt in a sauce pan as you bring them to a boil. Simmer for 5 minutes, or until the agar agar dissolves, whisking occasionally. Dissolve the arrowroot or kudzu in about ¼ cup cold water (enough water to cover). Whisk thickener into the simmering pot. Let cool. After 15 minutes, stir in the walnuts and vanilla. Pour filling into the baked pie crust. Allow it to cool and settle for 2 hours, or refrigerate it for an hour. Serve at room temperature.

Improvisation

You can substitute pecans for walnuts.

Cookies

These cookie recipes are variations of the pie crust recipes with additions of dried fruits, spices, carob, or chocolate chips. If you like, use one of these cookie recipes for a pie crust, or use a pie crust recipe for cookies.

Chocolate Chip Cookies

Kids love to shape these cookies.

2 cups spelt or whole wheat pastry flour, or a combination
⅓ cup maple syrup
⅓ cup canola oil
¼ teaspoon sea salt
½ cup Sunspire malted or Barats non-dairy chocolate chips

MAKES 2 DOZEN COOKIES
TIME: 25 MINUTES

Preheat the oven to 350 degrees. Without sifting, combine and mix all of the ingredients together. Shape into 2 dozen, 2-inch-round cookies. Bake them for 15 minutes. Let them cool for about 10 minutes before transferring to a cooling rack or platter.

Improvisations

1. **Carob Chip Cookies**: Substitute carob chips for chocolate chips.

2. **Date Cookies**: Substitute ½ cup dates (10 pitted dates) for chocolate chips.

3. **Chunky Chocolate-Nut Cookies**: Add 1 tablespoon vanilla and ½ cup of walnuts, pecans, or hazelnuts.

4. You can add some coconut.

5. Substitute kamut flour and increase the oil and maple syrup to ½ cup each.

[handwritten annotations:]
4x
whole wheat
4 8C 1.3 lb
⅔ C .5# barley malt
⅔ C .5# sorghum
1⅓ C .5# palm oil
1 tsp salt
2 C malt
.5 lb. choc chips
2 tsp vanilla

Carob Cookies

½ cup roasted carob
powder
2 cups whole wheat
pastry flour
¼ teaspoon sea salt
½ cup corn or canola oil
½ cup rice syrup
1 tablespoon vanilla

Preheat oven to 350 degrees. Sift the carob powder, flour, and salt into a large mixing bowl. Mix in the other ingredients and shape the cookies into 2-inch rounds. Place them on a lightly oiled cookie sheet. Bake 15 minutes. Take them out of the oven and let them cool for about 10 minutes. Then put them on a cooling rack or platter.

MAKES 18 COOKIES
TIME: 25 MINUTES

Fruit Cake Cookies

3 cups whole wheat
pastry flour
½ teaspoon sea salt
1 tablespoon vanilla
10 pitted dates (½ cup)
¼ cup raisins
½ cup canola or corn oil
½ cup water or fruit juice
½ cup rice syrup

Preheat oven to 350 degrees. Combine all the ingredients in a mixing bowl. Shape them with your hands into 2-3 dozen cookies, depending on how large (1-3 inches) you make them. Lightly oil a cookie sheet. Bake cookies for 15 minutes. Take them out of the oven and let them cool for about 10 minutes before putting them on a cooling rack or platter.

Improvisation

Change the sweetener and add ½ teaspoon cinnamon.

MAKES 2-3 DOZEN
TIME: 20 MINUTES

Apple Date Crisp

5 apples, rinsed and sliced
1 cup pitted dates
2 teaspoons cinnamon
2 cups rolled oats
⅓ cup canola or corn oil
⅔ cup teff or kamut
flour
½ teaspoon sea salt
3 cups apple juice

SERVES 6-8
TIME: 35 MINUTES

Preheat the oven to 350 degrees. Put sliced apples on the bottom of a large (9x13x2-inch) glass baking dish. Place pitted dates on top of apples, spaced evenly. Sprinkle 1 teaspoon of cinnamon over apples and dates. In a separate mixing bowl, combine rolled oats, flour, salt, oil, vanilla, and 1 teaspoon of cinnamon. Mix together and crumble mixture on top of apples and dates. Pour apple juice on top. Bake for 30 minutes.

Improvisations

1. Substitute peaches or pears for apples, or use a combination of seasonal fruits.

2. Try other types of dried fruits, or use a combination of fresh and dried.

3. Try other flavors of fruit juice.

4. You can add nuts.

Exotic Pear Crisp

Moist and sweet

5 pears, sliced
2 teaspoons cinnamon
2 cups kamut flakes
1 tablespoon vanilla
⅓ cup canola or corn oil
½ cup spelt flour
½ teaspoon sea salt
3¼ cups cherry
or apple juice
4 tablespoons date sugar

SERVES 6-8
TIME: 35 MINUTES

Follow the directions for the previous recipe, *Apple Crisp,* and sprinkle the date sugar on top of crisp before baking.

Improvisations

1. Substitute spelt flakes or rolled oats for kamut flakes.

2. You can use whole wheat pastry flour.

3. You can substitute apples for pears or other fruit in season.

Cakes

Ginger Bread Cake

2 cups spelt flour
1 cup barley flour
½ teaspoon sea salt
2 tablespoons non-aluminum baking powder
1½ tablespoons ginger powder
1 teaspoon cinnamon
1 teaspoon nutmeg
5 tablespoons flax seeds or Fortified Flax*
2 cups apple or pear juice
½ cup canola or corn oil
¾ cup maple syrup
1 tablespoon vanilla

Preheat oven to 350 degrees. Without sifting, combine flours, salt, cinnamon, nutmeg, ginger, and baking powder in a large mixing bowl. Grind flax seeds in a blender and add juice. Blend until gelatinous. Add oil, vanilla, and maple syrup to the blender. Blend briefly. Add wet ingredients to the dry ingredients and stir them together. Pour cake batter into a lightly oiled 9x13x2-inch cake pan. Bake for 40 minutes.

---

* Do not grind Fortified Flax; add it directly to the blender or food processor.

TIME: 45 MINUTES

Corn Bread Cake

A great complement to refried beans or chili

2 cups corn meal
2 cups whole wheat pastry
flour
½ teaspoon sea salt
2 tablespoons baking
powder
½ cup canola or corn oil
½ cup maple syrup
½ cup vanilla soy milk or
Rice Dream drink
1½ cup apple juice
1 tablespoon vanilla

OPTION #1:
*You can blend the wet
ingredients first in a food
processor or blender.*

OPTION #2:
*Add 1 cup blueberries
or strawberries.*

TIME: 35 MINUTES

Preheat oven to 350 degrees. Put all the ingredients in a large mixing bowl, and mix them all together. Pour batter into a lightly oiled 9x13x2-inch baking dish. Bake for 30 minutes.

Improvisations

1. Use 2 cups of vanilla soy milk and omit the vanilla and apple juice.

2. **Wheat-Free Corn Bread**: Substitute 2 cups of brown rice flour for whole wheat pastry flour. Add 5 tablespoons of flax seeds or Fortified Flax*. Grind the flax seeds in a blender until powdery. Add juice and blend until gelatinous. Otherwise, follow the same directions as above.

---

* Do not grind Fortified Flax; add it directly to the blender or food processor.

Mocha Walnut Cake

5 tablespoons flax seeds
or Fortified Flax*
2 cups apple juice
½ cup corn or canola oil
1 cup maple syrup
1 tablespoon vanilla
3 cups spelt flour
½ teaspoon sea salt
2 tablespoons non-
aluminum baking powder
⅔ cups walnuts
½ cup grain coffee

TIME: 45 MINUTES

Preheat oven to 350 degrees. Grind the flax seeds in a blender for 30 seconds. Add juice and blend until gelatinous. Add maple syrup, vanilla, and oil to the blender and mix briefly. Combine all the ingredients in a large mixing bowl. Stir. The batter is like a thick pudding. Lightly oil a 9-inch round or 9x13x2-inch baking pan. Pour batter into cake baking pan. Bake 40 minutes.

---

* Do not grind Fortified Flax; add it directly to the blender or food processor.

Banana Cake

4 cups whole wheat
pastry flour
2 tablespoons baking
powder
½ teaspoon sea salt
½ cup canola or corn oil
1 cup maple syrup
1 tablespoon vanilla
2 cups apple juice
2 ripe bananas
½ cup vanilla soy milk or
rice dream drink
¾ cup walnuts
1½ cups raisins, or
½ cup raisins with ¾ cup
other dried fruits, such as
pitted dates or chopped
dried pears

TIME: 50 MINUTES

Preheat oven to 350 degrees. Put flour, sea salt, and baking powder in a large mixing bowl. (Sifting is optional.) Blend the bananas, maple syrup, soy milk, vanilla, oil, and apple juice in a food processor. (You may need to do it in shifts, unless you have an extra large food processor.) Pour liquid ingredients on top of dry ingredients. Add nuts and dried fruits. Mix it all together. Oil a 9x13x2-inch baking dish. Pour batter in. Bake for 45 minutes.

Improvisation

Use only ¾ cup apple juice and add an extra banana. Bake for 30-40 minutes.

Layer Cakes

Great for birthday and dinner parties, these layer cakes are delicious and serve 24 slices. Cut the recipes in half for a smaller cake. Try making layer cakes with one kind of cake for the top and another kind for the bottom. For example, make the *Chocolate Cake Supreme* for the bottom layer and the *Hazelnut Cake* for the top. Mix and match icings, too. These cakes are great without frosting, too.

Carrot Coconut Cake

4 cups spelt flour
½ teaspoon sea salt
2 tablespoons baking powder
1 teaspoon cinnamon
½ teaspoon cardamom
½ teaspoon nutmeg
½ cup raisins or currants
½ cup walnuts
2 cups grated carrots
½ cup canola or corn oil
½ cup maple syrup
1 cup plain Rice Dream drink or vanilla soy milk
1 cup apple or pear juice
1 tablespoon vanilla

TIME: 45 MINUTES
(LET IT COOL AT LEAST AN
HOUR BEFORE FROSTING)

Preheat the oven to 350 degrees. In a large mixing bowl, combine the flour, baking powder, salt, cinnamon, nutmeg, cardamom, walnuts, raisins, and grated carrots. Blend the oil, maple syrup, apple juice, rice dream, and vanilla in a food processor or blender. Add the wet to the dry ingredients. Stir them all together until well blended. Lightly oil a 9x13x2-inch baking pan, or 2 9-inch round cake pans or 2 loaf pans. Pour batter into cake baking pan(s). Bake for 35 minutes, or until a toothpick inserted into the cake comes out dry. Cool on rack before frosting.

Coconut Icing

1 pound extra firm tofu
½ cup unsweetened
shredded coconut
½ cup maple syrup
1 teaspoon vanilla

TIME: 10 MINUTES

Blend all these ingredients in a food processor once the cake has cooled. Cut the carrot cake in half. Put one half of the cake on a large plate. Spread a little less than half the icing on this half of cake. Stack the other cake on top. Spread the rest of the frosting up, down, and around the sides of the two layers. Sprinkle an extra tablespoon of coconut on the top. Serve immediately, or refrigerate until it is time to serve.

Carob Fudge Layer Cake

**Take your pick of Caramel, Carob Fudge or
any other icing in this chapter.**

1¾ cups roasted carob powder
2¼ cups spelt flour, or
3 cups whole wheat
pastry flour*
2 tablespoons baking
powder
½ teaspoon sea salt
½ pound extra firm tofu
1¼ cups fruit juice (apple,
cherry, raspberry, or pear)
½ cup canola or corn oil
⅔ cup maple syrup
1 tablespoon vanilla

TIME: 35 MINUTES
(LET IT COOL AT LEAST AN
HOUR BEFORE FROSTING)

Preheat oven to 375 degrees. Sift roasted carob powder, sea salt, baking powder, and flour into a large mixing bowl. Blend all the other (wet) ingredients, including the tofu, in a food processor. Add the wet ingredients to the dry, and mix them all together until well blended. Pour into a lightly oiled, large glass baking dish (9x13x2-inch). Bake for 30 minutes. Cool on rack before frosting.

---

* Using 3 cups of whole wheat pastry flour makes the batter very thick, almost like fudge. The cake will be delicious.

Caramel Icing

½ pound soy cream cheese,
tofu, or nut or seed butter
½ cup barley malt
⅓ cup maple syrup

Blend these ingredients in a food processor. When the cake is cool, cut it in half. Put one half on a large plate or cake platter. Spread about ⅓ of the frosting on the top of it. Stack the other half on top, and frost it as well, plus the sides.

TIME: 10 MINUTES

Carob Fudge Icing

1 pound extra firm tofu
1 cup roasted carob powder
12 ounces rice nectar syrup
with blueberries*, or plain
rice syrup

Follow same directions as for *Caramel Icing*.

* Rice nectar is a natural rice syrup made with blueberries, available in 12-ounce jars. There are other flavors, too: strawberry, raspberry, and plain. Any one of them will do.

TIME: 10 MINUTES

Chocolate Cake Supreme

The batter resembles a pudding; it is thick and airy.
*Try it frosted with the **Cocoa Icing** on the next page, the*
Chocolate Hazelnut Pudding or Frosting *on page 260,*
or without frosting.

3 cups kamut flour, or 3½ cups whole wheat pastry flour, or 4 cups spelt flour
2 tablespoons baking powder
½ teaspoon sea salt
5 tablespoons flax seeds or Fortified Flax*
⅓ cup apple, cherry, or raspberry juice
⅔ cup water
1 tablespoon vanilla
1 cup maple syrup
½ cup canola oil
1 cup vanilla soy milk, or Rice Dream drink
8 ounces Rapunzel organic bittersweet chocolate, or 2 cups Sunspire malted or Barats non-dairy chocolate chips
1½ cups vanilla soy milk or Rice Dream drink

OPTIONAL:
Melt more chocolate chips and add them to the batter for a richer chocolate flavor, if desired.

TIME: 50 MINUTES
LET IT COOL AT LEAST AN HOUR
BEFORE FROSTING

Preheat the oven to 350 degrees. Combine flour, salt, and baking powder in a large mixing bowl. Grind flax seeds to a powder in a blender. Add juice and water and process 30 seconds, until gelatinous. Add vanilla, maple syrup, and canola oil and blend briefly. Add the wet ingredients to the dry ingredients in the mixing bowl. In a sauce pan, melt the baking chocolate or chips in soy milk. Stir constantly to avoid burning the chips; they melt quickly. Add the melted chocolate chips to the other ingredients in the large mixing bowl. Stir all of the ingredients together. Taste the batter. Transfer the batter to a 9x13x2-inch lightly oiled, glass baking pan. Bake 40 minutes. Cool on rack before frosting.

---

* Do not grind Fortified Flax; add it directly to the blender or food processor.

Cocoa Fudge Icing

1 cup cocoa powder
1 pound extra firm tofu
12 ounces strawberry rice
nectar (syrup) or plain rice
syrup

Blend these ingredients in a food processor. Taste and adjust the flavoring, if desired. When the cake is cool, cut it in half. Put one half on a large plate or cake platter. Spread about ⅓ of the frosting on the top. Stack the other half on top, and frost it and the sides.

TIME: 10 MINUTES

Outrageously Delicious Hazelnut Cake
Wheat-free and great without a frosting, too!

5 tablespoons flax seeds or
Fortified Flax*
2 cups apricot or
apple juice
¼ cup canola or
hazelnut oil
1 cup maple syrup
1 tablespoon vanilla
1 cup hazelnuts
2 cups brown rice flour
1 cup barley flour
2 tablespoons non-
aluminum baking powder
½ teaspoon sea salt

Preheat oven to 350 degrees. Grind the flax seeds in a blender until powdery. Add juice and blend until gelatinous. Add oil, maple syrup, and vanilla to the blender and mix briefly. Grind the hazelnuts in a food processor. Sift flours, baking powder, and salt. Combine all the ingredients in a large mixing bowl. Stir. The batter is like a thick pudding. Lightly oil a 9-inch round or 9x13x2-inch baking pan. Pour batter into pan. Bake 40 minutes. Cool on rack before frosting.

Improvisation

Omit flax seeds. Use 3 cups whole wheat pastry flour instead of barley and rice flours.

TIME: 50 MINUTES
(LET IT COOL AT LEAST AN
HOUR BEFORE FROSTING)

* Do not grind Fortified Flax; add it directly to the blender or food processor.

Hazelnut Butter Icing

½ cup hazelnut butter
1 pound firm tofu
½ cup honey
1 tablespoon vanilla

TIME: 10 MINUTES

Blend these ingredients in a food processor. When the cake is cool, cut it in half. Put one half on a large plate or cake platter. Spread about ⅓ of the frosting on the top of it. Stack the other half on top, and frost it as well, plus the sides.

Chocolate Hazelnut Pudding or Frosting

As a hot fudge, pudding or frosting, this versatile treat will please the sweetest tooth in town.

1 cup cocoa powder
1 cup water
pinch of sea salt
½ cup hazelnut butter
½ cup rice syrup
3 tablespoons kudzu or arrowroot
¼ cup cold water

TIME: 5 MINUTES

Dissolve the cocoa powder in the water by heating them together with a pinch of sea salt over medium heat for 1-2 minutes. Turn off the heat and stir in the hazelnut butter and rice syrup. If you are looking for a hot fudge sundae, stop here and serve it over cake or frozen desserts. To make a pudding or frosting, dissolve kudzu in ¼ cup cold water, and stir it into the hot fudge over low heat for 2 minutes. Stir continuously until it thickens. Let it cool to room temperature or refrigerate it before icing the cake or serving as a pudding.

Improvisations

1. You can substitute almond or peanut butter for hazelnut butter.

2. Use less water and omit the thickener.

3. Use other sweeteners, such as maple syrup.

4. Garnish with shredded coconut.

THE QUICK & EASY GOURMET

Kanten (Vegetable Gelatin)

1 quart fruit juice, such as
apple or cherry
4 tablespoons agar
agar flakes
pinch of sea salt

SERVES 4
TIME: 5 MINUTES AND
ABOUT AN HOUR TO COOL

Simmer all the ingredients for 5 minutes, or until the agar agar dissolves. Pour into individual dessert cups or into a loaf pan. Leave it on the counter for several hours to cool and gel.

Improvisation

1. Put a pint of rinsed berries or sliced fruits in the loaf pan or individual serving bowls before pouring the hot juice in.

2. Along with the berries, add thinly sliced lemon rounds and fresh mint leaves.

Apricot Compote

Try any fresh or dried fruit this way.

1 cup dried apricots
1 cup water
a pinch sea salt
1 tablespoon kudzu or
arrowroot

SERVES 3-4
TIME: 10 MINUTES

Simmer the apricots, ¾ cup of water, and sea salt together for 10 minutes, or until the apricots are tender. Dissolve the kudzu in ¼ cup of cold water. Add and stir it into the simmering apricots until thick. Serve as is or use as a topping for a pie or cake.

Hot Carob Fudge

Here's a great topping for frozen rice dream or soy-based frozen desserts. Or let it cool and enjoy it as a pudding.

²/₃ cup roasted carob powder
1¹/₃ cups water
1 tablespoon rice syrup
1 tablespoon tahini
1 tablespoon kudzu or arrowroot
pinch of sea salt

OPTIONAL:
½ teaspoon vanilla

SERVES 2-4
TIME: 5 MINUTES

Put the roasted carob powder in a small saucepan with a pinch of sea salt and 1¹/₈ cup of water. While you bring it to a boil, add rice syrup and tahini. Stir. When it boils, turn the flame down to a simmer. Dilute kudzu in remaining ¼ cup of cold water. Add it to the pot. Stir in vanilla and taste. If it is just right, pour it over individual servings of frozen Rice Dream or soy-based desserts. If not, add more rice syrup or vanilla, to taste.

Improvisations

1. Use a nut butter, such as almond, cashew, or hazelnut, instead of tahini.

2. Use another sweetener, such as maple syrup.

3. Omit the kudzu. Let the hot carob fudge simmer for another minute or two and it will thicken naturally.

4. Serve over banana cake, with or without frozen dessert.

Appendices

—⚜—

Glossary

—⚜—

Index

Appendix 1

—— ☙☙ ——

*Pesticides That Pose a High-risk for Children**

Mothers & Others considers the following pesticides to pose particularly high risks to children, because they have been found in ten or more foods heavily consumed by children, and because they are all either probable or possible carcinogens, neurotoxins, reproductive/developmental toxins, or may have other adverse health effects. (This list is not meant to be exhaustive.) Mothers & Others is asking supermarkets to discourage actively their suppliers from selling produce grown with any pesticides posing high risks to children. Pesticides are listed alphabetically.

ACEPHATE

Problem: *Organophosphate pesticide/toxic to the nervous system; possible carcinogen*

Permitted in:[†] beans, Brussels sprouts, cauliflower, celery, cranberries, eggs, lettuce, meat (cattle, goats, hogs, horses, poultry, sheep,) milk, peanuts, peppers, soybeans

AZINPHOSMETHYL (guthion)

Problem: *Organophosphate pesticide/toxic to the nervous system; also a high risk to farmer*

Permitted in: almonds, apples, apricots, artichokes, barley, beans (dry, snap), blackberries, blueberries, boysenberries, brachial, Brussels sprouts, cabbage, cauliflower, celery, cherries, citrus, crabapples, cranberries, cucumbers, eggplants, filberts, gooseberries, grapes, kiwi, loganberries, meat (cattle, goats, horses, sheep), melons, mushrooms, nectarines, oats, onions, parsley, peaches, pears, peas (black-eyed), pecans, peppers, pistachios, plums, potatoes, quinces, raspberries, rye, soybeans, spinach, strawberries, sugarcane, tomatoes, walnuts, wheat

---

* This list is available from: Mothers & Others, Shopper's Campaign for Better Food Choices, 40 West 20th Street, New York, NY, 10011, (212) 727-4474 under the title *High-risk Pesticides for Children.*

† The EPA permits the use of these pesticides on the listed crops; in practice, residues of these pesticides may not be found in all of these crops.

BENOMYL

Problem: *possible human carcinogen, reproductive toxin*

Permitted in: apples, apricots, avocados, bananas, barley, beans, beets, black-berries, blueberries, boysenberries, broccoli, Brussels sprouts, cabbage, carrots, cauliflower, celery, cherries, Chinese cabbage, citrus, collards, corn, cucumbers, currants, dandelions, dewberrries, eggplant, eggs, garlic, grapes, kale, kohlrabi, loganberries, mangoes, meat (cattle, goats, hogs, horses, poultry, sheep), melons, milk, mushrooms, mustard greens, nectarines, nuts, oats, papayas, peaches, peanuts, pears, peppers, pineapples, pistachios, plums, pumpkins, raspberries, rice, rutabagas, rye, soybeans, spinach, squash (summer and winter), strawberries, sweet potatoes, tomatoes, turnips, wheat, and sometimes in turnip greens and watercress.

CAPTAN

Problem: *probable human carcinogen*

Permitted in: apples, apricots, avocados, beets, blackberries, blueberries, broccoli, Brussels sprouts, cabbage, cantaloupes, carrots, cauliflower, celery, cherries, collards, corn, crabapples, cranberries, cucumbers, dewberrries, egg-plants, garlic, grapes, honeydew melons, kale, leeks, lettuce, mangoes, meat (cattle, hogs), muskmelons, mustard greens, nectarines, onions, peaches, pears, peas, peppers, pimentos, plums, pumpkins, quinces, raspberries, rhubarb, rutabagas, shallots, soybeans, spinach, squash (summer and winter), strawberries, taro (corn), tomatoes, turnips, watermelons

CARBARYL

Problem: *toxic to the nervous system; may cause birth defects*

Permitted in: almonds, apricots, asparagus, bananas, barley, beans, beets, blackberries, blueberries, boysenberries, broccoli, Brussels sprouts, cabbage, carrots, cauliflower, celery, cherries, chestnuts, Chinese cabbage, citrus, collards, corn, cowpeas, cranberries, cucumbers, dandelions, dewberrries, egg-plants, endive, filberts, grapes, horseradish, kale, kohlrabi, lentils, lettuce, loganberries, maple sap, melons, millet, mustard greens, nectarines, oats, okra, olives, oysters, parsley, parsnips, peaches, peanuts, peas, pecans, peppers, pistachio nuts, plums, potatoes (regular and sweet), poultry, prickly pear cactus, pumpkins, radishes, raspberries, rice, rutabagas, rye, salsify, sorghum, soybeans, spinach, squash (summer and winter), strawberries, sunflower seeds, Swiss chard, tomatoes, turnips, walnuts, wheat

CHLOROTHALONIL

Problem: *probable human carcinogen*

Permitted in: apricots, bananas, beans (dry, snap), broccoli, Brussels sprouts, cabbage, carrots, cauliflower, celery, cherries, cocoa beans, coffee beans, corn, cranberries, cucumbers, melons, nectarines, onions (bulb and green), papayas, parsnips, passion fruit, peaches, peanuts, plums, potatoes, prunes, pumpkins, soybeans, squash (summer and winter), tomatoes

CHLORPYRIFOS

Problem: *organophosphate pesticide/toxic to the nervous system*

Permitted in: almonds, apples, bananas, beans (lima and snap), beets, blueberries, cherries, citrus, corn, cranberries, cucumbers, eggs, figs, kiwi, legumes (succulent or dried, except soybeans), meat (cattle, goat, hog, horse, poultry, sheep) milk fat, mushrooms, nectarines, onions, peaches, peanuts, pears, peppers, plums, pumpkins, radishes, rutabagas, seed and pod vegetables, sorghum, soybeans, strawberries, sunflower seeds, sweet potatoes, tomatoes, tree nuts, turnips, leafy vegetables and sometimes in asparagus, dates, grapes, leeks, caneberries, cherimoya, feijoa (pineapple guava), sapote

DACTHAL (DCPA)

Problem: *data gaps for chronic, reproductive, and developmental effects; contains 2,3,7,8-TCDD(dioxin) and hexachlorobenzene(HCB) as impurities, both of which are suspected human carcinogens, toxic to the fetus, causing birth defects, and toxic to the immune system**

Permitted in: beans (dry and snap), corn, cress, cucumbers, eggplant, garlic, horseradish, lettuce, melons (cantaloupes, honeydew, watermelon) onions, peas (black-eyed), peppers, pimentos, potatoes, rutabagas, squash (winter and summer) soybeans, strawberries, sweet potatoes, tomatoes, turnips, leafy vegetables, yams

DIAZINON

Problem: *organophosphate pesticide/toxic to the nervous system*

Permitted in: almonds, apples, apricots, bananas, beans (guar, lima, snap), beets, blackberries, blueberries, boysenberries, carrots, celery, cherries, chicory, citrus, coffee beans, corn, cowpeas, cranberries, cucumbers, dandelions, dewberrries, endive, figs, filberts, ginseng, grapes, hops, kiwi, lettuce, loganberries, meat (cattle, sheep), melons, mushrooms, nectarines, olives, onions, parsley, parsnips, peaches, peanuts, pears, peas, pecans, peppers, pineapples, plums, potatoes (regular and sweet), radishes, raspberries, rutabagas, sorghum, soybeans, spinach, squash (summer and winter), strawberries, sugarcane, Swiss chard, tomatoes, turnips, leafy vegetables, walnuts, watercress

---

* The EPA requires certification that the levels of 2,3,7,8-TCDD and HCB in DCPA used to formulate products do not exceed 0.1 ppb and 0.3 percent, respectively.

DICHLORAN

Problem: *suspected mutage; effects on the eye*

Permitted in: apricots, beans, blackberries, boysenberries, carrots, celery, cherries, cucumbers, endive, garlic, grapes, kiwi, lettuce, nectarines, onions, peaches, plums, potatoes, raspberries, rhubarb, sweet potatoes

DICOFOL (KELTHANE)

Problem: *possible human carcinogen*

Permitted in: apples, apricots, beans (dry, snap, and lima), blackberries, boysenberries, bushnuts, butternuts, cantaloupes, cherries, chestnuts, crabapples, cucumbers, dewberries, eggplants, figs, filberts, grapefruits, grapes, hazelnuts, hickory nuts, hops, kumquats, lemons, limes, loganberries, melons, muskmelons, nectarines, oranges, peaches, pears, pecans, peppers, pimentos, plums, pumpkins, quinces, raspberries, squash (summer and winter), strawberries, tangerines, tomatoes, walnuts, watermelons

DIMENTHOATE

Problem: *organophosphate pesticide/toxic to the nervous system; possible carcinogen*

Permitted in: apples, bananas, beans (dry, lima, snap), broccoli, cabbage, cauliflower, celery, collards, corn, cottonseed, eggs, endive, grapefruit, grapes, kale, lemons, lentils, lettuce, meat (cattle, goat, horse, poultry, sheep), melons, milk, mustard greens, oranges, pears, peas, pecans, peppers, potatoes, sorghum, soybeans, spinach, Swiss chard, tangerines, tomatoes, turnips, wheat

EBDCs

EBDCs are listed as a probable carcinogen and reproductive toxin because of ETU, a breakdown product. The crops listed are for maneb, one of the EBDC fungicides.

Problem: *probable human carcinogen; reproductive toxin*

Permitted in: almonds, apples, apricots, bananas, beans, beets, broccoli, Brussels sprouts, cabbage, carrots, cauliflower, celery, Chinese cabbage, collards, corn, cranberries, cucumbers, eggplant, endive, figs, grapes, kale, kohlrabi, lettuce, melons, mustard greens, nectarines, onions, papayas, peaches, peppers, potatoes, pumpkins, rhubarb, spinach, squash (winter and summer), tomatoes, turnips

ENDOSULFAN

Problem: *very high acute toxicity to birds, fish, bees, crustaceans, and mammals (including humans)*

Permitted in: almonds, apples, apricots, artichokes, barley, beans, beets, blueberries, broccoli, Brussels sprouts, cabbage, carrots, cauliflower, celery, cherries, collards, corn, cucumbers, eggplants, filberts, grapes, kale, lettuce, macadamia nuts, meat (cattle, goats, horses, sheep), melons, milk (fat), mustard greens and seed, nectarines, oats, peaches, pears, peas, pecans, peppers, pineapples, plums, potatoes, prunes, pumpkins, raspberries, rye, spinach, squash (summer and winter), strawberries, sugarcane, sunflower seeds, sweet potatoes, tomatoes, turnips (greens), walnuts, watercress, wheat

IPRODIONE
Problem: *may cause blood abnormalities; data gaps for developmental effects*
Permitted in: almonds, apricots, beans, blueberries, boysenberries, broccoli, caneberries, carrots, cherries, currants, garlic, ginseng, grapes, kiwi, lettuce, nectarines, onions, peaches, peanuts, plums, potatoes, prunes, raspberries, rice, strawberries

MALATHION
Problem: *organophosphate pesticide/toxic to the nervous system*
Permitted in: almonds, apricots, asparagus, avocados, barley, beans, beets, blackberries, blueberries, boysenberries, carrots, chayote, cherries, chestnuts, corn, cranberries, cucumbers, currants, dates, dewberries, eggplants, eggs, figs, filberts, garlic, gooseberries, grapefruit, grapes, guavas, hops, horseradish, kumquats, leeks, lemons, lentils, limes, loganberries, macadamia nuts, mangoes, meat (cattle, goats, hogs, horses, poultry, sheep), melons, milk (fat), mushrooms, nectarines, oats, okra, onions (including green onions), oranges, papayas, parsnips, passion fruit, peaches, peanuts, pears, peas, pecans, peppermint, peppers, pineapples, plums, potatoes, prunes, pumpkins, quinces, radishes, raspberries, rice, rutabagas, rye, salify, shallots, sorghum, soybeans, spearmint, squash (summer and winter), strawberries, sunflower seeds, sweet potatoes, tangerines, tomatoes, turnips, leafy vegetables, walnuts, wheat

METHAMIDOPHOS
Problem: *organophosphate pesticide/toxic to the nervous system*
Permitted in: beets, broccoli, Brussels sprouts, cabbages, cauliflower, cucumbers, eggplants, lettuce, melons, peppers, potatoes, tomatoes

MEVINPHOS
Problem: *organophosphate pesticide/toxic to the nervous system; also a high risk to farmers*
Permitted in: apples, artichokes, beans, beets, broccoli, Brussels sprouts, cabbage, carrots, cauliflower, celery, cherries, chicory (radicchio), citrus, collards, corn, cucumbers, eggplant, grapes, kale, lettuce, melons (cantaloupes, honey-

dew, muskmelon, watermelon), mustard greens, okra, onions (green), parsley, peaches, pears, peas, peppers, plums, potatoes, raspberries, spinach, strawberries, summer squash, tomatoes, turnips, walnuts, watercress

PARATHION

Many uses of parathion on crops heavily consumed by children were voluntarily canceled in 1991.

Problem: *organophosphate pesticide/toxic to the nervous system; possible carcinogen; highly acutely toxic; a high risk to farmers*

Permitted in: barley, canola, cotton, sorghum, soybean, sunflower, wheat

PERMETHRIN

Problem: *possible human carcinogen*

Permitted in: almonds, apples, artichokes, asparagus, avocados, broccoli, Brussels sprouts, cabbage, cauliflower, celery, cherries, corn, eggplant, filberts, garlic, horseradish, kiwi, leafy vegetables, lettuce, mushrooms, onions, peaches, pears, peppers (bell), pistachios, potatoes, soybeans, spinach, tomatoes, curcurbit vegetables, walnuts, watercress

THIABENDAZOLE

Problem: *may cause birth defects*

Permitted in: apples, apricots, avocados, bananas, beans (dry), beets, cantaloupes, carrots, citrus, grapes, mangoes, mushrooms, papaya, pears, potatoes, soybeans, strawberries, sweet potatoes, squash (hubbard), wheat

The results of a 1992 USDA study reported that after washing and peeling the fruits and vegetables sampled, there were 25 pesticides detected in apples, 24 pesticides detected in green beans, 22 pesticides detected in peaches, 21 pesticides detected in celery, 21 in grapes, 11 in oranges, 7 in broccoli, 16 in potatoes, 9 in grapefruits, 10 in carrots, 4 pesticides in bananas, and 19 pesticides detected in lettuce. Of the 24 pesticides found in apples, 21 of those pesticides are either carcinogenic, toxic to the nervous system, and/or toxic to the endocrine system. 21 of the 24 pesticides found in green beans were either carcinogenic, or toxic to the nervous or endocrine systems.

As nutritionists encourage us to eat more fruits and vegetables, the EPA allows significant levels of cancer-causing pesticides in them. Pesticides are on the coatings of seeds and sprayed repeatedly during the growing season.

Caught in a giant bureaucracy during the Reagan and Bush presidencies, EPA's laboratories had inadequate funds, equipment, and staff. Standard testing methods used by the Food and Drug Administration does not detect many pesticides in current use.

The FDA only tests about 1% of domestic and imported fruits and vegetables for pesticide residues. By the time illegal or high amounts of pesticides are found in food samples, it is too late to recall the rest of the shipment.

Although banned in 1972, there are still DDT residues in conventionally grown carrots, onions, potatoes, spinach, and sweet potatoes. The international export of DDT and other pesticides banned in this country to unsuspecting underdeveloped countries goes on. The circle of poison is completed as imported foods such as coffee, vegetables, fruits, and flowers come back to America and naive consumers buy and eat them.

In 1989, the Natural Research Defense Council (NRDC) published *Intolerable Risks: Pesticides in Our Children's Foods.* It accused the EPA of setting dangerously high limits for pesticides in food. The NRDC claims that the EPA does not take into account the eating patterns of children and underestimates the produce consumption for the average child. This is particularly harmful to children because their digestive and nervous systems are still developing. They absorb toxic chemicals more readily than adults do. Congress asked the National Academy of Science (NAS) to respond to the NRDC's 1989 report.

In June 1993, the National Academy of Sciences reported that the current EPA-approved levels of pesticides in foods are unacceptable and unsafe for children. The NAS report, *Pesticides in the Diets of Infants and Children,* stated "exposure to pesticides early in life can lead to a greater risk of cancer, neurodevelopmental impairment, and immune dysfunction."

This should come as no surprise. Whatever is in the soil will be in the food. We must find logical ways to feed and protect ourselves and our families from the pesticides in food. The easiest solution is to grow and buy organically raised foods.

The EPA and the National Center for Policy Alternatives estimate that nearly fifteen percent of global warming is from toxic chemical agriculture. Organic farming techniques like cover cropping, building healthy soil, making compost (managing animal and plant waste), and farmscaping (planting trees and other perennial crops) can actually reverse global warming. The sensual pleasures of great tasting organic foods also serve our political palates and preserve our earth's vital resources.

Appendix 2

———— ❧ ————

The Ten Commandments

HUMANE SUSTAINABLE AGRICULTURE:
FARMERS', RANCHERS', AND CONSUMERS' PLEDGE

1. To make a covenant to transform conventional industrialized agriculture into a profitable and equitable system of food and fiber production that is humane and ecologically sound.

2. To practice and support agricultural methods that are good for all: for farmers, ranchers, the land, animals, and consumers.

3. To support local farms and farmers' markets in the community or region that offer produce from organic and other alternative sustainable methods of food production.

4. To purchase no animal produce from factory farms, where veal calves, pigs, and poultry are raised in complete confinement without having access to the outdoors, and factory feedlots, where thousands of cows and beef cattle are kept on dirt lots.

5. To support state and federal legislation and civil initiatives to encourage the adoption of humane sustainable agriculture (HSA) and discourage the proliferation of factory farming.

6. To stay informed and involved by joining the *Good for You, Good for All* campaign of The Humane Society of the United States.

7. To commit to informing others about why supporting HSA is Good for you and Good for All.

8. To reach out and encourage local institutions—schools, hospitals, church groups—to engage in community-supported agriculture.

9. To appeal to grocery stores and restaurants to provide certified organic foods, more humane animal products, like eggs from uncaged hens, free-range pork and beef, and rBGH-hormone free diary products.

10. To covenant between urban consumers and rural producers to farm
without harm and eat with conscience.

For more information, contact:

Howard Lyman, Director
Eating with Conscience Campaign
The Humane Society of the United States
700 Professional Drive
Gaithersburg, MD 20879
Tel: 301-258-3110
Fax: 301-258-3081

Appendix 3

——— ✧✧ ———

Reading Labels

What do they mean? Is "certified organic" the same as "biodynamic", "transitional" or "unsprayed"? What does "conventionally grown" mean? Should you buy foods labeled "sprayed with pesticides?"

Conventional is another word for grown with chemical fertilizers and pesticides. You can assume produce is conventionally grown, unless it is labeled otherwise.

Low spray means sprayed with some pesticides. Rather than using organic methods of pest control, some farmers use pesticides only when a crop has an insect problem.

Integrated Pest Management (IPM) uses pest-resistant plants, beneficial insects (natural enemies or predators), such as lady beetles and spiders, crop rotation and soil tillage, and minimal and prudent amounts of pesticides.

Locally Grown is conventionally grown, with no post-harvest pesticides because the crops do not have to travel far.

Transitional means no chemical fertilizers and pesticides used. The farm that grew it is in the process of obtaining organic certification. It recently stopped using chemical fertilizers and pesticides.

Unsprayed means organically grown, but not certified organic, because organic certification is too expensive for some organic gardeners and farmers.

Certified Organic generally means grown without pesticides for at least three years. Organic standards of certification will soon become law and uniform for all fifty states. Random inspections throughout the full production cycle insure certified organic foods are chemical-free. Some food retailers hire independent testing companies to analyze produce for traces of pesticides.

No Detected Residues applies to foods grown with chemicals and tested for pesticides after harvesting. They contain no detectable residues above 0.05 parts per million.

Biodynamically Grown grows foods organically. The spiritual philosophy of Rudolph Steiner determines the farmer's relationship to the earth, the sun, and the rhythms of the moon, planets, and stars. Farmers rotate crops, companion plant, make green manures, make compost with biodynamic herbal preparations, and plant and harvest crops by the natural cycles of the moon. Ideally biodynamic farms are self-sufficient ecosystems.

Currently, farmers are being subsidized to use pesticides, fungicides, and insecticides. If they want to switch to organic agriculture, they lose technical and financial government support. Farmers will convert their farms to sustainable agriculture as the demand for organic food grows. Many organic food companies, such as Arrowhead Mills, Cascadian Farm, and Earth's Best, pay farmers to grow organic crops for them. Thousands of farmers are growing organic foods with excellent crop yields and profits.

For maximum pleasure, ecology, health, and taste, I recommend eating and meal planning around the seasonal availability of organically grown foods.

The Gerson Institute in California treats and cures all types of cancer with a special diet rich in organic foods.

Appendix 4

Organic Mail Order Guide

I have personally tried products from these companies and highly recommend them. Quality organic foods are available at neighborhood natural food stores, gourmet shops, food coops, Oriental markets, supermarkets, and fruit and vegetable stores. If you can't find what you need at your local store, call or write to the following distributors. For many of them, no order is too small.

GENERAL

Arrowhead Mills
Box 2059
Hereford, TX 79045
800-858-4308
Beans, grains, flour (including quinoa, amaranth, teff, kamut, and spelt), peanut butter, tahini, oils, flax seeds, etc.

Community Mill and Bean
267 Rt. 89 S
Savannah, NY 13146
315-365-2664
Flours, beans, grains, and cereals

Garden Spot Distributors
438 White Oak Road
New Holland, PA 17557
800-829-5100 or 717-354-4936
Beans, grains, flour, pastas (including quinoa, teff, spelt, and kamut), date sugar, flax seeds, maple syrup, etc.

Gold Mine Natural Foods Co.
1947 30th St.
San Diego, CA 92102
800-475-FOOD
Grains, flours (including teff, kamut, spelt, amaranth, and quinoa), noodles, beans, oils, sea vegetables, miso, kudzu, mirin, sweeteners, shiitake mushrooms, ceramic pressure cooker inserts, ceramic

knives, pressure cookers, *Ohsawa America* —my favorite brand for organic rice vinegar, soy sauce, and umeboshi products.

Krystal Wharf Farms
Organic Food and Seed
RD 2 Box 2112
Mansfield, PA 16933
717-549-8194
Vegetables, fruits, beans, flour, grains, (including quinoa, spelt, and kamut), nuts, seeds, nut butters, oils, pasta, herbs, spices, garden seeds.

Kushi Institute
P.O. Box 7
Leland Road
Beckett, MA 01223
413-623-2102
Grains, noodles, sea vegetables, beans, miso, umeboshi products, shiitake mushrooms, kudzu.

Macrobiotic Company of America
799 Old Leicester Highway
Asheville, NC 28806
800-438-4730
Grain, flours, noodles, beans, oils, sea vegetables, miso, sweeteners, shiitake mushrooms, soy sauce, umeboshi products, cookware, ceramic pressure cooker inserts and cutlery.

McFadden Farm
Potter Valley, CA 95469
800-544-8230
Fresh and dried herbs, sun dried tomatoes, beans, potatoes, and wine grapes.

Mountain Ark Trading Company
120 South East Ave.
Fayetteville, AR 72701
800-643-8909
Grain, flours (including teff, spelt, kamut, quinoa, and amaranth), noodles, beans, dried fruits, nuts, seeds, peanut butter, tahini, oils, sea vegetables, miso, mirin, sweeteners, shiitake mushrooms, soy sauce, umeboshi products, garden seeds, cookware and cutlery.

Natural Lifestyles Supplies
16 Lookout Drive
Asheville, NC 28804
800-752-2775
Grain, flours, noodles, beans, oils, sea vegetables, miso, herbs, mirin, sweeteners, shiitake mushrooms, soy sauce, umeboshi products, cookware and cutlery.

Walnut Acres
Walnut Acres Road
Penns Creek, PA 17862
800-433-3998
Vegetables, fruits, dried fruits, fruit spreads, fruit juices, beans, grains, flours (including quinoa, kamut, and spelt), herbs, oils, sprouting seeds, nuts, nut butters, flax seeds, stainless steel bakeware.

ANCIENT GRAINS, FLOURS, AND PASTA
(See also those distributors listed under "general".)

Artesian Acres
Brian Smillie
R.R. #3
Lacombe, Alberta TOC 1SO
403-782-5075
Kamut flour, grain, and pasta.

Kamut Assn. of North America
2161 Meyers Avenue
Escondido, CA 92029
619-747-3008
Information on kamut and nearest sources to you.

Maskel Teff
Wayne and Elizabeth Carlson
1318 Willow
Caldwell, ID 83805
208-454-3330
Brown and ivory teff grain and flour.

Montana Flour and Grains
Robert M. Quinn
Ferry Rt. P.O. Box 808
Big Sandy, MT 59520
406-378-3105
406-622-5503
Kamut flour and grain, plus a list of growers and distributors for kamut flour, flakes, grain, and pasta.

Purity Foods, Inc.
2871 West Jolly Road
Okemos, MI 48864
517-351-9231
Spelt flour, grain, flakes, and pasta.

Quinoa Corporation
P.O. Box 1039
Torrance, CA 90505
310-530-8666
Quinoa grain, flour, and pasta.

DRIED FRUITS, SUN-DRIED TOMATOES, DRIED SHIITAKE MUSHROOMS, AND NUTS
(See also those distributors listed under "general".)

Ahler's Organic Date Garden
P.O. Box 726
Mecca, CA 92254-0726
619-396-2337
Several varieties of dates and date products.

Capay Fruits and Vegetables
Star Route, Box 3
Capay, CA 95607
916-796-4111
Sun-dried tomatoes and sun-dried tomatoes in organic olive oil.

Everything Under the Sun
P.O. Box 663
Winters, CA 95694
916-795-5256
Fresh and dried fruits, sun-dried tomatoes, and nuts.

Hard Scrabble Enterprises, Inc.
HC 71
Box 42
Circleville, WV 26804
202-332-0232

Dried shiitake mushrooms.

Living Tree Centre
P.O. Box 10082
Berkeley, CA 94709
510-420-1440
Almonds, almond butter, and pistachios.

Sun Gardens
P.O. Box 190
Bard, CA 92222
800-228-4690
Several varieties of dates and date products.

Timber Crest Farms
4791 Dry Creek Road
Healdsburg, CA 95448
707-433-8255
Dried fruits and nuts.

Williams Creek Farm
18843 Williams Highway
Williams, OR 97544
503-846-6481
Sun-dried tomatoes.

Windy River Farm
P.O. Box 312
Merlin, OR 97532
503-476-8979
Dried tomatoes, zucchini, leeks, and onions.

FARM-RAISED SEAFOOD &
SMOKED FISH

Aqua/Future
P.O. Box 783, Industrial Road
Turners Falls, MA 01376
413-863-3575
Farm-raised, hybrid striped bass and tilapia.

Bioshelters, Inc.
500 Sunderland Road
Amherst, MA 01002
413-549-3558
Farm-raised tilapia, hydroponic basil and wheat grass.

Ducktrap River Fish Farm, Inc.
57 Little River Drive
Belfast, ME 04915
800-828-3825
Several varieties of smoked fish and smoked farmed fish: trout, mackerel, salmon, mussels, tuna, scallops, shrimp.

Durham's Tracklements
117 Blue Hill Road
Amherst, MA 01002
800-844-7853; Fax: 413-256-8403

Several varieties of smoked salmon: New England, Thai, Mediterranean, and teriyaki; smoked farm-raised brook trout, tilapia, and, when available, mackerel.

Red-Wing Meadow Trout Farm
500 Sunderland Road
Amherst, MA 01002
413-549-4118
Farm-raised trout.

The Farm at Mount Walden, Inc.
Main Street
Box 189
The Plains, VA 22171
800-648-7688
Farm-raised & applewood smoked trout and salmon.

FRUITS AND VEGETABLES
Diamond Organics
P.O. Box 2159
Freedom, CA 95019
800-922-2396
Lettuces, greens, fresh herbs, roots, and fruits. Ships from the East and West Coasts.

Everything Under the Sun
P.O. Box 663
Winters, CA 95694
916-795-5256
Fruits.

Krystal Wharf Farms
Organic Food and Seed
RD 2 Box 2112
Mansfield, PA 16933
717-549-8194
Vegetables and fruits.

McFadden Farm
Potter Valley, CA 95469
800-544-8230
Potatoes and wine grapes.

Walnut Acres
Walnut Acres Road
Penns Creek, PA 17862
800-433-3998
Vegetables and fruits.

Williams Creek Farm
18843 Williams Highway
Williams, OR 97544
503-846-6481
Fruits and vegetables.

HERBS, SPICES, AND FLAX SEEDS
(See also those distributors listed under "general".)

Diamond Organics
P.O. Box 2159
Freedom, CA 95019
800-922-2396

Fresh herbs, garlic, and ginger.

Frontier Cooperative Herbs
Box 299
Norway, IA 52318
800-669-3275

Dried herbs, spices, flax seeds, dried burdock, and tea.

Jean's Greens
RR1 Box 55J
Hale Road
Rensselaerville, NY 12147
518-239-TEAS
Dried herbs, spices, dried burdock, flax seeds, and teas.

McFadden Farm
Potter Valley, CA 95469
800-544-8230
Fresh and dried herbs.

Omega-Life, Inc.
P.O. Box 208
Brookfield, WI 53008-0208
800-328-3529
Fortified Flax (ground flax seeds fortified with vitamins).

Pacific Botanicals
4350 Fish Hachery Road
Grants Pass, OR 97527
503-479-7777
Organically grown and wild-crafted herbs and spices.

Sunny Pine Farm
Rte 2, Box 280
Twisp, WA 98848
509-997-4811
Garlic and garlic products.

Williams Creek Farm
18843 Williams Highway
Williams, OR 97544
503-846-6481
Garlic, herbs, and spices.

Windy River Farm
P.O. Box 312
Merlin, OR 97532
503-476-8979
Dried herbs, herbal vinegars, sprinkles (salt-free seasonings made from herbs and vegetables), and herb teas.

KITCHENWARE

Leslie Cerier
58 Schoolhouse Road
Amherst, MA 01002
413-259-1695
Stainless steel cookware and pressure cookers, ceramic pressure cooker inserts, ceramic and stainless steel vegetable knives, vegetable scrubbers, grater plates, suribachis, ceramic dinnerware, sushi mats.

Gold Mine Natural Foods Company
1947 30th St.
San Diego, CA 92102
800 475-FOOD
Stainless steel cookware and pressure cookers, ceramic pressure cooker inserts, ceramic and stainless steel vegetable knives, vegetable scrubbers, grater plates, sushi mats.

Kushi Institute

P.O. Box 7
Leland Road
Beckett, MA 01223
413-623-2102
Ceramic pressure cooker inserts, stainless steel pressure cookers, knives, ceramic dinnerware, vegetable scrubbers, grater plates, sushi mats.

Macrobiotic Company of America
799 Old Leicester Highway
Asheville, NC 28806
800-438-4730
Ceramic pressure cooker inserts, stainless steel pressure cookers, vegetable knives, grater plates, sushi mats, bamboo and stainless steel steamers, cast-iron wok.

Mountain Ark Trading Company
120 South East Ave.
Fayetteville, AR 72701
800-643-8909
Stainless steel cookware and pressure cookers, pressure cooker inserts, vegetable knives.

Natural Lifestyles Supplies
16 Lookout Drive
Asheville, NC 28804
800-752-2775
Stainless steel and enamel cookware and pressure cookers, sushi mats, vegetable scrubbers, water filters, stainless steel bakeware, cutlery.

MISO

(See also those distributors listed under "general".)

South River Miso Company
South River Farm
Conway, MA 01341
413-369-4057
Mellow and aged misos: barley, brown rice, millet, chick pea, aduki rice, black soybean barley, and dandelion leek.

NUT FLOURS

Omega Nutrition U.S.A. Inc.
1720 Labounty Road
Ferndale, WA 98248
800-661-3529
Hazelnut, pistachio, almond.

OILS, OLIVES, AND CAPERS

(See also those distributors listed under "general".)

Gaeta Itri
141 John Street
Babylon, NY 11702
800-669-2681
Extra virgin olive oil, olives, and capers.

Greek Gourmet
5 Pond Park Road
Hingham, MA 02043
617-749-1866
Extra virgin olive oil and olives.

Omega Nutrition U.S.A. Inc.
1720 Labounty Road
Ferndale, WA 98248
800-661-3529
Canola, flax, almond, safflower, extra virgin olive, sesame, and sunflower oils; apple cider vinegar, nut flours.

PASTA

(See also those distributors listed under "general".)

Mrs. Leeper's Inc.
11035 Technology Place
Suite 300
San Diego, CA 92127
619-673-0073
Kamut, wheat, rice, and vegetable pasta in many shapes and sizes.

SEA VEGETABLES

(See also those distributors listed under "general".)

Island Herbs
Waldron Island, WA 98297-9999
Sea Vegetables: kelp (fronds or powder), nori, wakame, bladderwrack (whole or flakes), grapestone, sagassum mutica, and sea lettuce. Also fresh sea vegetables: grapestone, bladderwrack, sea lettuce, and nori.

Maine Coast Sea Vegetables
Shore Road
Franklin, Maine 04634
207-565-2907
Sea vegetables: sea palm, digitata, kelp, dulse, alaria, nori laver, sea seasonings: 1.5 oz. shakers of dulse/garlic, kelp/cayenne, nori/ginger, nori, dulse, kelp, sea chips, sea pickles.

Maine Seaweed Company
P.O. Box 57
Steuben, ME 04680
207-546-2875
Sea vegetables: alaria, dulse, digitata, wild nori, and kelp. Minimum order: 3 pounds.

Ocean Harvest Sea Vegetables
P.O. Box 1719
Mendocino, CA 95460
707-937-1923
Sea vegetables: sea palm, silky sea palm, sweet kombu, ocean ribbons, wakame, wild nori, and kombu.

SWEETENERS

(See also those distributors listed under "general".)

T&A Gourmet
P.O. Box 5179
Somerset, NJ 08875-5179
800-762-2135
Rice syrup (plain, blueberry, strawberry, and raspberry), barley malt, sorghum, honey, conserves, and maple syrup.

Barat Chocolate
P.O. Box 609
112 Main Rd.
Montville, NJ 07045
Tofu chocolates and chocolate chips.

WINES

Four Chimneys Farm Winery
211 Hall Road
Himrod, NY 14842
607-243-7502
Wines, grape juice, vinegars, and cooking wines.

Frey Vineyards
14000 Tomki Road
Redwood Valley, CA 95470
707-485-5177

The Organic Wine Company
54 Genoa Place
San Francisco, CA 94133
415-433-0167
French Wines with minimal amounts of added sulfites.

ORGANIZATIONS TO JOIN AND FOR INFORMATION

Attra
P.O. Box 3657
Fayetteville, AR 72702
800-346-9140
Nonprofit organization that promotes sustainable agriculture through workshops and newsletters; funded by a grant from the U.S. Fish and Wildlife Service.

Bio-Dynamic Farming and Gardening Association, Inc.
P.O. Box 550
Kimberton, PA 19442
215-983-3196
Sells books and literature, supports training and research, sponsors conferences and lectures, publishes a newsletter and quarterly magazine about bio-dynamic agriculture.

California Action Network
P.O. Box 464
Davis, CA 95617
916-756-7857

Publishes a directory of organic products and produce, organic farmers and wholesalers.

Center for Science in the Public Interest (CSPI) and Americans for Safe Food
1875 Connecticut Ave., NW, Suite 530
Washington, DC 20009
202-332-9110
Consumer organization working for and publishing information on food safety and nutrition issues.

CHEFS Coalition (Chefs Helping To Enhance Food Safety)
c/o Public Voice for Food and Health Policy
1101 14th Street, NW, Suite 710
Washington, DC 20005
202-371-1840
National nonprofit research, education and advocacy organization that promotes safer, healthier, and more affordable foods to protect the environment. It links chefs with organic food sources, meets with Congress, sends letters to legislators, organizes educational events and press conferences, writes and distributes pamphlets to alert the public to critical food issues.

Committee for Sustainable Agriculture
P.O. Box 1300
Colfax, CA 95713
916-346-2777
Nonprofit educational organization providing information and sponsoring events on ecological farming, food safety, and environmental issues to farmers, retailers, and consumers.

Demeter Association, Inc.
1090 Rock Creek Canyon Road
Colorado Springs, CO 80926
719-579-8082
Information about certification procedures and guidelines for biodynamic farming.

Eating with a Conscience Campaign
Howard Lyman, Director
The Human Society
    of the United States
700 Professional Drive
Gaithersburg, MD 20879
301-258-3110; Fax: 301-258-3081

Food and Water, Inc.
Depot Hill Road
RR1 Box 114
Marshfield, VT 05658
802-426-3700

Nonprofit consumer advocacy organization working for safe food and a cleaner environment that publishes *Safe Food News* and sends timely updates and action alerts to members.

Mothers & Others
40 West 20th Street
New York, NY 10011
212-242-0010

A national organization working on environmental and food safety issues affecting children that publishes a newsletter and excellent books, such as *For Our Kid's Sake: How to Protect Your Child Against Pesticides in Food* and *The Way We Grow.*

National Coalition Against Misuse of Pesticides
701 E Street, SE, Suite 200
Washington, DC 20003
202-543-5450

Provides information on pesticides and alternatives to them.

Organic Food Production Association of North America (OFPANA)
P.O. Box 1078
23 Ames Street
Greenfield, MA 01301
413-774-7511

A nonprofit organization linking organic growers, manufacturers, distributors, retailers and consumers that promotes organic products in the marketplace, protects the honesty of organic standards, and publishes a newsletter for members.

Appendix 5

—— ✺✺ ——

Grow Your Own Herbs

The end of the growing season doesn't have to mean the end of fresh herbs. Herbs make fragrant and attractive house plants. Whether you live in the country and have your own organic garden or live in the city, consider growing your own herbs.

House-bound herbs need:

Light. If your most convenient window doesn't get much light, supplement it with a special bulb called a grow light. (Two hours of grow light equal one hour of natural sunlight.) Below are the requirements for house-bound herbs:

  v Chives, basil, anise, marjoram, borage, chervil, coriander, caraway, dill, rosemary, and savory need all-day sun.

  v Mint, bay leaf, parsley, rosemary, thyme, myrtle need partial sun.

  v Ginger and lemon balm do not need direct light. However, if the foliage turns yellow, the plant needs more light.

Moisture. Use lukewarm water or the rinse water from sprout- making.

  v Mints, lemon balm, rosemary, ginger, scented geraniums need to be kept moist.

  v Bay leaf, marjoram, sage, oregano, thyme need to be dried out between waterings.

  v Aloe (the very useful "burn plant") seldomly needs to be watered; it thrives on dry soil and little light.

To increase humidity, set potted herbs on trays filled with water and gravel. Make sure the plants are *over* the water, not in it.

Fresh air. Herbs thrive at 50 degrees to 70 degrees F. On cold days, a slightly open window in an *adjoining* room will provide cool air without a draft.

Pest protection. Although herbs are usually pest-free, indoor conditions can sometimes attract bugs. If they do, make a soap spray by dissolving two tablespoons of Ivory Soap Flakes in lukewarm water. Spray both sides of the leaves once a week. *Note:* Rinse leaves thoroughly before cooking or eating.

Space. Use a container with a diameter of one-half to one-third the ultimate height of the plant. Group plants together (this creates humidity), but not so close that they touch.

Plant an indoor window box. Place large plants (rosemary and tarragon) at the edges. Put smaller plants (basil, chives, thyme, parsley, and marjoram) in the center. Not good in boxes: Sage needs a deep container; lemon balm and mint spread like crazy.

Decorate with herbs. Put parsley, basil, thyme, marjoram, savory, and nasturtium in hanging baskets. Put tall plants (bay leaf and lovage) in decorative pots in corners. Place miniature plants (oregano, parsley, thyme) on tables or shelves.

Trimming. Keep plants cut back for a uniform, attractive appearance.

To get started, herbs can be grown from:

Seeds.* Clean your containers and fill them one-fourth to one-third full with drainage material (bits of broken bricks or clay pots, pebbles). Then fill them to within one inch of the top with sterile commercial potting soil. Label. Mist daily until germination, then water as needed. Fertilize with liquid seaweed or fish emulsion one week after germination and again in one month. When the plants grow their first set of true leaves, thin them by leaving only the healthiest plant in each pot.

Cuttings. Get cutting from friends with outdoor herb gardens. Many herbs (chives, mint, oregano, lemon balm, etc.) spread so quickly that gardeners are happy to give some plants away. If you can't plant the cuttings immediately, put them in water. When time permits, prepare a pot with a drainage layer, then fill it about halfway with soil, tapping firmly. Soak the soil.

Small plants from a nursery. These are the easiest to deal with, but the most costly—about $2.50 each.

---

* The best seeds (open-pollinated and chemically untreated) are available in natural food and gardening stores and by mail:

Johnny's Selected Seeds, Foss Hill Rd., Dept. 530, Albion, ME 04910
Seeds of Change, 621 Old Sante Fe Trail #10, Sante Fe, NM 87501
Abundant Life Seeds, Box 772, Port Townsend, WA 98368
Krystal Wharf Farms, RD 2 Box 2112, Mansfield, PA 16933
Ecology Action, 5798 Ridgewood Road, Willits, CA 95490
Mountain Ark Trader, P.O. Box 3170, Fayetteville, AR 72702

Glossary

These are some of the ingredients that I frequently use in this book that may be new to you. You can find them in natural food stores, gourmet shops, food co-ops, Oriental markets, fruit and vegetable stores, supermarkets, and mail order natural food catalogues.

ANCIENT GRAINS

Exotic super-grains worshipped by ancient civilizations have reemerged as alternatives to corn, wheat, rice, and other grains we know so well.

Amaranth has more fiber, iron, and protein than most grains. It contains lysine, an essential amino acid, which, when combined with corn, wheat, or brown rice, creates a complete protein. Amaranth tastes slightly nutty. Try it cooked in combination with other grains in pilafs, puddings, and banana bread. Sprout it as alfalfa seeds or toast it. Boiled in water and chilled, it makes a nutritious thickening agent that can replace corn starch.

Kamut is a nonhybridized ancient relative of wheat that is easy to digest, even for most people allergic to wheat. Kamut has more protein, fiber, fat, iron, zinc, copper, potassium, and vitamins B1 and B2 than wheat.

Quinoa (keen-Wa) is the only grain that is a complete protein. It has a light sesame-like flavor and is quick cooking. Serve quinoa as a side dish, or mixed with other grains, vegetables, herbs, or spices.

Spelt is a nonhybridized ancient relative of wheat that is quicker and easier to digest than most grains, even for most people allergic to wheat. Spelt tastes rich and nutty. It has more protein, fiber, fat, iron, zinc, copper, and vitamins B1 and B2 than wheat.

Teff has a moist, poppy-seed like texture and a mildly sweet flavor reminiscent of chocolate and molasses. An eight-ounce serving of teff is equal to 40% of the USRDA for calcium and 100% of the USRDA for iron. Teff has only traces of gluten, an advantage for people who are allergic to gluten or wheat. Teff blends well with vegetables, other grains, tofu, herbs, spices, and fresh and dried fruit. See chapter 12.

BEANS AND SOY FOODS

Aduki Beans are small, dark red beans, and lowest in fat of all the beans.

Anasazi Beans. Maroon and white speckled beans, similar to pinto beans, but sweeter.

Tempeh, made from cooked and fermented soybeans, has a firm, tender meat-like texture. It is high in protein, easy to digest, cholesterol-free, and delicious. You can sauté, bake, broil, steam, or simmer tempeh with vegetables, herbs, and spices. It is very versatile. You can add it to soups, stews, casseroles, and sandwiches.

Tofu, also known as bean curd, is a staple of Oriental cooking. Made from soybeans and nigari (a coagulant extracted from sea salt), it is cholesterol-free, low-calorie, high in protein and calcium. Its mildly sweet flavor picks up whatever spice you cook it with. Available in firm, extra firm, soft, and silky textures, you can slice it and add it to soups, stews, stir-fries, and salads, or whip it into creamy sauces, dressings, pie fillings, and puddings.

COOKING OILS

Unrefined, expeller-pressed oils are the best. Extracted from nuts, grains, seeds, fruits, and beans, they are rich in color, nutritious, and aromatic.

Canola Oil is versatile and the oil lowest in saturated fats. Try it for baking, frying, and salad dressings.

Corn Oil pressed from whole corn has a buttery flavor. Try corn oil for baking, sautéing, making sauces, and refrying grains.

Extra Virgin Olive Oil is the most flavorful of all the olive oils and has the best aroma. It is from the first pressing of the highest quality olives. Its natural acidity cannot exceed 1%. Extra virgin olive oil is delicious for sautés, salad dressings, and sauces.

Hot Pepper Sesame Oil is a fiery hot toasted sesame oil made with chili peppers. Use it to make hot and spicy soups, stir-fries, salads, and fish entrees.

Sesame Oil is ideal for Oriental stir-fries, marinades, sauces, and salad dressings. It can withstand high heat. Use it also for frying and deep frying (tempura). Naturally pressed from sesame seeds, it has a delicate sesame aroma and is low in saturated fats.

Toasted Sesame Oil has a strong toasted sesame seed aroma and flavor. Naturally pressed from toasted sesame seeds, it brings an Oriental flair to salads, stir-fries, marinades, sauces, grains, beans, and pasta.

Safflower Oil is odorless and flavorless. Use it when you don't want to overpower the flavors of other foods. Try it in salad dressings, or for baking and sautéing.

FLOURS AND BAKING SUPPLIES

Arrowroot Powder added to pastry recipes (try a tablespoon) can make pastries lighter and fluffier. Arrowroot is also a thickener for stews, sauces, and puddings.

Barley Flour can substitute for whole wheat pastry flour. It is sweeter and lighter. See *Ginger Bread Cake* on page 252.

Brown Rice Flour can substitute for whole wheat pastry flour. It makes breads and pastries sweet, moist, dense, and smooth. See *Outrageous Hazelnut Cake* on page 259 and *Wheat-Free Corn Bread* on page 253.

Carob Powder and Chips can substitute for chocolate to make cakes, fudge, hot drinks, and cookies. Carob is caffeine-free, low in fat, and rich in calcium, magnesium, iron, and Vitamins A and B. Carob tastes sweeter than chocolate.

Corn Meal is sweet and coarse. It gives breads a crumbly texture. If your bread batter is too moist, add some corn meal.

Flax Seeds ground into a meal makes a good binder for eggless baking. They are high in vitamin E, Omega-3 fatty acids, and aid in the digestion of fiber-rich whole grains.

Kamut Flour is ideal for pasta making and pastries. It has a low gluten content. Kamut has a lighter and richer taste than its ancient relative, wheat.

Rolled Oats, also known as oatmeal, add sweetness to baked goods. They make breads chewy and moist. Buzz them in a blender to make your own oat flour. Besides breakfast cereal, you can add rolled oats to soups and sauces for a creamy consistency without dairy.

Spelt Flour uses about a quarter less liquid than its ancient relative, wheat (flour). It is an excellent substitute for whole wheat flour in bread and pastry recipes. Tolerated by many sensitive to wheat, spelt flour is also popular because of its delightful, nutty taste.

Teff Flour gives pastries a chocolatety, molasses-like flavor. It is low in gluten and well tolerated by those sensitive to wheat. Use teff flour in place of whole wheat pastry flour to make pancakes, muffins, granola, cookies, pie crusts, and gravies. See chapter 12.

Whole Wheat Flour is excellent for breads and making seitan.

Whole Wheat Pastry Flour is excellent for making pastries. It is lighter and has less bran than whole wheat flour.

Noodles

Bifun, also known as rice vermicelli, are Chinese quick-cooking clear noodles made from rice flour and potato starch. They are delicious in soups, salads, and stir-fries.

Soba are Japanese noodles made from buckwheat flour or a combination of buckwheat flour and whole wheat. Some brands also add iron-rich, green, mugwort leaf or wild yam (jinejo).

Somen are thin Japanese wheat flour noodles.

Udon are flat Japanese wheat or rice flour noodles.

Nut and Seed Butters

Nut and seed butters are pastes made from ground raw or roasted nuts and seeds. They are rich, creamy, and they spread like dairy butter; but they contain no cholesterol. Use them for spreads, making sauces, dips, dressings, pastries, and main dishes. Besides peanut butter, there is almond, hazelnut, pistachio, cashew, sunflower, and sesame butter.

Tahini, popular in Middle Eastern cooking, is a paste or seed butter made by grinding sesame seeds. Tahini contains iron and calcium. Add tahini to sauces, spreads, and stews for a rich, creamy, texture and flavor. See *Chickpea Vegetable Pâté* on page 163, and *Greens With Tahini Sauce* on page 165.

Rice

There are many varieties of rice available in many flavors and sizes.

Brown Basmati Rice is an aromatic long brown rice that cooks up light and fluffy.

Brown Rice is available in short-, medium-, and long-grain varieties. Short-grain brown rice is more moist and glutinous than medium- or long-grain brown rice. Long-grain brown rice is excellent for pilafs and salads. It is fluffier than short-grain brown rice.

Sweet Brown Rice is glutinous and can be made into amasake and mochi. A little sweet brown rice cooked with short-grain brown rice makes great sushi and grain balls.

Wehani Rice is an aromatic red-brown rice that smells like hot buttered peanuts.

Wild Rice is nutty-flavored, black, and slender. Blended with other varieties of rice, sautéed vegetables, spices, or nuts, wild rice makes a meal a special occasion. See *Wild and Wonderful* on page 207.

Salty Seasonings

Bragg Liquid Aminos is a tasty soy sauce-like condiment and an ideal substitute for tamari or shoyu for those sensitive to yeast and fermented foods. Made by extracting amino acids from soybeans without adding salt, Bragg Liquid Aminos has a naturally salty flavor from the sodium in soybeans. Try it on potatoes, grains, salads, stir-fries, etc. instead of salt or tamari.

Gomasio is a sesame-salt condiment for grains and vegetables.

Miso is a sweet-salty fermented paste made from beans and/or grains, and sea salt. The light, mellow, sweet, and white miso varieties, aged 3-6 months, have a subtle flavor, excellent for salad dressings, creamy sauces, dips and delicate soups. Aged 1-3 years, darker miso varieties—barley, brown rice, red, and hatcho—are saltier, stronger in flavor, and delicious in soups, casseroles, and stews.

Sea Salt, when naturally dried, contains more trace minerals and less sodium chloride than commercial salt, which has added iodine, chemicals, stabilizers, or free-flowing agents. Solar-dried sea salt is moist, with a crystalline structure. I keep mine in a jar near the stove and use my fingers to take a pinch when I need it. It is excellent for baking. Use a spoon for adding more at the table, because it does not pour from a shaker.

Shoyu is a natural soy sauce made with wheat. It has a more delicate flavor than tamari.

Shiso (Beef Steak Leaf) is an herb high in calcium and iron. Add one to cooking grains. Use them to season tofu dips, spreads, and vegetable pie fillings. See *Elegant Vegetable Quiche* on page 227.

Tamari is a natural soy sauce made without wheat. It is the liquid that rises to the surface in miso making. Tamari is delicious in stir-fry dishes.

Umeboshi Plums are small, sweet, sour, salty, pickled plums aged for several years. They are an excellent seasoning for grain dishes, sauces, salad dressings, and as a condiment.

Umeboshi Paste is a puree of umeboshi plums, commonly used as a spread on toasted nori when making sushi. It is especially useful when you are looking for a thick, salty, and sour seasoning to flavor salad dressings, sauces, and dips.

Sea Vegetables

Agar agar powder, bars, and flakes are flavorless. Use it to gel jams, aspics, and gelatins (kantens).

Alaria is similar to Japanese wakame and harvested in Maine. Its mild flavor is delicious when simmered for a long time in stews and miso soup.

Arame is a thin, black Japanese sea vegetable with a mild, sweet taste. To cook, rinse and soak it for 5 minutes. Add it to soup, stews, sautés, or marinate it for salads.

Digitata (Horsetail Kelp) is a tough-textured Maine sea vegetable that softens and melts in long cooking soups, stews, and bean dishes.

Dulse is a soft, leafy, reddish-purple-brown Maine sea vegetable, perfect for a snack. It melts in your mouth. Kids love it. You can also add it to oatmeal, soups, stews, bean dishes, or rinse it and add it to a salad in place of spinach. Dulse is high in potassium, phosphorus, iron, protein, vitamin C, and fat. It is unusual for seaweed to be so high in fat (3.2 grams per 100). Its combination of fat and protein yields a nutty flavor.

Hijiki is a spaghetti-like Japanese sea vegetable. It is highest in calcium of all the sea vegetables, and very rich in iron and vitamin A, too. Rinse and soak it for 5 minutes. Add it to soups, stews, sautés, or marinate it for salads.

Kelp is a quick cooking, sweet, delicate, thin, leafy variety of kombu from Maine. Add it to soups, stews, and bean dishes. Also, try toasting and grinding it into a powder, to use as a condiment for soups and popcorn.

Kombu is a Japanese sea vegetable that looks like a narrow, olive-brown lasagna noodle. It is a real flavor enhancer and tenderizer. In fact, monosodium glutamate (MSG) is a synthetic version. Kombu becomes tender when cooked for a long time. Beans cooked with kombu are less likely to give you gas. Kombu isolates radioactive substances in the body for elimination. Kombu and other varieties of kombu (kelp, ocean ribbons, and sweet kombu) cleanse the circulatory system, and reduce hypertension and high blood pressure. Kombu is high in calcium, iron and iodine. Kombu, kelp, ocean ribbon, and sweet kombu are excellent in soups, stews, and bean dishes.

Nori (Sea Lettuce) is a delicate purplish-black sheet that turns green when lightly toasted. Wrap it around rice, cooked and raw vegetables, pickles, noodles, tofu, seitan, tempeh, or fish to make sushi, a great lunch, appetizer, or traveling snack. Toasted and crumbled nori is a tasty garnish and condiment. Of all the seaweeds, it is the highest in protein, iron, and vitamins A and B2, and is the only one without sodium.

Ocean Ribbon is a quick cooking, sweet, delicate, thin, Californian variety of kombu.

Sea Palm, the fettuccine of sea vegetables, is from California. It is dark green, versatile, and sweet. It is delicious in salads, sautés, stews, and noodle dishes.

Wakame is a dark green sea leaf harvested in California and Japan. It is the seaweed highest in alginic acid, which cleanses heavy metals such as lead, mercury, and cadmium from the intestines. Use it in miso soup, salads with fresh or marinated vegetables, or in tender-root vegetable and bean dishes. Roasted and ground with toasted sesame seeds, it makes a delicious seasoning and substitute for table salt. Wakame is high in calcium and vitamin B12.

SWEETENERS

Amasake is a sweet, thick, creamy, fermented, rice drink. Try it over cereal and in pancake batters in place of milk or juice. Thicken it with arrowroot or kudzu to make a delicious pudding.

Barley Malt, made from sprouted roasted barley, has a caramel flavor. Substitute it for honey or molasses in bean dishes, pie fillings, sauces, and pastries. Barley malt is about 60 % as sweet as sugar.

Brown Rice Syrup or **Rice Honey** is thick and amber-colored. Made from cooked brown rice and sometimes sprouted barley, too, it is about half as sweet as sugar. Use it in sauces, salad dressings, puddings, frostings, pie fillings, and as a topping for pancakes.

Date Sugar made of dried crushed dates is ½-²/₃ as sweet as regular sugar. Grind it in food processor or coffee grinder for a smooth consistency, or use it coarse.

Maple Syrup is my favorite sweetener. Made from boiling down the sap from maple trees, maple syrup is 65% sucrose. There are three grades of syrup: A, B, and C. You can bake with any of them. "C" has the richest flavor, darkest color, and is least expensive.

Mirin is a sweet cooking wine made from rice. Use it to sweeten stir-fries, soups, stews, marinades, dips, dressings, sauces, and puddings.

Sucanat, made by evaporating organic sugar cane juice, is coarse like brown sugar. All the vitamins, minerals, and other nutrients are intact. You can substitute sucanat cup for cup for sugar in any recipe.

VEGETABLES

Bok choy or **Bok Choi** is a dark green and white leafy vegetable used in Chinese and Japanese soups and stir-fries.

Burdock is a hardy, wild, long brown root vegetable revered in Oriental medicine for its strengthening properties. Buy firm burdock roots instead of rubbery ones. To prepare burdock, scrub it with a vegetable scrubber until it turns white. Slice it thin and add it to sautés, stews, or sauces. It is delicious with ginger, carrots, and onions.

Chinese Cabbage (Napa) is a light green and white leafy vegetable resembling a romaine lettuce. It has a subtle mustard flavor without the tang. Chinese cabbage is quicker cooking than head cabbage. Use it in stir-fries, soups, and if it is young and tender, try a few leaves in a salad.

Collards (collard greens) are high in calcium, iron, and vitamins A and C. Collards are delicious steamed, added to soups, stews, and stir-fries. Select whole collard leaves without yellow spots or tears.

Daikon is a long white radish. Grate it into salads or use it as a condiment. Add sliced daikons to salads, stir-fries, soups, and stews. According to Oriental medicine, eating daikon dissolves excess fat and mucus.

Frisee (Curly Endive) is in the chicory family. It has frilly green leaves and crisp sturdy ribs. Frisee adds texture and an elegant design to salads. Try substituting frisee for lettuce.

Jicama is a delicately sweet root vegetable that has a crisp texture like a water chestnut, even after cooking. Enjoy it raw for a snack, in dips and salads, or add it to stews and stir-fries.

Mizuna is a Japanese leafy mustard green with a delicate and peppery flavor. Try it in a salad or as a quick cooking addition to stir-fries.

Mustard Greens are hot and spicy, especially when fresh picked. Mustard greens are high in calcium, iron, and vitamin A. These curly-edged greens are great in salads, vegetarian sushi, stir-fries, and soups. There is also a red mustard variety.

Tat soi (Chinese flat cabbage), is a little green leafy vegetable with spoon-shaped leaves (like miniature spinach), but with sweet white crunchy stalks. Use it in stir-fries and salads.

Vinegar

Tangy vinegar adds zest to sauces, salads and marinades. Besides the familiar wine vinegar and apple cider vinegar, there are the following:

Balsamic Vinegar is Italian, rich, and slightly sweet. Try it in salad dressings, sauces, and even Oriental marinades.

Brown Rice Vinegar is golden in color and mellow tasting, low in acid content, and ideal for Oriental salad dressings, stir-fries, sauces, and marinades.

Umeboshi Plum Vinegar (Ume) is my favorite. I often use it in place of tamari or lemon and salt. Ume has a sour (lemony) and salty flavor and a deep ruby color. Ume vinegar is technically not really a vinegar, but can be used like one. It is the extracted juices from pickled Japanese plums or apricots, shiso (beefsteak) leaves, and sea salt. It is alkalizing instead of acidic and aids digestion. For quick, delicious salad dressings, try olive oil and umeboshi vinegar, or umeboshi vinegar, sesame oil, and rice vinegar.

MISCELLANEOUS

Dried Chestnuts, added to grains, beans, breads and desserts, create a delicious smoky flavor.

Capers are pickled flower buds that are delicious in salads and sauces. See *Spinach and Potato Salad With Capers* on page 78 and *The Ultimate Pasta and Bean Salad* on page 87.

Kudzu (Kuzu) like arrowroot, is a thickener for soups, stews, sauces, jellies, and jam. Oriental medicine recommends kudzu for its calming antacid effect on digestion.

Lotus Seeds have a delicate, nutlike flavor. They are rich in minerals. Try them in soups, grain, and vegetable dishes.

Mochi, made of cooked sweet brown rice, pounded into a cake, can substitute for cheese. You can also heat sliced mochi in a waffle iron for a quick breakfast or snack.

Seitan (Wheat Gluten or Wheat Meat) is a meat substitute high in protein and made from whole wheat flour, tamari, and kombu. Try seitan in sandwiches, stews, and stir-fries. To make your own seitan, see page 136.

Shiitake Mushrooms are brown, large-capped mushrooms. A few added to a soup stock or vegetable sauté makes a concentrated, rich flavor.

Index

A Taste of India, 204
A Taste of Japan, 155
Aduki bean
    Chestnutty Rice, 213
    Gyspy Bean Soup, 129
Agar agar
    Kanten, 261
    Walnut Pie, 247
Almond butter
    Creamy Chocolate Truffle Pie, 246
Almond milk, To Make Your Own, 16
Almond Pesto, 53
Almonds
    Almond Pesto, 53
    Banana Date Tofu Pie, 244
    Heavenly Potato Leek Soup, 126
    Pasta Salada with Pesto, 54
    Tofu Stroganoff, 50
Amaranth
    Aztec Two-step, 209
Amasake
    Chocolatey Pancakes, 240
Angel hair pasta
    Colorful Ginger Noodle Soup, 41
Ancient Goddess Spring Tabouli, 74
Another Great Pesto, 55
Appetizers
    Any Bean Pâté, 163
    Babaghanoush, 81
    Chickpea Vegetable Pâté, 163
    Cutlets, 137
    Herb Pâté, 168
    Mediterranean Tofu Dip, 85
    Smoked Fish Hors d'Oeuvres, 189
    Sunny Mushroom Pâté, 164
    2-Bean Vegetable Pâté, 163
    Vegetarian Sushi, 161
Apple
    Apple Crumb Pie, 233

Apple Date Crisp, 250
    Fruit Paradise, 238
    Millet Apple Raisin Cake, 212
    Teff Applesauce Cake, 229
Apple Cider Vinegar
    Creamy Garlic, 92
    Will's Dressing, 94
Apple Crumb Pie, 233
Apple Date Crisp, 250
Apple juice
    Apple Date Crisp, 250
    Banana Cake, 254
    Corn Bread Cake, 253
    Exotic Pear Crisp, 251
    Ginger Bread Cake, 252
    Kanten, 261
    Lemon Poppy Seed Cake, 230
    Mocha Walnut Cake, 254
    Outrageously Delicious Hazelnut Cake, 259
Applesauce
    Teff Applesauce Cake, 229
Apricot Compote, 261
Apricot juice
    Outrageously Delicious Hazelnut Cake, 259
Apricots
    Apricot Compote, 261
    Coffee Apricot Tofu Pie, 228
    Espresso Scones, 236
Arame
    Japanese Rainbow Salad, 82
    Ruby Red Salad, 83
    Udon Noodle Soup, 42
Arrowroot
    Chocolate Hazelnut Pudding or Frosting, 260
    Cutlets, 137
    Quick Ginger Scallion Sauce, 144

Arugola
  Italiano Arugola Salad with Cauliflower, 75
Arugula, *see* Arugola
Asparagus
  Red Lentil Asparagus Soup, 122
  Sunny Mushroom Pâté, 164
Autumn Minestrone, 120
Aztec Two-step, 209

Babaghanoush, 81
Banana
  Banana Cake, 254
  Banana Date Tofu Pie, 244
  Bananarama Tofu Pie, 236
Banana Cake, 254
Banana Date Tofu Pie, 244
Bananarama Tofu Pie, 236
Barley
  Barley Rice, 205
  Brown Rice and Barley Bread, 218
  Shiitake Barley Mushroom Soup, 112
  Split Pea Barley Soup, 125
Barley flour
  Brown Rice and Barley Bread, 218
  Ginger Bread Cake, 252
  Outrageously Delicious Hazelnut Cake, 259
Barley malt
  Caramel Icing, 257
  Emperor's Sweet-and-Sour Tempeh, 139
  Sweet-and-Sour Everything, 140
  Sweet-and-Sour Tempeh and Vegetables, 140
  Sweet-and-Sour Tofu, 51
  Walnut Pie, 247
Basic Beans, 119
Basic Brown Rice, 204
Basic Teff, 223
Basil
  Almond pesto, 53
  Another Great Pesto, 55
  Autumn Minestrone, 120
  Country-style Broccoli, 65
  Creamy Mushroom Basil Sauce, 147
  Elegant Vegetable Quiche, 227-228
  Green Queen, 93
  Herb Pâté, 168
  It Must Be Chili, 133

  Pasta Salada with Pesto, 54
Basmati rice
  A Taste of India, 204
Bass
  Quick-fried Bass with Tartar Sauce, 196
  Striped Bass, Trout, or Tilapia Stuffed with Herbed Croutons, 195
Bay scallops
  Dorothy's Steamed Bay Scallops, 194
Bean Cookery, 117
Beans
  Any Bean Pâté, 163
  Autumn Minestrone, 120
  Basic Beans, 119
  Brazilian Black Bean Soup, 130
  Chickpea Vegetable Pâté, 163
  Chickpeas in Garlic Sauce, 164
  Creamy Beans, 119
  French Peasant Stew, 134
  Ginger Mustard Beans, 119
  Gypsy Bean Soup, 129
  Indian Red Bean Sauce, 143
  It Must Be Chili, 133
  Lentil Soup, 124
  Paradise of India, 123
  Pinto Beans and Tortillas, 176-177
  Pinto Parsley Salad, 95
  Quick Bean Soaking Method, 117
  Red Lentil Asparagus Soup, 122
  Refried Beans, 69
  Roasted Eggplant and Pepper Salad, 80
  Spanish Dancer, 45
  Split Pea Barley Soup, 125
  Sweet Bean Stew, 132
  Sweet Split Pea Soup
  Thanks, Grandma, 121
  The Ultimate Pasta and Bean Salad, 87
  3-Bean Dill Salad, 88
  3-Bean Summer Salad with Cilantro and Capers, 88
  2-Bean Vegetable Pâté, 163
  Using a Ceramic Pressure Cooker Insert (Rice Crock), 118
Beets
  Ruby Red Salad, 83
  Sweet Borscht, 111
Berry Good Tofu Pie, 235
Black Bean
  Brazilian Black Bean Soup, 130

THE QUICK & EASY ORGANIC GOURMET

Black, White, and Greens, 160
Blueberry
  Berry Good Tofu Pie, 235
  Blueberry Crumb Pie, 234
  Topless Blueberry Pie, 234
Blueberry Crumb Pie, 234
Boiled Salads, 100
Bok choy
  A Taste of Japan, 155
  Chinese Cabbage and Watercress Soup, 38
  Juicy Ginger Vegetables, 47
  Oriental Express, 61
Brazilian Black Bean Soup, 130
Bread Making Improvisations, 218-219
Breads
  Bread Making Improvisations, 218-219
  Brown Rice and Barley Bread, 218
  Corn Bread Cake, 253
  Garlic Bread, 179
  Ginger Bread Cake, 252
  Herb Croutons, 110
  Rice Bread #1, 216
  Rice Bread #2, 217
  Wheat-Free Corn Bread, 253
Breakfast
  Chocolatey Pancakes, 240
  Coffee Cake and Cupcakes, 180
  Deluxe Morning Breakfast, 226
  Emily's Strawberry Drink, 175
  French Toast, 173
  Good Morning Strawberry Muffins, 174
  Scrumptious Muffins, 239
  Vanilla Hazelnut Granola, 239
Broccoli
  Children's Special Soup, 154
  Country-style Broccoli, 65
  Creamy Broccoli Soup, 128
  Shiitakes in a Wok, 167
  Sunset Casserole, 135
  Szechwan Broccoli, 60
Broiled Farm-raised Trout, 194
Bronze Delight, 215
Brown basmati rice
  A Taste of India, 204
Brown rice
  Barley Rice, 205
  Basic Brown Rice, 204
  Brown Rice and Barley Bread, 218

Chestnutty Rice, 213
Festive Rice Salad, 86
Japanese Fried Rice, 61
Rice Bread #1, 216-217
Rice Bread #2, 217
Short and Sweet, 205
Spelt Good, 206
Sunny Mountain Rice, 210
Three Sisters Grains, 208
Vegetable Fried Rice, 157
Vegetarian Sushi, 161-163
Wild and Wonderful, 207
Brown rice flour
  Outrageously Delicious Hazelnut Cake, 259
Brown Rice and Barley Bread, 218
Brussel sprouts
  Holiday Tempeh, 138
  Sweet-and-Sour Tempeh and Vegetables, 140
Buckwheat Groats, see Kasha
Bulgar
  It Looks Like Meatloaf, 70-71
  Ancient Goddess Spring Tabouli, 74
Burdock
  Fat-free, 63
  Ginger Burdock Sauce, 145
  Juicy Ginger Vegetables, 47
Butternut squash
  Lentil Soup, 124
  Millet and Teff with Squash and Onions, 225
  Sunset Casserole, 135
  Sweet Bean Stew, 132
  Sweet Millet, 211

Cabbage
  Brazilian Black Bean Soup, 130
  Colorful and Crunchy, 55,
  Fragrant Indian Cabbage, 66
  Ginger Vegetables, 158
  Homemade Saurakraut, 104
  Japanese Rainbow Salad, 82
  Pressed Cabbage Salad, 103
  Sauerkraut with Carrots and Onions, 104
Cakes
  Banana Cake, 254

Carob Fudge Layer Cake, 256
Carrot Coconut Cake, 255
Chocolate Cake Supreme, 258
Coffee Cake and Cupcakes, 180
Corn Bread Cake, 253
Ginger Bread Cake, 252
Lemon Poppy Seed Cake, 230
Mocha Walnut Cake, 254
Outrageously Delicious Hazelnut Cake, 259
Canola oil
    Apple Crumb Pie, 233
    Banana Cake, 254
    Banarama Tofu Pie, 236
    Berry Good Tofu Pie, 235
    Blueberry Crumb Pie, 234
    Carob Cookies, 249
    Carob Fudge Layer Cake, 256
    Carrot Coconut Cake, 255
    Chocolate Cake Supreme, 258
    Corn Bread Cake, 253
    Dessert Pie Crust, 231
    Espresso Scones, 236
    Fruit Cake Cookies, 249
    Fruit Paradise, 238
    Ginger Bread Cake, 252
    Hazelnut Butter Cookies, 238
    Lemon Poppy Seed Cake, 230
    Luscious Strawberry Pie, 245
    Mocha Walnut Cake, 254
    Peach Crumb Pie, 234
    Peanut Butter Chocolate Chip Cookies, 237
    Peanut Butter Cookies, 237
    Scrumptious Muffins, 239
    Super Chocolate Chip Cookies, 232
    Topless Blueberry Pie, 234
    Vanilla Hazelnut Granola, 239
Capers
    Festive Rice Sald, 86
    Spinach and Potato Salad with Capers, 78
    The Ultimate Pasta and Bean Salad, 87
    3-Bean Summer Salad with Cilantro and Capers, 88
Caramel Icing, 257
Carob
    Carob Cookies, 249
    Carob Fudge Icing, 257
    Carob Fudge Layer Cake, 256
    Hot Carob Fudge, 262

Carob Chip Cookies, 248
Carob Chips
    Carob Chip Cookies, 248
Carob Cookies, 249
Carob Fudge Icing, 257
Carob Fudge Layer Cake, 256
Carrot
    Cashew Carrot Curry Sauce, 52
    Cashew Florentine Sauce, 53
    Carrot Coconut Cake, 255
    Gyspy Bean Soup, 129
    Lemony Carrot and Radish Salad, 99
    Pickles, 105
    Sauerkraut with Carrots and Onions, 104
    Sweet Bean Stew, 132
    Sweet Millet, 211
    Vegetables in Indian Spices, 141
Carrot Coconut Cake, 255
Cashew Carrot Curry Sauce, 52
Cashew Florentine Sauce, 53
Cashew milk, To Make Your Own, 16
Cashews
    Cashew Carrot Curry Sauce, 52
    Cashew Florentine Sauce, 53
    Cashew milk, To Make Your Own, 16
    Curried Vegetables with Cashews, 142
Casseroles Plus
    Elegant Vegetable Quiche, 227
    It Looks Like Meat Loaf, 70-71
    Roasted Potatoes, 177
    Sunset Casserole, 135
    Tempting Tempeh Casserole, 166
Cauliflower
    Black, White, and Greens, 160
    Brazilian Black Bean Soup, 130
    Creamy Cauliflower Soup, 127
    Curried Tempeh with Tomatoes, 67
    Curried Vegetables with Cashews, 142
    French Peasant Stew, 134
    High Energy, 68
    Italiano Arugola Salad with Cauliflower, 75
    New England Fish Chowder, 188
    Paradise of India, 123
    Steamed Cauliflower, 178
Celery
    French Patty Pan Stew...and Soup, 131
    New England Fish Chowder, 188

Cherry juice
    Exotic Pear Crisp, 251
Chestnut
    Chestnutty Rice, 213
Chestnutty Rice, 213
Chickpea Vegetable Pâté, 163
Chickpeas
    Chickpea Vegetable Pâté, 163
    Chickpeas in Garlic Sauce, 164
    French Peasant Stew, 134
    The Ultimate Pasta and Bean Salad, 87
    3-Bean Dill Salad, 88
Chickpeas in Garlic Sauce, 164
Children's Special Soup, 154
Chili
    It Must Be Chili, 133
Chinese cabbage
    Chinese Cabbage and Watercress Soup, 38
    Oriental Express, 61
Chinese Cabbage and Watercress Soup, 38
Chinese Hot and Spicy Soup, 111
Chinese Stir-fry, 192
Chocolate
    Chocolate Cake Supreme, 258
    Chocolate Hazelnut Pudding or Frosting,
      260
    Chocolate Pudding, 246
    Chunky Chocolate-Nut Cookies, 248
    Creamy Chocolate Truffle Pie, 246
Chocolate chip
    Chocolate Cake Supreme, 258
    Chocolate Chip Cookies, 248
    Chocolate Pudding, 246
    Creamy Chocolate Truffle Pie, 246
    Peanut Butter Chocolate Chip Cookies, 237
    Super Chocolate Chip Cookies, 232
Chocolate Cake Supreme, 258
Chocolate Chip Cookies, 248
Chocolate Hazelnut Pudding or Frosting, 260
Chocolate Pudding, 246
Chocolatey Pancakes, 240
Chunky Chocolate-Nut Cookies, 248
Cilantro
    Brazilian Black Bean Soup, 130
    Cilantro Pesto Pasta, 77
    Fragrant Indian Cabbage, 66
    Green Queen, 93
    3-Bean Summer Salad with Cilantro and
      Capers, 88

Cocoa
    Chocolate Hazelnut Pudding or Frosting,
      260
    Cocoa Fudge Icing, 259
Coconut
    Carrot Coconut Cake, 255
    Coconut Icing, 256
Coconut Icing, 256
Coconut Milk, To Make Your Own, 16
Cod
    Chinese Stir-fry, 192
    New England Fish Chowder, 188
Coffee Apricot Tofu Pie, 228
Coffee Cake and Cupcakes, 180
Collard greens
    Black, White, and Greens, 160
    Colorful Ginger Noodle Soup, 41
    Miso Vegetable Soup, 114
Colorful and Crunchy, 55
Colorful Ginger Noodle Soup, 41
Cookies
    Carob Chip Cookies, 248
    Carob Cookies, 249
    Chocolate Chip Cookies, 248
    Chunky Chocolate-Nut Cookies, 248
    Date Cookies, 248
    Fruit Cake Cookies, 249
    Hazelnut Butter Cookies, 238
    Peanut Butter Chocolate Chip Cookies, 237
    Peanut Butter Cookies, 237
    Super Chocolate Chip Cookies, 232
Corn
    It Must Be Chili, 133
    Wheat-free Corn Bread, 253
Corn Bread Cake, 253
Corn meal
    Corn Bread Cake, 253
    Fritters, 224
Corn oil
    Apple Crumb Pie, 233
    Banana Cake, 254
    Bananarama Tofu Pie, 236
    Berry Good Tofu Pie, 235
    Blueberry Crumb Pie, 234
    Carob Cookies, 249
    Carob Fudge Layer Cake, 256
    Carrot Coconut Cake, 255
    Corn Bread Cake, 253

Dessert Pie Crust, 231
Fruit Cake Cookies, 249
Fruit Paradise, 238
Ginger Bread Cake, 252
Hazelnut Butter Cookies, 238
Lemon Poppy Seed Cake, 230
Mocha Walnut Cake, 254
Peach Crumb Pie, 234
Peanut Butter Chocolate Chip Cookies, 237
Peanut Butter Cookies, 237
Scrumptious Muffins, 239
Super Chocolate Chip Cookies, 232
Country-style Broccoli, 65
Couscous
   Couscous and Teff, 215
   Hot or Cold Salad, 46
   Kasha Cous, 214
   Quinoa Pepper Pilaf, 45
Couscous and Teff, 215
Creamy Beans, 119
Creamy Broccoli Soup, 128
Creamy Cauliflower Soup, 127
Creamy Chocolate Truffle Pie, 246
Creamy Garlic, 92
Creamy Mushroom Basil Sauce, 147
Create your own
   green salad, 89
   quick cooking soup, 33
   stir-fry, 58
Cucumber
   Pickles, 105
   Pressed Cucumber Salad, 103
Curried Summer Vegetables, 142
Curried Tempeh with Tomatoes, 67
Curried Vegetables with Cashews, 142
Cusk
   New England Fish Chowder, 188

Daikon
   Emperor's Sweet-and-Sour Tempeh, 139
   Ginger Vegetables, 158
   Lemony Carrot and Radish Salad, 99
Date Cookies, 248
Dates
   Apple Date Crisp, 250
   Banana Date Tofu Pie, 244
   Date Cookies, 248
   Fruit Cake Cookies, 249

Date sugar
   Banana Date Tofu Pie, 244
   Exotic Pear Crisp, 251
   Topless Blueberry Pie, 234
Delicata squash
   Holiday Tempeh, 138
   Lentil Soup, 124
   Sunset Casserole, 135
   Sweet Bean Stew, 132
   Sweet Split Pea Soup, 125
Deluxe Morning Breakfast, 226
Dessert Pie Crust, 231
Desserts
   Apple Crumb Pie, 233
   Apple Date Crisp, 250
   Apricot Compote, 261
   Banana Cake, 254
   Banana Date Tofu Pie, 244
   Bananarama Tofu Pie, 236
   Berry Good Tofu Pie, 235
   Blueberry Crumb Pie, 234
   Carob Chip Cookies, 248
   Carob Cookies, 249
   Carob Fudge Layer Cake, 256
   Carrot Coconut Cake, 255
   Chocolate Cake Supreme, 258
   Chocolate Chip Cookies, 248
   Chocolate Hazelnut Pudding or Frosting, 260
   Chocolate Pudding, 246
   Chunky Chocolate-Nut Cookies, 248
   Coffee Apricot Tofu Pie, 228
   Coffee Cake and Cupcakes, 180
   Creamy Chocolate Truffle Pie, 246
   Date Cookies, 248
   Dessert Pie Crust, 231
   Espresso Scones, 236
   Exotic Pear Crisp, 251
   Fruit Cake Cookies, 250
   Fruit Paradise, 238
   Ginger Bread Cake, 252
   Hazelnut Butter Cookies, 238
   Hot Carob Fudge, 262
   Kanten (Vegetable Gelatin), 261
   Lemon Poppy Seed Cake, 230
   Luscious Strawberry Pie, 245
   Mocha Walnut Cake, 254
   Outrageously Delicious Hazelnut Cake, 259

THE QUICK & EASY ORGANIC GOURMET

Peach Crumb Pie, 234
Peanut Butter Chocolate Chip Cookies, 237
Peanut Butter Cookies, 237
Scrumptious Muffins, 239
Super Chocolate Chip Cookies, 232
Teff Applesauce Cake, 229
Topless Blueberry Pie, 234
Walnut Pie, 247
Dill
 Easy Potato Salad, 79
 Elegant Vegetable Quiche, 227-228
 Herb Pâté, 168
 Sautéed Kale with Leeks and Dill, 156
 Thanks, Grandma, 121
 The Ultimate Pasta and Beans Salad, 87
 3-Bean Dill Salad, 88
Dips
 Any Bean Pâté, 163
 Babaghanoush, 81
 Chickpea Vegetable Pâté, 163
 Herb Pâté, 168
 Mediterranean Tofu Dip, 85
 Sunny Mushroom Pâté, 164
 2-Bean Vegetable Pâté, 163
Dorothy's Steamed Bay Scallops, 194

Easy Potato Salad, 79
Edible flowers
 Composed Green Salads, 89-90
Eggplant
 Babaghanoush, 81
 Roasted Eggplant and Pepper Salad: 80,
Elegant Vegetable Quiche, 227-228
Emily's Strawberry Drink, 175
Emperor's Sweet-and-Sour Tempeh, 139
Espresso Scones, 236
Exotic Pear Crisp, 251
Extra virgin olive oil
 Almond Pesto, 53
 Ancient Goddess Spring Tabouli, 74
 Designing an Italian Sauté, 64
 Green Queen, 93
 Len's Sunny Macaroni Salad, 76
 Pasta Salada with Pesto, 54
 Special Marianade for Sun-dried Tomatoes,
  84
 The Ultimate Pasta and Bean Salad, 87
 Will's Dressing, 94

Fancy French Onion Soup with Herb Crou-
 tons, 110
Fat-free, 63
Festive Rice Salad, 86
Fig
 Espresso Scones, 236
Fish
 Broiled Farm-raised Trout, 194
 Chinese Stir-fry, 192
 Dorothy's Steamed Bay Scallops, 194
 Honey Shrimp Kabobs, 193
  in stir-fry, 58
 Japanese Poached Salmon, 191
 New England Fish Chowder, 188
 Pan Fry Fish: Cajun-Style, French, Italian,
 Japanese, American, 197
 Quick Fried Bass with Tartar Sauce, 196
 Savory Fish Stew, 191
 Smoked Fish Hors D'Oeuvres, 189
 Smoked Fish Salads, 190
 Striped Bass, Trout, or Tilapia Stuffed with
  Herbed Croutons, 195
Fragrant Indian Cabbage, 66
Flax seeds
 Chocolate Cake Supreme, 258
 Ginger Bread Cake, 252
 Mocha Walnut Cake, 254
 Outrageously Delicious Hazelnut Cake,
  259
 Wheat-free Corn Bread, 253
Freckles, 208
Free Play
 create your own green salad, 89
 create your own quick cooking soup, 33
 International Free Play, 58
French Patty Pan Stew...and Soup, 131
French Peasant Stew, 134
French Style
 Designing a French Sauté, 70
 Fancy French Onion Soup with Herb Crou-
  tons, 110
 French Patty Pan Stew...and Soup, 131
 French Peasant Stew, 134
 Mushroom Leek Sauce, 146
 Pan Fry Fish, 197
 Soups with International Themes, 34
 Sweet Split Pea Soup, 125
 The Ultimate Pasta and Bean Salad, 87
French Toast, 173

Fritters, 224
Fruit Cake Cookies, 249
Fruit Paradise, 238

Garlic
    Almond Pesto, 53
    Autumn Minestrone, 120
    Chickpeas in Garlic Sauce, 164
    Creamy Garlic, 92
    Designing an Italian Sauté, 64
    Designing a Mexican Stir-fry, 68
    French Patty Pan Stew...and Soup, 131
    Garlic Bread, 179
    Roasted Potatoes, 177
    Seitan making Party and Pot Roast, 136
    Soups with International Themes, 33-34
    Szechwan Broccoli, 60
Garlic Bread, 179
Ginger
    Brazilian Black Bean Soup, 130
    Colorful Ginger Noodle Soup, 41
    Designing an Oriental Stir-fry, 60
    Ginger Bread Cake, 252
    Ginger Burdock Sauce, 145
    Ginger Mustard Beans, 119
    Ginger Tempeh, 48
    Ginger Vegetables, 158
    Herb Pâté, 168
    Juicy Ginger Vegetables, 47
    Paradise of India, 123
    Quick Ginger Scallion Sauce, 144
    Seitan making Party and Pot Roast, 136
    Soups with International Themes, 33-34
    Tamari-ginger Gravy, 137
    Udon Noodle Soup, 42
Ginger Bread Cake, 252
Ginger Burdock Sauce, 145
Ginger Tempeh, 48
Ginger Vegetables, 158
Golden Goddess, 93
Good Morning Strawberry Muffins, 174
Green Queen, 93
Grains
    A Taste of India, 204
    Ancient Goddess Spring Tabouli, 74
    Aztec Two-step, 209
    Barley Rice, 205
    Basic Brown Rice, 204

Basic Teff, 223
Bronze Delight, 215
Chestnutty Rice, 213
Cooking Grains, 199-200
Couscous and Teff, 215
Creamy Broccoli Soup, 128
Creamy Cauliflower Soup, 127
Deluxe Morning Breakfast, 226
Festive Rice Salad, 86
Freckles, 208
Fritters, 224
Greens and Grains, 43
High Energy, 68
Hot or Cold Salad, 46
How to Use a Rice Crock in a Pressure
    Cooker, 201
It Looks Like Meat Loaf, 70-71
Japanese Fried Rice, 61
Kasha, 214
Kasha Cous, 214
King Tut Special, 209
Millet and Teff with Squash and Onions,
    225
Millet Apple Raisin Cake, 212
Millet Croquettes, 211
Millet Veggie Loaf, 211
Nutty Grain Balls, 205
Quinoa Pepper Pilaf, 45
Quinoa Veggie Pilaf, 44
Shiitake Barley Mushroom Soup, 112
Short and Sweet, 205
Spanish Dancer, 45
Special Ways of Cooking Grains, 202
Spelt Good, 206
Sunny Mountain Rice, 210
Sweet Millet, 211
Tahini Cream Sauce, 144
Teff Applesauce Cake, 229
Teff Plus Other Grains, 223
Three Sisters Grains, 208
Vegetarian Sushi, 161-163
Vegetable Fried Rice, 157
Wild and Wonderful, 207
Grain coffee
    Coffee Apricot Tofu Pie, 228
    Espresso Scones, 236
    Mocha Walnut Cake, 254
Granola
    Vanilla Hazelnut Granola, 239

Green leafy vegetables
    Cashew Florentine Sauce, 53
    Chinese Cabbage and Watercress Soup, 38
    Chinese Stir-fry, 192
    Composed Green Salads, 89
    Fat-free, 63
    Green Noodle Sauté, 62
    Greens and Grains, 43
    Greens with Shiitake, 157
    Greens with Tahini Sauce, 165
    Italiano Green Sauté, 156
    Juicy Ginger Vegetables, 47
    Oriental Express, 61
    Pinto Parsley Salad, 95
    Sauté of Garden Greens, 64
    Sautéed Kale with Leeks and Dill, 156
    Spinach and Potato Salad with Capers, 78
    Sprouts, 90
Green Noodle Sauté, 62
Greens and Grains, 43
Greens with Shiitake, 157
Greens with Tahini Sauce, 165
Gyspy Bean Soup, 129

Hazelnut
    Chocolate Hazelnut Pudding or Frosting, 260
    Outrageously Delicious Hazelnut Cake, 259
    Vanilla Hazelnut Granola, 239
Hazelnut butter
    Creamy Chocolate Truffle Pie, 246
    Hazelnut Butter Cookies, 238
    Hazelnut Butter Icing, 260
Hazelnut Butter Cookies, 238
Hazelnut Butter Icing, 260
Heavenly Potato Leek Soup, 126
Herb Pâté, 168
Herbs
    (as a garnish), Composed Green Salads, 89
    Herb Croutons, 110
    Striped Bass, Trout, or Tilapia Stuffed with Herbed Croutons, 195
Hijiki
    Black, White, and Greens, 160
Homemade Saurakraut, 104
Honey
    Honey Shrimp Kabobs, 193

Honey Shrimp Kabobs, 193
Hot Carob Fudge, 262
Hot or Cold Salad, 46

Icings
    Caramel Icing, 257
    Carob Fudge Icing, 257
    Chocolate Hazelnut Pudding or Frosting, 260
    Cocoa Fudge Icing, 259
    Coconut Icing, 256
    Hazelnut Butter Icing, 260
Indian Red Bean Sauce, 143
Indian Style
    A Taste of India, 204
    Cashew Carrot Curry Sauce, 52
    Cashew Florentine Sauce, 53
    Curried Summer Vegetables, 142
    Curried Tempeh with Tomatoes, 67
    Curried Vegetables with Cashews, 142
    Designing an Indian Stir-fry, 66
    Fragrant Indian Cabbage, 66
    Indian Red Bean Sauce, 143
    Paradise of India, 123
    Soups with International Themes, 34
    Sweet Split Pea Soup, 125
    Vegetables in Indian Spices, 141
International Free Play, 58
Invent Your Own Miso Soup, 113
Invent Your Own Soups, Stews and Sauces, 116-117
It Looks Like Meat Loaf, 70-71
It Must Be Chili, 133
Italian Style
    Almond Pesto, 53
    Another Great Pesto, 55
    Autumn Minestrone, 120
    Country-style Broccoli, 65
    Creamy Mushroom Basil Sauce, 147
    Designing an Italian Sauté, 64
    Festive Rice Salad, 86
    Garlic Bread, 179
    Italiano Arugola Salad with Cauliflower, 75
    Italiano Green Sauté, 156
    Marinated Sun-dried Tomatoes, 84
    Mediterranean Tofu Dip, 85
    Pan Fry Fish, 197

Pasta Salada with Pesto, 54
Roasted Eggplant and Pepper Salad, 80
Sauté of Garden Greens, 64
Soups with International Themes, 33
Special Marinade for Sun-dried Tomatoes, 84
Spinach and Potato Salad with Capers, 78
Italiano Arugola Salad with Cauliflower, 75

Japanese Fried Rice, 61
Japanese Noodles in Tamari Broth, 39
Japanese Poached Salmon, 191
Japanese Rainbow Salad, 82
Juicy Ginger Vegetables, 47

Kale
    Chickpeas in Garlic Sauce, 164
    Fat-free, 63
    Ginger Vegetables, 158
    Green Noodle Sauté, 62
    Greens and Grains: 43
    Greens with Shiitake, 157
    Greens with Tahini Sauce, 165
    Sautéed Kale with Leeks and Dill, 156
    Sauté of Garden Greens, 64
    Sweet Vegetables Lo Mein, 157
    The Works, 159
Kamut
    King Tut's Special, 209
    Three Sisters Grains, 208
Kamut flakes
    Creamy Cauliflower Soup, 127
    Deluxe Morning Breakfast, 226
    Exotic Pear Crisp, 251
Kamut flour
    Apple Date Crisp, 250
    Chocolate Cake Supreme, 258
    Chocolate Chip Cookies, 248
Kamut pasta
    Pasta Salada with Pesto, 54
    The Ultimate Pasta and Bean Salad, 87
Kanten, 261
Kasha
    Bronze Delight, 215
    Greens and Grains, 43
    Kasha, 214

Kasha Cous, 214
    Sautéed Kale with Leeks and Dill, 156
Kasha, 214
Kasha Cous, 214
Kidney beans
    It Must Be Chili, 133
Kid's Favorites
    Apricot Compote, 261
    Carob Cookies, 249
    Children's Special Soup, 154
    Chocolate Cake Supreme, 258
    Chocolate Chip Cookies, 248
    Chocolatey Pancakes, 240
    Coffee Cake and Cupcakes, 180
    Corn Bread Cake, 253
    Easy Potato Salad, 79
    Emily's Strawberry Drink, 175
    Fancy French Onion Soup with Herb Croutons, 110
    French Toast, 173
    Fritters, 224
    Garlic Bread, 179
    Ginger Bread Cake, 252
    Good Morning Strawberry Muffins, 174
    Grains and breads — see Chapter 11
    Greens in Tahini Sauce, 165
    Japanese Noodles in Broth, 39
    Japanese Poached Salmon, 191
    Kanten (Vegetable Gelatin), 261
    Luscious Strawberry Pie, 245
    Millet Apple Raisin Cake, 212
    Miso Vegetable Soup, 114
    New England Fish Chowder, 188
    Peanut Butter Cookies, 237
    Pickles, 105
    Pinto Beans and Tortillas, 176-177
    Roasted Potatoes, 177
    Sauerkraut, 104
    Shiitake Barley Mushroom Soup, 181
    Shiitake in the Wok, 167
    Smoked Fish Hors d'oeuvres, 189
    Steamed Cauliflower, 178
    Steamed Vegetables, 178
    Super Chocolate Chip Cookies, 232
    Sweet Split Pea Soup, 125
    Sweet Vegetables Lo Mein, 157
    Teff Applesauce Cake, 229
    Thanks, Grandma, 121
    Vanilla Hazelnut Granola, 239

King Tut's Special, 209
Kudzu
    Chocolate Hazelnut Pudding or Frosting,
        260
    Macro Mushroom Sauce, 115
    Quick Ginger Scallion Sauce, 144
    Sweet-and-Sour Everything, 140
    Sweet-and-Sour Tempeh and Vegetables,
        140
    Sweet-and-Sour Tofu, 51
    Tamari-ginger Gravy, 137
    Tempting Tempeh Casserole, 166

Leek
    Fat-free, 63
    Green Noodle Saute, 62
    Greens with Tahini Sauce, 165
    Heavenly Potato Leek Soup, 126
    Mushroom Leek Sauce, 146
    Quinoa Veggie Pilaf, 44
    Sautéed Kale with Leeks and Dill, 156
    Sunset Casserole, 135
    Sweet Bean Stew, 132
Lemon
    Ancient Goddess Spring Tabouli, 74
    Italiano Arugola Salad with Cauliflower,
        75
    Lemon Fire, 95
    Lemon Poppy Seed Cake, 230
    Lemony Carrot and Radish Salad, 99
    The Ultimate Pasta and Bean Salad, 87
Lemon Fire, 95
Lemon Poppy Seed Cake, 230
Lemony Carrot and Radish Salad, 99
Len's Sunny Macaroni Salad, 76
Lentil Soup, 124
Lentils, see also Red lentils
    Lentil Soup, 124
    Red Lentil Asparagus Soup, 122
Lettuce
    Composed Green Salads, 89
Lima beans
    Thanks, Grandma, 121
Luscious Strawberry Pie, 245

Macaroni
    Autumn Minestrone, 120

Len's Sunny Macaroni Salad, 76
Macro Mushroom Sauce, 115
Maple syrup
    Apple Crumb Pie, 233
    Banana Cake, 254
    Banarama Tofu Pie, 236
    Berry Good Tofu Pie, 235
    Blueberry Crumb Pie, 234
    Carob Fudge Layer Cake, 256
    Carrot Coconut Cake, 255
    Chocolate Cake Supreme, 258
    Coconut Icing, 256
    Corn Bread Cake, 253
    Creamy Chocolate Truffle Pie, 246
    Dessert Pie Crust, 231
    Espresso Scones, 236
    Fruit Paradise, 238
    Ginger Bread Cake, 252
    Hazelnut Butter Cookies, 238
    Lemon Poppy Seed Cake, 230
    Luscious Strawberry Pie, 245
    Mocha Walnut Cake, 254
    Outrageously Delicious Hazelnut Cake,
        259
    Peach Crumb Pie, 234
    Peanut Butter Chocoalte Chip Cookies, 237
    Peanut Butter Cookies, 237
    Scrumptious Muffins, 239
    Super Chocolate chip Cookies, 232
    Vanilla Hazelnut Granola, 239
Marinated Salads, 100
Marinated Sun-dried Tomatoes, 84
Marinated Tofu, 101
Mediterranean Tofu Dip, 85
Mexican Style
    Designing a Mexican Stir-fry, 68
    Green Queen, 93
    High Energy, 68
    It Must Be Chili, 133
Pinto Beans and Tortillas, 176
    Quinoa Pepper Pilaf, 45
    Quinoa Veggie Pilaf, 44
    Refried Beans, 69
Soups with International Themes, 34
    Spanish Dancer, 45
Millet
    Aztec Two-step, 209
    Freckles, 208

INDEX

King Tut's Special, 209
Millet and Teff with Squash and Onions, 225
Millet Apple Raisin Cake, 212
Spelt Good, 206
Sweet Millet, 211
Three Sisters Grains, 208
Millet and Teff with Squash and Onions, 225
Millet Apple Raisin Cake, 212
Millet Croquettes, 211
Millet Veggie Loaf, 211
Mint
    Festive Rice Salad, 86
Mirin
    as a cooking liquid, 16
    Designing An Oriental Stir-fry, 60
    Fat-free, 63
    Ginger Tempeh, 48
    in Oriental Soups, 33
    Japanese Poached Salmon, 191
    Juicy Ginger Vegetables, 47
Miso
    Another Great Pesto, 55
    Invent Your Own Miso Soup, 113
    It Looks Like Meatloaf, 70-71
    Miso Vegetable Soup, 114
Mizuna
    Chinese Stir-fry, 192
Monkfish
    New England Fish Chowder, 188
Muffins
    Good Morning Strawberry Muffins, 174
    Scrumptious Muffins, 239
Mushrooms
    Chinese Stir-fry, 192
    Creamy Broccoli Soup, 128
    Creamy Mushroom Basil Sauce, 147
    Elegant Vegetable Quiche, 227-228
    Lentil Soup, 124
    Macro Mushroom Sauce, 115
    Mushroom Leek Sauce, 146
    Shiitake Barley Mushroom Soup, 112
    Sunny Mushroom Pâté, 164
    Sunset Casserole, 135
    Tofu Stroganoff, 50
    Vegetable Gravy, 147
Mushroom Leek Sauce, 146
Mustard
    Ginger Mustard Beans, 119

Mustard greens
    Indian Red Bean Sauce, 143
    Vegetarian Sushi, 161-163

Napa cabbage
    see Chinese cabbage
Navy beans
    Thanks, Grandma, 121
    3-Bean Dill Salad, 88
New England Fish Chowder, 188
Noodles and Pasta
    Almond Pesto, 53
    Another Great Pesto, 55
    Chinese Hot and Spicy Soup, 111
    Cilantro Pesto Pasta, 77
    Colorful Ginger Noodle Soup, 41
    Green Noodle Sauté, 62
    Japanese Noodles in Tamari Broth, 39
    Len's Sunny Macaroni Salad, 76
    Pasta Salada with Pesto, 54
    Sweet Vegetables Lo Mein, 157
    The Ultimate Pasta and Bean Salad, 87
    Tofu Stroganoff, 50
    Udon Noodle Soup, 42
Nori
    Vegetarian Sushi, 161-163
Nuts and Nuts—and Seeds, Too, 91
Nutty Grain Balls, 205

Oats
    Freckles, 208
Ocean ribbons
    Seitan making Party and Pot Roast, 136
Oil-free salads
    Exciting Oil-free Salads, 98-105
Oil-free Stir-fry, 63
Oils
    for baking, 8
    for salads, 8
    for sautéing and stir-fry, 8
    storing, 8
Olive oil
    see extra virgin olive oil
Olives
    Ancient Goddess Spring Tabouli, 74
    Festive Rice Salad, 86

THE QUICK & EASY ORGANIC GOURMET

Onions
  Cashew Carrot Curry Sauce, 52
  Cashew Florentine Sauce, 53
  Fancy French Onion Soup with Herb Croutons, 110
  French Patty Pan Stew...and Soup, 131
  Juicy Ginger Vegetables, 47
  Millet and Teff with Squash and Onions, 225
  Sauerkraut with Carrots and Onions, 104
  Sweet-and-Sour Tofu, 51
  Sweet Bean Stew, 132
  Tofu Stroganoff, 50
  Vegetable Gravy, 147
Oriental Style
  A Taste of Japan, 155
  Black, White, and Greens, 160
  Chinese Cabbage and Watercress Soup, 38
  Chinese Hot and Spicy Soup, 111
  Chinese Stir-fry, 192
  Colorful and Crunchy, 55
  Colorful Ginger Noodle Soup, 41
  Designing an Oriental Stir-fry, 60
  Emperor's Sweet-and-Sour Tempeh, 139
  Fat-Free, 63
  Ginger Burdock Sauce, 145
  Ginger Tempeh, 48
  Ginger Vegetables, 158
  Greens with Shiitake, 157
  Invent Your Own Miso Soup, 113
  Japanese Fried Rice, 61
  Japanese Noodles in Tamari Broth, 39
  Japanese Poached Salmon, 191
  Japanese Rainbow Salad, 82
  Juicy Ginger Vegetables, 47
  Lemon Fire, 95
  Macro Mushroom Sauce, 115
  Marinated Tofu, 101
  Miso Vegetable Soup, 114
  Oriental Express, 61
  Oriental Vegetable Salad, 83
  Pan Fry Fish, 197
  Quick Ginger Scallion Sauce, 144
  Ruby Red Salad, 83
  Shiitake In the Wok, 167
  Soups with International Themes, 33
  Stir-fry Vegetables with Tofu, 49
  Sweet Vegetables Lo Mein, 157

  Szechwan Broccoli, 60
  Tamari-ginger Gravy, 137
  The Works, 159
  Udon Noodle Soup, 42
  Vegetable Fried Rice, 157
  Vegetarian Sushi, 161-163
  Winds of Japan, 97
Oriental Express, 61
Oriental Vegetable Salad, 83
Outrageously Delicious Hazelnut Cake, 259

Pan Fry Fish, 197
Paradise of India, 123
Parsley
  Ancient Goddess Spring Tabouli, 74
  Chickpea Vegetable Pâté, 163
  Creamy Garlic, 92
  French Patty Pan Stew...and Soup, 131
  Herb Pâté, 168
  Japanese Rainbow Salad, 82
  Mediterranean Tofu Dip, 85
  Pinto Parsley Salad, 95
  Tahini Parsley Sauce, 166
Pasta
  see noodles
Patty pan squash
  French Patty Pan Stew...and Soup, 131
Peach
  Peach Crumb Pie, 234
Peach Crumb Pie, 234
Peanut butter
  Peanut Butter Chocolate Chip Cookies, 237
  Peanut Butter Cookies, 237
Peanut Butter Chocolate Chip Cookies, 237
Peanut Butter Cookies, 237
Peanut oil
  Creamy Garlic, 92
Pears
  Exotic Pear Crisp, 251
Peas
  Fragrant Indian Cabbage, 66
  Vegetables in Indian Spices, 141
Peppers
  High Energy, 68
  Quinoa Pepper Pilaf, 45
  Roasted Eggplant and Pepper Salad, 80
  Vegetables in Indian Spices, 141
Pesto, 53-55

Pickles, 105
Pies
    Apple Crumb Pie, 233
    Banana Date Tofu Pie, 244
    Banarama Tofu Pie, 236
    Berry Good Tofu Pie, 235
    Blueberry Crumb Pie, 234
    Creamy Chocolate Truffle Pie, 246
    Dessert Pie Crust, 231
    Luscious Strawberry Pie, 245
    Peach Crumb Pie, 234
    Topless Blueberry Pie, 234
    Walnut Pie, 247
Pignola nuts
    Another Great Pesto, 55
Pinto beans
    It Must Be Chili, 133
    Pinto Beans and Tortillas, 176-177
    Pinto Parsley Salad, 95
Pinto Beans and Tortillas, 176-177
Pinto Parsley Salad, 95
Poppy seeds
    Lemon Poppy Seed Cake, 230
Potatoes
    Curried Summer Vegetables, 142
    Curried Vegetables with Cashews, 142
    Easy Potato Salad, 79
    Heavenly Potato Leek Soup, 126
    High Energy, 68
    New England Fish Chowder, 188
    Roasted Potatoes, 177
    Spinach and Potato Salad with Capers, 78
    Sweet Borscht, 111
    Vegetables in Indian Spices, 141
Pressed Cabbage Salad, 103
Pressed Cucumber Salad, 103
Pressed Salads, 102
Pressure Cooking With Confidence, 200-201
    How to Use a Rice Crock in a Pressure
    Cooker, 201-202
Pumpkin seeds
    Colorful and Crunchy, 55

Quick and Easy Vegetable Sauce, 40
Quick Bean Soaking Method, 117
Quick-fried Bass with Tartar Sauce, 196
Quick Ginger Scallion Sauce, 144

Quick Recipes
    A Taste of Japan, 155
    Almond Pesto, 53
    Another Great Pesto, 55
    Apricot Compote, 261
    Basic Teff, 223
    Broiled Farm-raised Trout, 194
    Bronze Delight, 215
    Cashew Carrot Curry Sauce, 52
    Cashew Florentine Sauce, 53
    Chinese Cabbage and Watercress Soup, 38
    Chinese Stir-fry, 192
    Cilantro Pesto Pasta, 77
    Chocolate Hazelnut Pudding or Frosting, 260
    Chocolatey Pancakes, 240
    Colorful and Crunchy, 55
    Colorful Ginger Noodle Soup, 41
    Country-style Broccoli, 65
    Couscous and Teff, 215
    Creamy Mushroom Basil Sauce, 147
    Curried Tempeh with Tomatoes, 67
    Dorothy's Steamed Bay Scallops, 194
    Easy Potato Salad, 79
    Emily's Strawberry Drink, 175
    Fat Free, 63
    Fragrant Indian Cabbage, 66
    Freckles, 208
    French Toast, 173
    Ginger Tempeh, 48
    Ginger Vegetables, 158
    Green Noodle Sauté, 61
    Greens and Grains, 43
    Greens with Shiitake, 157
    Greens with Tahini Sauce, 165
    Herb Pâté, 168
    Hot Carob Fudge, 262
    Hot or Cold Salad, 46
    Italiano Arugola Salad with Cauliflower, 75
    Japanese Fried Rice, 61
    Japanese Noodles in Tamari Broth, 39
    Japanese Rainbow Salad, 82
    Juicy Ginger Vegetables, 47
    Kasha, 214
    Kasha Cous, 214
    Lemony Carrot and Radish Salad, 99
    Mediterranean Tofu Dip, 85

Millet Apple Raisin Cake, 212
Mushroom Leek Sauce, 146
Oriental Express, 61
Oriental Vegetable Salad, 83
Pasta Salada with Pesto, 54
Quick Fried Bass with Tartar Sauce, 196
Quick Ginger Scallion Sauce, 144
Quinoa Veggie Pilaf, 44
Refried Beans, 69
Ruby Red Salad, 83
Sauté of Garden Greens, 64
Sautéed Kale with Leeks and Dill, 156
Smoked Fish Hors D'Oeuvres, 189
Smoked Fish Salads, 190
Spanish Dancer, 45
Spinach and Potato Salad with Capers, 78
Steamed Cauliflower, 178
Steamed Vegetables, 178
Stir-Fry Vegetables with Tofu, 49
Sunny Mushroom Pâté, 164
Sweet-and-Sour Tofu, 51
Sweet Vegetables Lo Mein, 157
Szechuan Broccoli, 60
Tahini Parsley Sauce, 166
The Works, 159
3-Bean Dill Salad, 88
3-Bean Summer Salad with Cilantro and
    Capers, 88
Tofu Stroganoff, 50
Udon Noodle Soup, 42
Vegetable Gravy, 147
Quinoa
  High Energy, 68
  Quinoa Pepper Pilaf, 45
  Quinoa Veggie Pilaf, 44
  Spanish Dancer, 45
  Sunny Mountain Rice, 210
Quinoa Pepper Pilaf, 45
Quinoa Veggie Pilaf, 44

Radish
  Emperor's Sweet-and-Sour Tempeh, 139
  Lemony Carrot and Radish Salad, 99
  Ruby Red Salad, 83
  3-Bean Dill Salad, 88
Raisins
  Banana Cake, 254

Carrot Coconut Cake, 255
Millet Apple Raisin Cake, 212
Teff Applesauce Cake, 229
Raspberry
  Berry Good Tofu Pie, 235
Red lentils
  Indian Red Bean Sauce, 143
  Red Lentil Asparagus Soup, 122
Refried Beans, 69
Rice, see Basmati Rice and Brown Rice
Rice Bread #1, 216-217
Rice Bread #2, 217
Rice crock
  How to Use a Rice Crock in a Pressure
      Cooker, 201-202
  Using A Ceramic Pressure Cooker Insert
      (Rice Crock), 118
Rice Dream drink
  Carrot Coconut Cake, 255
  Chocolate Cake Supreme, 258
  Chocolatey Pancakes, 240
  Corn Bread Cake, 253
  Emily's Strawberry Drink, 175
  French Toast, 173
Rice flour
  Wheat-free Corn Bread, 253
Rice syrup
  Berry Good Tofu Pie, 235
  Carob Cookies, 249
  Carob Fudge Icing, 257
  Chocolate Hazelnut Pudding or Frosting,
      260
  Cocoa Fudge Icing, 259
  Coffee Apricot Tofu Pie, 228
  Fruit Cake Cookies, 249
  Luscious Strawberry Pie, 245
  Walnut Pie, 247
Rice vinegar
  Emperor's Sweet-and-Sour Tempeh, 139
  Japanese Rainbow Salad 82
  Oriental Vegetable Salad, 83
  Ruby Red Salad, 83
  Sweet-and-Sour Everything, 140
  Sweet-and-Sour Tempeh and Vegetables,
      140
  Sweet-and-Sour Tofu 51
Roasted Eggplant and Pepper Salad, 80
Roasted Potatoes, 177

Rolled oats
  Apple Date Crisp, 250
  Deluxe Morning Breakfast, 226
  Fruit Paradise, 238
  Scrumptious Muffins, 239
  Tahini Cream Sauce, 144
  Vanilla Hazelnut Granola, 239
Ruby Red Salad, 83
Rutabaga
  Green Noodle Sauté, 62
  Sweet Bean Stew, 132

Salad dressings
  Creamy Garlic, 92
  Golden Goddess, 93
  Green Queen, 93
  Lemon Fire, 95
  Pinto Parsley Salad, 95
  Tofu Mayo, 96
  Will's Dressing, 94
  Winds of Japan, 97
Salads
  Ancient Goddess Spring Tabouli, 74
  Babaghanoush, 81
  Boiled Salads, 100
  Cilantro Pesto Pasta, 77
  Colorful and Crunchy, 55
  Composed Green Salads, 89
  Easy Potato Salad, 79
  Festive Rice Salad, 86
  Grated Salads, 98
  Hot or Cold Salad, 46
  Italiano Arugola Salad with Cauliflower, 75
  Japanese Rainbow Salad, 82
  Lemony Carrot and Radish Salad, 99
  Len's Sunny Macaroni Salad, 76
  Marinated Salads, 100
  Marinated Sun-dried Tomatoes, 84
  Marinated Tofu, 101
  Mediterranean Tofu Dip, 85
  Oriental Vegetable Salad, 83
  Pasta Salada with Pesto, 54
  Pickles, 105
  Pinto Parsley Salad, 95
  Pressed Cabbage Salad, 103
  Pressed Cucumber Salad, 103

Pressed Salads, 102
Roasted Eggplant and Pepper Salad, 80
Ruby Red Salad, 83
Sauerkraut with Carrots and Onions, 104
Smoked Fish Salads, 190
Spinach and Potato Salad with Capers, 78
Sprouts, 90
The Ultimate Pasta and Bean Salad, 87
3-Bean Dill Salad, 88
3-Bean Summer Salad with Cilantro and Capers, 88
Salmon
  Japanese Poached Salmon, 191
Salsa
  Spanish Dancer, 45
Sauces
  Cashew Carrot Curry Sauce, 52
  Cashew Florentine Sauce, 53
  Chickpeas in Garlic Sauce, 164
  Creamy Mushroom Basil Sauce, 147
  Ginger Burdock Sauce, 145
  Greens with Tahini Sauce, 165
  Indian Red Bean Sauce, 143
  Macro Mushroom Sauce, 115
  Mushroom Leek Sauce, 146
  Quick and Easy Vegetable Sauce, 40
  Quick Ginger Scallion Sauce, 144
  Sweet-and-Sour Everything, 140
  Sweet-and-Sour Tofu, 51
  Tahini Cream Sauce, 144
  Tahini Parsley Sauce, 166
  Tamari-ginger Gravy, 137
  Tartar Sauce, 196
  Tofu Stroganoff, 50
  Vegetable Gravy, 147
Sauerkraut with Carrots and Onions, 104
Sauté of Garden Greens, 64
Sautéed Kale with Leeks and Dill, 156
Savory Fish Stew, 191
Scallions
  Herb Pâté, 168
  Quick Ginger Scallion Sauce, 144
  Udon Noodle Soup, 42
Scallops
  Dorothy's Steamed Bay Scallops, 194
Scrumptious Muffins, 239
Sea palm
  Children's Special Soup, 154

Sea salt
    Pickles, 105
    Sauerkraut with Carrots and Onions, 104
Sea Vegetables
    Black, White, and Greens, 160
    Children's Special Soup, 154
    Colorful Ginger Noodle Soup, 41
    Japanese Rainbow Salad, 82
    Ruby Red Salad, 83
    Seitan making Party and Pot Roast, 136
    Udon Noodle Soup, 42
    Vegetarian Sushi, 161-163
Secrets
    of Soups, Stews, and Sauces, 108
Seitan
    Cutlets, 137
    Seitan making Party and Pot Roast, 136
    Tofu Stroganoff, 50
Seitan-making Party and Pot Roast, 136
Sesame oil
    Creamy Garlic, 92
    Designing an Oriental Stir-fry, 60
Sesame seed milk, To Make Your Own, 16
Shiitake In the Wok, 167
Shiitake mushrooms
    A Taste of Japan, 155
    Children's Special Soup, 154
    Chinese Hot and spicy Soup, 111
    Greens with Shiitake, 157
    Lentil Soup, 124
    Macro Mushroom Sauce, 115
    Miso Vegetable Soup, 114
    Seitan making Party and Pot Roast, 136
    Shiitake Barley Mushroom Soup, 112
    Shiitake In the Wok, 167
    Udon Noodle Soup, 42
Short and Sweet, 205
Shrimp
    Honey Shrimp Kabobs, 193
Smoked Fish Hors d'Oeuvres, 189
Smoked Fish Salads, 190
Soba noodles
    Japanese Noodles in Tamari Broth, 39
    Sweet Vegetables Lo Mein, 157
Soups
    A Taste of Japan, 155
    Autumn Minestrone, 120
    Brazilian Black Bean Soup, 130

Children's Special Soup, 154
Chinese Cabbage and Watercress Soup, 38
Chinese Hot and Spicy Soup, 111
Colorful Ginger Noodle Soup, 41
Creamy Broccoli Soup, 128
Creamy Cauliflower Soup, 127
Creamy Squash Soup, 126
Fancy French Onion Soup with Herb Croutons, 110
French Patty Pan Stew...and Soup, 131
Gypsy Bean Soup, 129
Heavenly Potato Leek Soup, 126
Invent Your Own Miso Soup, 113
Japanese Noodles in Tamari Broth, 39
Lentil Soup, 124
Miso Vegetable Soup, 114
New England Fish Chowder, 188
Paradise of India, 123
Red Lentil Asparagus Soup, 122
Shiitake Barley Mushroom Soup, 112
Split Pea Barley Soup, 125
Sweet Borscht, 111
Sweet Split Pea Soup, 125
Thanks, Grandma, 121
Udon Noodle Soup, 42
Vegetable Stocks, 108
Soy cream cheese
    Caramel Icing, 257
Soy mayonnaise see Tofu Mayo, 79
Soy milk
    Banana Cake, 254
    Carrot Coconut Cake, 255
    Chocolate Cake Supreme, 258
    Chocolatey Pancakes, 240
    Corn Bread Cake, 253
    Emily's Strawberry Drink, 175
    French Toast, 173
    Lemon Poppy Seed Cake, 230
Spanish Dancer, 45
Special Marinade for Sun-dried Tomatoes, 84
Spelt
    Spelt Good, 206
Spelt cous
    Ancient Goddess Spring Tabouli, 74
    It Looks Like Meatloaf, 70-71
Spelt flakes
    Creamy Broccoli Soup, 128
    Deluxe Morning Breakfast, 226

Spelt flour
  Banana Date Tofu Pie, 244
  Carob Chip Cookies, 248
  Carob Fudge Layer Cake, 256
  Carrot Coconut Cake, 255
  Chocolate Cake Supreme, 258
  Chocolate Chip Cookies, 248
  Chunky Chocolate-Nut Cookies, 248
  Date Cookies, 248
  Exotic Pear Crisp, 251
  Ginger Bread Cake, 252
  It Looks Like Meatloaf, 70-71
  Mocha Walnut Cake, 254
  Walnut Pie, 247
Spelt Good, 206
Spelt pasta
  Pasta Salada with Pesto, 54
Split pea
  Split Pea Barley Soup, 125
  Sweet Split Pea Soup, 125
Spinach
  Cashew Florentine Sauce, 53
  Spinach and Potato Salad with Capers, 78
Spinach and Potato Salad with Capers, 78
Sprouts, 90
Squash, *see also* butternut squash, delicata
  squash, patty pan squash, summer squash,
  and zucchini
  Millet and Teff with Squash and Onions,
  225
Steamed Cauliflower, 178
Stews
  Curried Summer Vegetables, 142
  Curried Vegetables with Cashews, 142
  French Patty Pan Stew...and Soup, 131
  French Peasant Stew, 134
  Holiday Tempeh, 138
  It Must Be Chili, 133
  Savory Fish Stew, 191
  Seitan making Party and Pot Roast, 136
  Sweet Bean Stew, 132
  Vegetables in Indian Spices, 141
Stir-fry
  Chinese Stir-fry, 192
  Country-style Broccoli, 65
  Curried Tempeh with Tomatoes, 67
  Fat-Free, 63
  Fragrant Indian Cabbage, 66

Ginger Vegetables, 158
Green Noodle Sauté, 61
High Energy, 68
It Looks Like Meat Loaf, 70-71
Italiano Green Sauté, 156
Japanese Fried Rice, 61
Juicy Ginger Vegetables, 47
Oriental Express, 61
Refried Beans, 69
Sauté of Garden Greens, 64
Sautéed Kale with Leeks and Dill, 156
Shiitake In the Wok, 167
Stir-fry Vegetables with Tofu, 49
Sweet Vegetables Lo Mein, 157
Szechwan Broccoli, 60
The Works, 159
Stir-fry Vegetables with Tofu, 49
Strawberry
  Berry Good Tofu Pie, 235
  Emily's Strawberry Drink, 175
  Good Morning Strawberry Muffins, 174
  Luscious Strawberry Pie, 245
String beans
  Curried Summer Vegetables, 142
  Pickles, 105
  Sunset Casserole, 135
  3-Bean Dill Salad, 88
Striped bass
  Striped Bass, Trout, or Tilapia Stuffed with
  Herbed Croutons, 195
Striped Bass, Trout, or Tilapia Stuffed with
  Herbed Croutons, 195
Summer squash
  Sweet-and-Sour Tofu, 51
Sun-dried tomatoes
  Festive Rice Salad, 86
  Marinated Sun-dried Tomatoes, 84
  Mediterranean Tofu Dip, 85
  Special Marinade for Sun-dried Tomatoes,
  84
  Sunflower seed milk, To Make Your Own,
  16
Sunflower seeds
  Cilantro Pesto Pasta, 77
  It Looks Like Meatloaf, 70-71
  Len's Sunny Macaroni Salad, 76
  Pasta Salada with Pesto, 54
  Sunny Mountain Rice, 210

Sunny Mushroom Pâté, 164
Sunny Mountain Rice, 210
Sunny Mushroom Pâté, 164
Sunset Casserole, 135
Super Chocolate Chip Cookies, 232
Sweet-and-Sour Everything, 140
Sweet-and-Sour Tempeh and Vegetables, 140
Sweet-and-Sour Tofu, 51
Sweet Bean Stew, 132
Sweet Borscht, 111
Sweet brown rice
   Short and Sweet, 205
Sweet Millet, 211
Sweet Potato
   Sweet Bean Stew, 132
Sweet Split Pea Soup, 125
Sweet Vegetables Lo Mein, 157
Szechwan Broccoli, 60

Tahini
   Babaghanoush, 81
   Chickpea Vegetable Pâté, 163
   Coffee Apricot Tofu Pie, 228
   Greens with Tahini Sauce, 165
   Tahini Cream Sauce, 144
   Tahini Parsley Sauce, 166
Tahini Cream Sauce, 144
Tahini Parsley Sauce, 166
Tamari
   Creamy Garlic, 92
   Japanese Noodles in Tamari Broth, 39
   Seitan-making Party and Pot Roast, 136
   Sweet-and-Sour Tofu, 51
   Tamari-ginger Gravy, 137
   Tempting Tempeh Casserole, 166
Tamari-ginger Gravy, 137
Tartar Sauce
   Quick-fried Bass with Tartar Sauce, 196
Teff flour
   Apple Crumb Pie, 233
   Apple Date Crisp, 250
   Banarama Tofu Pie, 236
   Berry Good Tofu Pie, 235
   Blueberry Crumb Pie, 234
   Chocolatey Pancakes, 240
   Creamy Chocolate Truffle Pie, 246
   Dessert Pie Crust, 231
   Espresso Scones, 236

Fruit Paradise, 238
Hazelnut Butter Cookies, 238
Lemon Poppy Seed Cake, 230
Peach Crumb Pie, 234
Peanut Butter Chocolate Chip Cookies, 237
Peanut Butter Cookies, 237
Scrumptious Muffins, 239
Super Chocolate chip Cookies, 232
Topless Blueberry Pie, 234
Vanilla Hazelnut Granola, 239
Teff grain
   Basic Teff, 223
   Bronze Delight, 215
   Coffee Apricot Tofu Pie, 228
   Couscous and Teff, 215
   Deluxe Morning Breakfast, 226
   Elegant Vegetable Quiche, 227-228
   Freckles, 208
   Fritters, 224
   Lemon Poppy Seed Cake, 230
   Millet and Teff with Squash and Onions, 225
   Teff Applesauce Cake, 229
   Teff Plus Other Grains, 223
Teff Applesauce Cake, 229
Tempeh
   Curried Tempeh with Tomatoes, 67
   Emperor's Sweet-and-Sour Tempeh, 139
   Ginger Tempeh, 48
   Holiday Tempeh, 138
   Sweet-and-Sour Tempeh and Vegetables, 140
   Tempting Tempeh Casserole, 166
Tempting Tempeh Casserole, 166
Thanks, Grandma, 121
The Ultimate Pasta and Beans Salad, 87
The Works, 159
3-Bean Dill Salad, 88
3-Bean Summer Salad with Cilantro and Capers, 88
Three Sisters Grains, 208
Tilapia
   Striped Bass, Trout, or Tilapia Stuffed with Herbed Croutons, 195
Toasted sesame oil
   Colorful and Crunchy, 55
   Japanese Rainbow Salad, 82
   Ruby Red Salad, 83

Tofu
  Banana Date Tofu Pie, 244
  Bananarama Tofu Pie, 236
  Berry Good Tofu Pie, 235
  Caramel Icing, 257
  Carob Fudge Icing, 257
  Carob Fudge Layer Cake, 256
  Cocoa Fudge Icing, 259
  Coconut Icing, 256
  Children's Special Soup, 154
  Chinese Hot and Spicy Soup, 111
  Chocolate Hazelnut Pudding or Frosting,
    260
  Chocolate Pudding, 246
  Coffee Apricot Tofu Pie, 228
  Creamy Chocolate Truffle Pie, 246
  Creamy Garlic, 92
  Elegant Vegetable Quiche, 227-228
  Hazelnut Butter Icing, 260
  Herb Pâté, 168
  Luscious Strawberry Pie, 245
  Marinated Tofu, 101
  Mediterranean Tofu Dip, 85
  Shiitake In the Wok, 167
  Stir-fry Vegetables with Tofu, 49
  Sweet and Sour Tofu, 51
  Tofu Mayo, 96
  Tofu Stroganoff, 50
Tofu Mayo, 96
Tofu Stroganoff, 50
Tomatoes
  Autumn Minestrone, 120
  Curried Tempeh with Tomatoes, 67
  It Must Be Chili, 133
Topless Blueberry Pie, 234
Trout
  Broiled Farm-raised Trout, 194
  Striped Bass, Trout, or Tilapia Stuffed with
    Herbed Croutons, 195
2-Bean Vegetable Pâté, 103

Udon Noodle Soup, 42
Udon noodles
  Japanese Noodles in Tamari Broth, 39
  Sweet Vegetables Lo Mein, 157
  Udon Noodle Soup, 42,
Umeboshi paste

  definition, 290
  Tofu Stroganoff, 50
Umeboshi Plums
  definition, 290
  It Looks Like Meat Loaf, 70-71
Umeboshi vinegar
  Almond Pesto, 53
  as a cooking liquid, 16
  definition, 294
  Greens and Grains, 43
  Greens with Tahini Sauce, 165
  Japanese Rainbow Salad, 82
  Len's Sunny Macaroni Salad, 76
  Oriental Vegetable Salad, 83
  Pasta Salada with Pesto, 54
  Ruby Red Salad, 83
Using A Ceramic Pressure Cooker Insert
  (Rice Crock), 118

Vanilla Hazelnut Granola, 239
Vegetable Fried Rice, 157
Vegetable Gravy, 147
Vegetables in Indian Spices, 141
Vegetarian Sushi, 161-162

Walnut Pie, 247
Walnuts
  Banana Cake, 254
  Carrot Coconut Cake, 255
  Cilantro Pesto Pasta, 77
  Coffee Cake and Cupcakes, 180
  It Looks Like Meatloaf, 70-71
  Mocha Walnut Cake, 254
  Walnut Pie, 247
Watercress
  Chinese Cabbage and Watercress Soup, 38
  Chinese Stir-fry, 192
Wheat-free Baking
  With Spelt Flour, 244, 247, 248, 252, 254-
  256, 258
  With Teff Flour, 231-239, 246
Wheat-free Corn Bread, 253
Whole oats
  Freckles, 208
Whole wheat bread flour
  Brown Rice and Barley Bread, 218

Rice Bread #1, 216-217
Rice Bread #2, 217
Seitan making Party and Pot Roast, 136
Whole wheat couscous
Quinoa Pepper Pilaf, 45
Whole wheat pastry flour
Banana Cake, 254
Carob Chip Cookies, 248
Carob Fudge Layer Cake, 256
Chocolate Cake Supreme, 258
Chocolate Chip Cookies, 248
Chunky Chocolate-Nut Cookies, 248
Coffee Cake and Cupcakes, 180
Corn Bread Cake, 253
Date Cookies, 248
Fruit Cake Cookies, 249
Good Morning Strawberry Muffins, 174
Luscious Strawberry Pie, 245
Outrageously Delicious Hazelnut Cake,
259
Walnut Pie, 247
Wild and Wonderful, 207
Wild greens

Composed Green Salads, 89
Wild rice
Sunny Mountain Rice, 210
Wild and Wonderful, 207
Winds of Japan, 97
Wine
Smoked Fish Hors D'Oeuvres, 189
Special Marinade for Sun-dried Tomatoes,
84

Yam
High Energy, 68
Lentil Soup, 124
Sweet Bean Stew, 132
Sweet Split Pea Soup, 125

Zucchinni
Cashew Carrot Curry Sauce, 52
Fat-free, 63
Roasted Eggplant and Pepper Salad, 80

About the Author

Leslie Cerier is a chef, caterer, cooking teacher, and national authority on cooking with teff. She has written numerous articles on nutrition, cooking, and natural living for *Bottom Line/Personal, Natural Health,* and local newspapers. She has developed recipes for the Maskel Teff company and for Dr. Gene A. Spiller's upcoming book: *Nutrition Secrets of the Ancients.* She lives in Western Massachusetts with her husband and two daughters.